Learner-Centred Education for Adult Migrants in Europe

International Issues in Adult Education

Series Editor

Peter Mayo (*University of Malta, Msida, Malta*)

Editorial Advisory Board

Stephen Brookfield (*University of St Thomas, Minnesota, USA*)
Waguida El Bakary (*American University in Cairo, Egypt*)
Budd L. Hall (*University of Victoria, BC, Canada*)
Astrid von Kotze (*University of Western Cape, South Africa*)
Alberto Melo (*University of the Algarve, Portugal*)
Lidia Puigvert-Mallart (CREA-*University of Barcelona, Spain*)
Daniel Schugurensky (*Arizona State University, USA*)
Joyce Stalker (*University of Waikato, Hamilton, New Zealand/Aotearoa*)
Juha Suoranta (*University of Tampere, Finland*)

VOLUME 33

The titles published in this series are listed at *brill.com/adul*

Learner-Centred Education for Adult Migrants in Europe

A Critical Comparative Analysis

Edited by

Maria N. Gravani and Bonnie Slade

BRILL
SENSE

LEIDEN | BOSTON

Cover illustration: Artwork by Oscar Dickson

All chapters in this book have undergone peer review.

The Library of Congress Cataloging-in-Publication Data is available online at http://catalog.loc.gov

Typeface for the Latin, Greek, and Cyrillic scripts: "Brill". See and download: brill.com/brill-typeface.

ISSN 2352-2372
ISBN 978-90-04-46150-5 (paperback)
ISBN 978-90-04-46151-2 (hardback)
ISBN 978-90-04-46152-9 (e-book)

Copyright 2021 by Koninklijke Brill NV, Leiden, The Netherlands.
Koninklijke Brill NV incorporates the imprints Brill, Brill Hes & De Graaf, Brill Nijhoff, Brill Rodopi, Brill Sense, Hotei Publishing, mentis Verlag, Verlag Ferdinand Schöningh and Wilhelm Fink Verlag.
All rights reserved. No part of this publication may be reproduced, translated, stored in a retrieval system, or transmitted in any form or by any means, electronic, mechanical, photocopying, recording or otherwise, without prior written permission from the publisher. Requests for re-use and/or translations must be addressed to Koninklijke Brill NV via brill.com or copyright.com.

This book is printed on acid-free paper and produced in a sustainable manner.

Contents

Foreword   VII
  Peter Mayo
Acknowledgements   XII
Notes on Contributors   XIII

PART 1
Conceptualisation

1 Setting the Context for a Comparative Exploration of Learner-Centred Education (LCE) in Programmes for Adult Migrants in Europe   3
    Maria N. Gravani and Bonnie Slade

2 Learner-Centred Education: Debating Conceptual, Theoretical and Empirical Approaches   18
    Maria N. Gravani and Pavlos Hatzopoulos

PART 2
Contextualisation

3 Comparative Cartography of Adult Education for Migrants in Cyprus, Estonia, Malta and Scotland   43
    Maria Brown, Maria N. Gravani, Bonnie Slade and Larissa Jõgi

4 Learner-Centred Education and Adult Education for Migrants in Estonia   54
    Larissa Jõgi and Katrin Karu

5 Learner-Centred Education and Adult Education for Migrants in Glasgow   79
    Bonnie Slade and Nicola Dickson

6 Learner-Centred Education and Adult Education for Migrants in Malta   100
    Maria Brown

7 Learner-Centred Education and Adult Education for Migrants in Cyprus   121
    Maria N. Gravani, Pavlos Hatzopoulos and Eleni Papaioannou

PART 3
Comparative Analysis & Reflections

8 Learner-Centred Education and Adult Education for Migrants: A Cross-Case Analysis of the Cypriot, Estonian, Maltese and Scottish Cases   151
    Pavlos Hatzopoulos, Maria N. Gravani, Bonnie Slade, Larissa Jõgi and Maria Brown

9 Reading the Migrants' World through Emancipatory Learner-Centred Education: Parting Reflections on the Micro Pedagogical Contexts   168
    Carmel Borg

Index   183

Foreword

It gives me great satisfaction to see a book, in a series such as this, covering adult education with respect to one of the most burning issues in this day and age. Adult Education and Migration is one of the key areas prevalent today. People have been migrating since time immemorial. This is therefore not a new phenomenon. It has probably been a feature of human life since its very inception. Some countries have been built on the dispossession of Indigenous peoples and on immigration from different parts of the world (English & Mayo, 2019, p. 217). Other nations have been characterised by internal migration (e.g., from Italy's *Mezzogiorno* [Southern regions and islands] to its North) or displacement (social engineering such as that involving Kurds in Turkey). What has been significant in more recent times is the exponential rate at which people are relocating to other territories. We speak of mass migration which has implications for learning on both sides of the main global migration divide, primarily the proverbial North-South divide and of course the East-West divide, though we should also note the South-South and North-North migration flows. Coverage of this phenomenon is increasing in the adult education literature, albeit not at the rate one expects. I expect it to grow significantly in the years to come and constitute a feature of the book series I initiated at the end of the first decade of this new Millennium. This is, to date, the first comprehensive book on Migration in the series.

It arose out of frequent gatherings of a group of scholars based in the UK (some with North American experiences of migration and work-skills education), Cyprus, Estonia and Malta, in connection with an Erasmus Mundus International Master programme in Adult Education for Social Change (IMAESC). Many of these are small countries, some with a small landmass, and populations that range from officially a quarter of a million to about two million or thereabouts. Scotland, home of the lead partner in the IMAESC project, is the odd one out in terms of population with the figure traditionally established as around 5 million. Of course, undocumented clandestine immigration makes us tread cautiously when banding about population figures. All of these countries have histories of mass emigration towards other countries with hubs of migrants giving rise to regions, districts and communities branded by names associated with the country of origin. Nova Scotia comes to mind. There are concentrations of ethnic groups in certain districts: e.g. Sunshine in Melbourne, Victoria (for Maltese). London is a traditional hub for Greek-Cypriots and for migrants from most of the countries under review in this book. Great personalities have emerged from the migrant communities involved. We can think of Cat Stevens/Yusuf Islam and George Michael (Georgios Kyriakos

Panayiotou), regarding Greek Cypriots (both sons of Greek-Cypriot restaurateurs) in London, and Presidential hopeful Pete Buttigieg (Maltese father) and graphic journalist Joe Sacco (Maltese) in the United States. People of Scottish ancestry making their mark abroad are countless. Make no mistake, Greek-Cypriots, Maltese, Scots and Estonians are found everywhere and not just in these visible spots.

Like most countries in the European South or East, many of the countries in question were traditionally centres of emigration in the pre or post World War (First and Second) years. The emergence of service based economies in addition to other forms of economic growth in these countries, besides the location of some of them at the borders between regions of the world, e.g. the central Mediterranean route between Africa and Europe or Middle East and Europe, and therefore the perception of these countries being gateways into the Eldorado that is Europe, have transformed some of these countries from net exporters of labour power into net importers of this same type of power.

Cyprus is an interesting case as it is politically divided with one part recently witnessing migration from Turkey to swell the ranks of one ethnic group in the Northern part. Many people from Greece avail themselves of a stronger economy and per capita income in Cyprus to migrate there, an island which once vociferously called for *enosis* with the 'mother country' (i.e., Greece itself). Nowadays workers from the North, consisting of Turkish-Cypriots, avail themselves of relaxed boundaries to migrate internally and therefore spend working hours in the more affluent Greek populated Southern part of the island. The island has people who were granted refugee status for having been dislocated from their communities north of what became known as the 'green line' following the Turkish invasion in 1974. The Cyprus situation is one exceptional case which demonstrates the level of complexity involved when we speak of migration.

The most visible case, however, is that concerning the massive waves of migration from 'South' to 'North', relative terms as demonstrated by any map dating back to the 'Golden Years' of Arab presence in places such as Cordoba and Seville. Arabs are represented as having moved down from North to South rather than vice versa. South-North, Centre etc. are terms that are relative to who wields power, material or symbolic. There is an unequal exchange between today's perceived geographically global South and North which is at the heart of the major migration flow. People migrate from 'South' to 'North' (taken globally) for many different reasons.

We are witnessing and shall continue to witness an exponential increase in migration from 'South' to 'North', and from 'South' to 'South'. Capitalism, via corporations, exacerbates the 'greenhouse effect' as individual sustainable living has minimal effects on climate improvement when contrasted with efforts expected of corporations and other similarly powerful entities. It is predicted that climate change will render life unbearable for people in the 'South'. 2015 was the hottest year to date and the UN Intergovernmental Panel on Climate Change predicts a 1.5 degrees centigrade increase (a conservative estimate with some going so far to envisage a 4.5% rise by the century's end), with 20–30% of the planet's species at risk of extinction. During the 2015–2016 summers, the southern parts of Africa faced unprecedented droughts, causing millions to starve. One envisages increase in famine, calamitous weather conditions, heatwaves, spread of malaria hitting regions hitherto untouched, droughts and floods. These will affect millions. Clashes over resources will, in all probability, lead to wars (Empson, 2016, pp. 1–2), fuelled further by a Western-based arms industry. As far as migration attempts go, we 'ain't seen nothing yet'. Droughts have, historically, not been assisted by appropriate famine relief from Western powers and corporations owing to potential destabilisation of market prices. This is a scary look into the future for which adult education and other efforts (education does not bring change on its own as it is not an independent variable) must brace themselves.

As I argue in a very recent book (Mayo, 2019, p. 82), many will reach and enter, perhaps clandestinely, 'Fortress Europe' and other Western places, while others will be left stranded in transit places such as Libya. Some will try to eke out a living on the margins of the country of disembarkation, without papers (*sans papiers*) and haunted by the threat of deportation. Others will have drowned in a sea, a raging sea, they would have never witnessed before as they would hail from a landlocked area. Many will have perished in the Sahara Desert, with their bones sending a chilling reminder regarding the fate that can await those who follow them. For many, however, there is no turning back.

Migration's growth on a massive scale is bound to touch and alter the demographic composition of communities. The survivors will have their own stories to tell, some tragic and others less so. In addition to the scars of missing loved ones, they have stories of day-to-day marginalisation and racism to tell. The hegemonic populist discourses render them scapegoats for most existing ills, as they are perceived as the cause of depressing local wages and diminishing employment prospects for locals, never mind the fact that we live in a capitalist system that causes 'jobs crises' that are constantly presented as 'skills crises'. Migrants are said to be responsible for changing the 'national' (read hegemonic) 'identity' and 'ethos' – monolithically conceived, a blanket construction which smothers any language of social difference that speaks of complex shifting identities.

These stories should be the staple of different forms of dialogical adult education or education in general in encounters which pose the important education-power question: who dialogues with whom and from which position of power or powerlessness? How are people, engaged in the discussion, discursively located materially and symbolically? To what extent do most of the adult education projects looked at in the various chapters go beyond *assistencialismo* (welfarism) to address these questions? Does adult education present the newcomer as 'object' or 'subject'? No doubt a modicum of learning for survival, in terms of second language acquisition (Jõgi & Karu, Chapter 4, this volume) and skills transmission, is extremely important. A progressive adult education analysis would, in my view, go further and address the power-dynamics involved and address deep epistemological questions.

How and where do established local knowledge, wisdoms and learning traditions *meet* the new knowledge, wisdoms and learning traditions brought by the newcomers to the locality? How much do members of the autochthonous group appreciate that the newcomers, whose subjectivities extend beyond the economic to include a broader range, have had their own knowledge dismissed colonially through *epistemicide* or unabashedly stolen and patented from them in a process of *cognitive injustice*, misappropriation and accumulation? Migration through forced dislocation brings with it trans-mobility and therefore 'portability of cultures' and life-worlds in addition to labour power. To appreciate this, we must heed Antonio Gramsci's advice in various places to gain cognizance of not only the conditions in which newcomers find themselves in the borrowed context but also those prevailing in the context of origin – the conditions that led them to migrate in the first place (Gramsci, 1975, Q. 23 Note 9, pp. 2198–2202). This can guard us against stock generalisations and stereotypical constructions of migrants from various regions or countries. It can help us to understand the people concerned in all their complexities, rather than to regard them as forming part of an undifferentiated mass. Unless adult education, and all education for that matter, deals substantially with this, it remains a faithful servant to an omnivorous capitalism segregating on ethnic and national lines and fails to contribute, with other variables, to change on social justice grounds. Looking comparatively at the situations concerning migrants, their various subjectivities and provision in different contexts, one can provide contrasting pictures of how these issues are tackled or overlooked. The call is for analyses of adult education involving people at the interface between ever changing life-worlds and system-worlds. The data that can trigger these discussions, hopefully leading to action, are here in this most welcome volume.

References

Empsom, M. (2016). *Marxism and ecology: Capitalism, socialism and the future of the planet*. Socialist Workers' Party.

English, L., & Mayo, P. (2019). Lifelong learning challenges: Responding to migration and the sustainable development goals. *International Review of Education, 65*(2), 213–231.

Gramsci, A. (1975). *Quaderni del Cercere* (Prison Notebooks, Vol. IV) (V. Gerratana, Ed.). Einaudi.

Mayo, P. (2019). *Higher education in a globalising world: Community engagement and lifelong learning.* Manchester University Press.

Peter Mayo
Faculty of Education
Department of Arts, Open Communities and Adult Education
University of Malta

Acknowledgements

We would like to acknowledge the support of the Open University of Cyprus, Cyprus, for funding, through its internal funding programme, the research that it is the basis for this book.

This project is associated with the (Erasmus Mundus) International Master in Adult Education for Social Change (IMAESC). All of the partners in the project have been collaborating on IMAESC since 2014. We want to thank the EACAE for funding our programme which to date has 74 graduates from over 35 countries. This is our first major collaborative research project addressing adult education and social change.

We would also like to thank colleagues and friends, including George Zarifis, Michele Schweisfurth and Mike Osborne, for being supportive interlocutors over many years. We thank too the many and diverse adult migrant learners, adult educators and policymakers who shared with us their experiences, perspectives and understandings of the courses in which they participated and allowed us to observe their classes.

Finally, we would like to thank Peter Mayo for encouraging us to prepare and submit this book to the series he is editing for Brill | Sense, *International Issues in Adult Education*, and for writing the foreword, as well as John Bennett, Brill | Sense, for his patience and support in editing this volume.

Notes on Contributors

Carmel Borg
is Associate Professor in the Department of Arts, Open Communities and Adult Education, at the Faculty of Education, University of Malta. He is a former Head of Department and ex-Dean of the Faculty of Education. He lectures in: sociology of education, curriculum theory, development and design; critical pedagogy; adult education for community development; and parental involvement in education. He is the author, co-author and editor of a number of books, papers in academic journals and chapters in books that foreground the relationship between education, democracy and social justice. He is also involved in a number of community-based projects focusing on critical literacy and critical active citizenship. He sits on a number of editorial boards and is founding editor of the *Malta Review of Educational Research* (MRER) and the Education Research Monograph Series (ERMS).

Maria Brown
lectures in Adult Education, Community-based Education and in Sociology. She is based at the Faculty of Education of the University of Malta. Her research interests include community action and community development, social equality, social policy, sustainable development, methodology and research methods. Her research includes contributions for the European Commission, Eurydice, the Council of Europe, the European Co-operation in Science & Technology (COST) and the Ministry for Education and Employment (Malta). She contributed to a number of EU-funded projects and published academic peer-reviewed publications.

Nicola Dickson
is an early-career researcher and PhD student at University of Glasgow. Her main research interests include the exploration of feminist, non-formal, community-based forms of adult education and the use of innovative arts-based methodologies to engage hard-to-reach groups. Nicola is the co-editor of a special issue of *Studies in the Education of Adults* on adult education, the arts and creativity (Autumn, 2021), and has published peer-reviewed articles on inclusive education and arts-informed research, including a chapter in the ebook, *Feminist Adult Educators' Guide to Aesthetic, Creative and Disruptive Strategies in Museums and Community*. She is currently the Honorary Secretary of the Standing Conference on University Teaching and Research in the Education of Adults.

Maria N. Gravani

is an Associate Professor in Continuing & Adult Education at the Open University of Cyprus (OUC); Academic Coordinator of the International Masters in Adult Education for Social Change (Erasmus Mundus). She has been an elected Member of the European Society for the Research in the Education of Adults (ESREA) Presidium, since 2017, and a co-convener of the ESREA network 'Adult Educator, Trainer Professional Development'. Her main research interests include the: teaching and learning of adults, across a variety of contexts (distance education, higher education, second chance education, education for migrants), as a means of individual empowerment and social change; and the adult educators and their professionalisation.

Pavlos Hatzopoulos

is a part-time Lecturer for the Masters in Continuing Education and Lifelong Learning at the School of Humanities and Social Sciences of the Open University of Cyprus. He has been involved in several international comparative research projects. His current research interests focus on the politics of migration and asylum in Europe and on education policies and practices for the integration of migrants.

Larissa Jõgi

is a Professor of Andragogy in the School of Educational Sciences at Tallinn University, Academic Coordinator of the International Masters in Adult Education for Social Change (Erasmus Mundus) at Tallinn University. She is a member of the ESREA and one of the conveners of the ESREA network 'Adult Educator, Trainer Professional Development'. She has been involved in many national and international development and comparative research projects. Her current research interests include: learning and migration, adult learning, professional identity and professionalisation of adult educators, learning during the life course, teaching and learning in university, methodology of qualitative research.

Katrin Karu

is a Lecturer in Andragogy at the School of Educational Sciences at Tallinn University (Estonia) and Academic Coordinator of the bachelor programme in 'Adult Education'. Her doctoral thesis is titled, 'Students' comprehension of learning: An andragogical view'. She has been involved in different research projects related to the competencies and training needs of adult educators, learning and andragogical principles in the university context and meanings of non-formal learning from the perspectives of practice and practitioners. Her current research interests include changing the learning culture in the university and academics' learning networks.

Peter Mayo

is a Professor of Sociology of Education and Adult Education at the Faculty of Education, University of Malta, Malta. His main research interests include: Critical Pedagogy, Critical Adult Education, Gramsci, Lorenzo Milani, Cultural Studies, Paulo Freire, Migration, Museum Education. He is Series Editor of Brill | Sense's *International Issues in Adult Education,* Editor of *Postcolonial Directions in Education,* and has been inducted into the International Adult Continuing Education Hall of Fame.

Eleni Papaioannou

is a part-time Lecturer for the Masters in Continuing Education and Lifelong Learning at the School of Humanities and Social Sciences of the Open University of Cyprus. Her main research interests include: adult education and lifelong learning, qualitative research, European policies.

Bonnie Slade

is a Professor in Adult Education at the School of Education, University of Glasgow, Scotland, and Programme Leader of the International Masters in Adult Education for Social Change (Erasmus Mundus). Her main research focus is on how adult education, across a variety of contexts (workplace, higher education, community) can work as a tool for social change and individual empowerment. She sits on the Editorial Boards of the *International Journal of Lifelong Education,* the *European Journal for Research on the Education and Learning of Adults* (RELA), and the *Malta Review of Educational Research* and is the Reviews Editor for the *Journal of Adult and Continuing Education.* From 2020 to 2023 she is serving as the Chair of the Standing Conference on University Teaching and Research in the Education of Adults.

PART 1

Conceptualisation

CHAPTER 1

Setting the Context for a Comparative Exploration of Learner-Centred Education (LCE) in Programmes for Adult Migrants in Europe

Maria N. Gravani and Bonnie Slade

Abstract

The first chapter of the book sets the background for the comparative exploration of learner-centred education (LCE) in language learning programmes for adult migrants in four European countries (Cyprus, Scotland, Malta, Estonia). It presents the rationale of the research project, upon which the book is built, its objectives, the research methodology and the comparative approach adopted. The design of the four case studies, the research questions as well as a brief introduction to the concept of learner-centred education, as a policy and practice, and its constituting elements, are discussed. The chapter concludes with a synopsis of the content of the book.

Keywords

learner-centred education – adult education – migrants – Europe – comparative study

1 Introduction

Learner-Centred Education (LCE) is a 'travelling policy' (Ozga & Jones, 2006) which has been endorsed by international agencies, national governments and local innovators (Schweisfurth, 2013). The Scottish Government's *Statement of Ambition on Adult Learning* (2014, p. 6) identifies LCE as one of its core principles by arguing that 'the educational process must build around the interests and motives of the learner and seek to fulfil the purposes and goals he or she sees as relevant and important'. Additionally, international organisations (UNESCO, UNICEF) promote LCE within a rights framework or make LCE a part of their definitions of quality education (Schweisfurth, 2013). It is argued that all learners can benefit from LCE in improved processes and outcomes and it can also be used as a foundation for the building of democratic citizens and societies, suitable for economies of the future (Schweisfurth, 2013). The value of a comparative and international perspective in the study of travelling policies and global orthodoxies like LCE is also highlighted. At the same time there is a growing realisation that we are deprived of research in the area of Adult Education investigating in what ways LCE is being enacted and implemented, while no comparative research has been done on the extent to which LCE is used in adult education as a tool for social change across different contexts. At the national level in many countries such research is non-existent.

In the light of the above, the study reported in this book explores the extent to which LCE is a sound choice for policy and practice in the four countries under exploration (Cyprus, Glasgow, Malta, Estonia), two countries from Northern Europe and two from the South, in bringing about social change in adult education. The study investigates how learner-centred is adult education in the above four countries by using the experiences and perceptions of adult learners and their educators as they embark on various adult education language learning programmes for migrants. Particularly, the objectives of the research study are to:

1. Unravel further the complex interplay of structure, culture and policies in the four European countries regarding the use of LCE as a tool for social change in adult education (AE);
2. Make a distinctive contribution to the discipline of adult comparative education by looking at LCE in AE programmes for migrants;
3. Identify practices of adult teaching and learning which might have general application to the AE sector in Europe and beyond; and
4. Provide information and provoke insights which will be of value to policymakers, researchers, and practitioners, and those involved in designing AE programmes for migrants for social change in Europe.

The research reported in this book complements and builds on previous research conducted by the researchers on LCE and, adult education, social change and migration. It adopts as a working definition for LCE drawing on Schweisfurth's (2013, p. 20) explanation 'as a pedagogical approach which gives learners, and demands from them, a relatively high level of active control over the contents and processes of learning. What is learnt, and how, are therefore shaped by learners' needs, capacities and interests'. Following this, the study draws on Schweisfurth's (2013) theoretical continuum of learner-centred approaches that recognises three 'justificatory' narratives: (1) the cognitive narrative, suggesting that the learner has control over the content and process of learning; (2) the emancipation, according to which learners not only have more control over what they learn and the process of learning, but are encouraged to question critically canons of received knowledge and the unequal structures of society and; the (3) preparation narrative, implying that the skills developed through inquiry-based self-regulated learning such as flexibility, critical independent thought and entrepreneurship are believed to support the development and sustaining of an effective knowledge economy. This research explores both adult learners' and educators' perceptions, experiences and their understandings of the AE programmes under exploration, as well as the policy context of migration and adult education in each case study.

2   Methodology

The research project purports to make a contribution to the field of Adult Education by investigating the ways in which learner-centred education (LCE) is being enacted, implemented or neglected in specific settings. The project attempts to address the relative lack of recent comparative research on if and how LCE is used in adult education as a tool for social change across different national contexts. The research presented in this book in on migrant adult learners and the pedagogies used for their education. By focusing on migration as a social process and migrants as active citizens, the research attempts to evaluate whether LCE practices can become a motor for empowering migrant adult learners. As Guo (2013, p. 3) identifies lifelong learning has failed to recognise and integrate diversity of migrants in the educational context. Instead, adult education has become a means of assimilation of migrants. Saville (2014) in his article 'How have we failed to integrate our migrant population?', referring to the English context, stigmatises the 'one-size fits all' approach to teaching English as a second language and stresses 'the need to consider the varying needs of all groups of migrants, and to tease apart what kind of support is needed in different cases'. Adult education for migrants must be reset on a new basis, beginning from the recognition of their diverse educational and learning needs, which will enable policymakers to take constructive pedagogical decisions on migrant adult education. The case studies focused on adult language learning programmes for migrants, since (a) language learning forms a key educational priority area for policies of migrant integration in all the four countries and (b) language courses are characterised by a high rate of participation for adult migrants.

3   Design of the Case Studies

The comparative approach of the research was put into practice in the design of four research case studies that were conducted in the four participating

countries: Scotland, Malta, Estonia, and Cyprus. Their design was informed by a survey of the current situation in these four countries in relation to existing adult education policies and programmes, migration policies and the provision of adult education programmes for migrants. Specifically, the four research teams collected data on:
– The political context and legal framework in relation to migration in each country, placing emphasis on (a) the variations of the legal status of migrants residing in the respective territories, (b) the degree of visibility of migrants in the respective education systems, and (c) the existence or lack of education policies for migrants that have been adopted, implemented or are under discussion.
– The political context and legal framework in relation to adult education, investigating (a) the extent to which migrant learners are targeted by adult educational policies and programmes and (b) the level of adoption of learner-centred pedagogies in the respective adult education system.
– The demographic context in respect to migrant populations, in relation to (a) the number of migrants residing in the respective countries, (b) the main nationalities of the migrants, and (c) the participation rate of migrants attending adult education programmes.
– The educational context: resources and human capacity. In relation to (a) the state expenditure on education and adult education in particular, (b) the number of teachers in early, primary, secondary education and adult education, and (c) the type of education providers in the field of adult education.

The four cartographies (Fejes & Wildemeersch, 2015) that were drafted depicted some similarities, but we found wide variations amongst the four countries under study in all the above areas, echoing what has been observed in recent relevant literature as the significant divergences and disparities amongst European education systems and migration policies.

Based on these findings, the research teams attempted to ensure that the four case studies are comparable on the basis of a clear set of common criteria. The common approach adopted by the four research teams comprised of the following main principles:
– The case studies did not form the basis for the comparison of national or local educational systems. Instead, the proposed comparative approach took as its unit of analysis the level of adult education programmes. The synthesis of the four case studies rests on a comparison of the four selected adult education programmes, rather than that of four national educational systems.

– The case studies focused on adult language programmes for migrants, since (a) language learning forms a key educational priority area for policies of migrant integration in all the four countries and (b) language courses are characterised by a high rate of participation for adult migrants.
– The case studies adopted an empirical qualitative approach, employing two principal methods: (a) semi-structured interviews with learners, teachers, and policymakers, as well as (b) observation conducted in the classes of the adult education programmes under study.

The four 'cartographies' explored the provision of adult education programmes for migrants, and pay particular emphasis to language learning. Based on the above criteria, and taking into account questions of gaining access to the adult education programmes and their participants, the four research teams selected the following adult education language programmes:

– In Scotland, the research team focused on English for Speakers of Other Languages' (ESOL) programmes for migrants that are organised at a centre run by a housing association in a densely populated area of Glasgow, one of the most ethnically diverse in Scotland (approximately a third of the population are from an ethnic minority).
– In Malta, the case study involved two language programmes formulated, managed, and provided by the Directorate for Research, Lifelong Learning and Innovation (DRLLLI) of the Ministry for Education and Employment (MEDE) (Malta). the two language programmes under investigation were: (a) English as a Foreign Language Level 1 (of 2) (EFL1); and (b) Maltese as a Foreign Language Level 1 (of 2) (MFL1). Both programmes are state provided against payment of a nominal fee and run once a year between October and May.
– In Estonia, the case study focused on the implementation of the module 'Language training', which is part of the Welcoming programme (WP) for migrants, started in Estonia in 2014 and provided by non-governmental organisation Expat Relocation Estonia OÜ. The target group of the Welcoming programme are adult new immigrants arriving to live in Estonia from third countries who have lived in Estonia less than three years and who own legitimate grounds for being in Estonia.
– In Cyprus, the research team chose to focus on the Greek language courses offered by state educational institutions, via the Adult Education Centres. These programmes, named 'Greek language for foreigners' are open to all non-native Greek speakers, including EU citizens who may be working in Cyprus, but are mainly attended by migrants. The research was conducted

in the context of one such 'Greek for Foreigners' course, as it is officially named, which was organised between November 2016 to May 2017 in the city of Larnaca, in one of the state-run Adult Education Centres hosted at the Kathari Elementary School.

4 Research Methods

The qualitative approach adopted by the research project was critical in orienting the case studies towards an extensive investigation of the different experiences, perspectives and understandings of migrant learners, educators, administrators and policymakers participating in the discourse and practice of adult education for migrants in the four countries. Qualitative methods are appropriate for researching and evaluating learner-centred educational practices, since they are capable of launching an investigation on whether what is learnt corresponds to learners' needs, capacities and interests (Lattimer, 2015). Qualitative research methods were also appropriate for this specific project, which aimed at critically exploring the extent to which the adult language learning programmes under study have been informed by the learner-centred education (LCE) paradigm, as opposed to the traditional teacher-centred delivery model.

All the four case studies employed two principal research methods: (a) research interviews with learners, teachers, and policymakers, as well as (b) observation conducted in the class of the language programmes under study. The research teams conducted 18 semi-structured interviews overall with three types of stakeholders:
– Migrant adult learners who attended the four respective language learning courses.
– Educators or tutors working in the language courses under study.
– Policymakers. This category is quite diverse since it involved education programme designers, coordinators, or inspectors working for state or non-governmental institutions depending on the type of institution that acted as the educational provider of the language course under study.

All the research interviews were semi-structured, following the protocol and guidelines agreed upon by the four research teams participating in the project. They were organised along the following six principal research questions:
– In what ways are the adult education programmes engaging to migrants and motivate them to learn?
– To what extent are learning challenges in the adult education programmes built on migrants' existing knowledge?

SETTING THE CONTEXT FOR A COMPARATIVE EXPLORATION OF LCE

- To what extent is dialogue used in adult teaching and learning?
- In what ways do the atmosphere and conduct of the programmes reflect mutual respect between migrants as adult learners and their educators?
- To what extent is the curriculum relevant to migrants' lives and perceived future needs, in a language accessible to them, and it is also based on skills and attitude outcomes as well as content?
- To what extent does assessment follow up these principles by testing skills and by allowing for individual differences, rather than being purely content-driven with success based only on rote learning?

All these questions were related to the issues of motivations for participation, the organisation of the course, teaching practices that are employed in class, the learning climate/atmosphere, and evaluation practices that correspond to the four elements which comprise LCE practice, according to Michele Schweisfurth's approach, namely: techniques, relationships, motivation, epistemology (2013, p. 11).

Observation was conducted before, during, but in some cases also after the language courses that were selected in the four locations. Overall, the research teams attended four classes. Observation provided an opportunity for a more nuanced analysis of the data collected by allowing the research team to:
- Focus on concrete educational practices and consider how these compare with the discourse of teachers, migrant learners and policymakers as was articulated in the research interviews.
- An in-depth analysis of the learner-centred dimensions of the language programme under study and their impact as motors for social change.

Researchers drafted field notes, detailing of what was observed and paying particular attention to:
- Space: the physical place of the classroom.
- Objects: the physical things which are present.
- Actors: the people involved in the class.
- Interactions: events that take place amongst these actors.
- Dialogue: what is being said between teachers and learners and also amongst learners during these interactions.
- Non-verbal communication: what is shown rather than said in these interactions.
- Time: the sequencing of educational practices that takes place over time.

Data from the interviews and observations are presented in Chapters 4 to 7 of this book.

5 Operationalising the Concept of Learner-Centred Education (LCE)

The research project is organised around the concept of learner-centred education (LCE) and has attempted to operationalise it by going beyond existing criticisms that raise, for example, its fuzziness and the fact that it is often associated with confusion or misunderstanding (e.g. Guthrie, 2016; Kliebard, 1995). The study endorses to this effect, Schweisfurth's conceptualisation of LCE. Schweisfurth views educational practice as existing along a continuum from less learner-centred to more learner-centred, with LCE at one end of the continuum. At that LCE end, learners have more control not just over content of learning, but over how they learn and what is learnt and how what is learnt is shaped by learners' needs, capacities, and interests.

In the above continuum, Schweisfurth (2013, p. 11) identifies four main elements which comprise LCE practice, namely: (a) Motivations, (b) Epistemology, (c) Techniques and (d) Relationships. These were employed heuristically in the present study as a conceptual framework to unveil the extent to which LCE is used as a tool for enhancing adult teaching and learning in the contexts under exploration.

The first element comprises of the motivation of learners, but also other participants to the educational process (Schweisfurth, 2013, p. 12). Learning is best achieved through internal rather than external motivation and learners need to be intrinsically motivated to be involved successfully in the education process. Similarly, adult learning theory designates that people tend to feel uncommitted to any decision or activity that they feel is imposed on them. Indeed, the most potent motivators for adults are the internal pressures (Knowles, 1980).

Second, part of LCE's constellation, according to Schweisfurth (2013, p. 12), is the nature of knowledge. She calls this element epistemology and sees this as a continuum. On one end of this continuum, is the fixed knowledge and curriculum to be taught; on the other end, knowledge is fluid and changes over time, thus the content is negotiable with learners. Schweisfurth's conceptualisation of learner-centred education raises thus the critical importance of the relevance of the curriculum and of educational practices to the learners' present and future lives, as well as the need that what is taught needs to build on learners' existing knowledge and skills (2013, p. 21). A key question to address in this respect, as she points out is that of 'who decides what is relevant to learners' (2015, p. 264) and one might add also those of 'how this relevance or non-relevance is perceived by all participants in the educational process' and how it is 'negotiated in a piecemeal fashion in the context of everyday learning practices'.

The third element relates to techniques and activities that teachers use in the classroom with learners, such as group work, independent inquiry, project-or problem-based learning, and 'scaffolding' based on individual learners' needs. This overlaps remarkably with Knowles' (1980) andragogical principle that focuses on selecting appropriate formats, such as individual, group and mass activities for learning; designing units of experiential learning; utilising indicated methods and materials and putting them in order, according to learners' needs. Brookfield (1986), similarly, comments on the concept of self-directed learning which assumes a high degree of responsibility for learning taken by the learner. Small (2011, cited in Schweisfurth, 2013) created a Teacher's Checklist to mark a learning environment where LCE is successfully implemented and practiced which among others include the following: learners are actively engaged in an experiential learning process; tasks, activities and projects are related to the learners' life experiences and interests; links between the new knowledge acquired and practical applications are directly drawn; creativity plays a major role and all concepts are connected to each other, thus weaving the web of meaningful and relevant knowledge; higher-order thinking, critical and analytical thinking and problem-solving skills are developed and enhanced; learners feel free to question and discuss anything; there is a wide range of activities employed (Small, 2011, cited in Schweisfurth, 2013).

According to Schweisfurth's conceptualisation of learner-centred education, the role of teaching techniques and methods should not be treated in a reductionist sense (2013, p. 12), as if the mere adoption of collaborative methods or group work can automatically lead to active learning. The critical task is to incorporate the question of choosing methods within the wider framework of fostering dialogic teaching, as a set of practices element that can both empower learners and serve their rights of expression and participation as well as enhance their personal and social development (2015).

Finally, the fourth element which comprises the LCE practice as identified by Schweisfurth (2013, p. 12), refers to the range of possible relationships between educators and learners. She suggests that in the continuum that extends from less learner-centred to more learner-centred education, relationships between educators and learners can similarly be various extending in a continuum from authoritarian to democratic. The kind of relationship affects the amount of control that learners do or do not have over their learning. Democratic relationships between educator and learners though, do not suggest freedom of action in the learning environment (Davies et al., 2001, cited in Schweisfurth, 2013). This also resembles the andragogical notion of a climate of mutual respect, collaboration, mutual trust, supportiveness, openness, authenticity, and pleasure that is conducive to adult learning (Knowles, 1980).

All the four case studies conducted in the context of the research reported were designed to investigate educational practices in adult education programmes along these four elements that constitute LCE practice. In this respect, the studies managed to address the questions of the extent to which the adult education programmes for migrants are learner-centred and how this affects the migrant learners' ability to take control over their learning but also over their integration in local host societies.

6 Learner-Centred Education: A Comparative Approach

Studies of learner-centred education have highlighted for some time the global emergence of LCE as a 'travelling policy' (Ozga & Jones, 2006) widely promoted by international agencies and national governments and local innovators. This development strengthens the need for employing a comparative perspective in the study of travelling policies and global orthodoxies like LCE (Phillips & Schweisfurth, 2014).

For one thing, the comparative approach is crucial, first for exploring the complex global, regional, national and local dynamics that account for varying implementations (or non-implementations) of LCE at different settings, for appreciating the thin or wide differences in practices of implementation, and for assessing the successes, failures and needs for improvement of diverse LCE programmes. Even more, the study's primary focus on migration and migrants pushes further for the adoption of a comparative approach, as it can be useful in unravelling the convergences and divergences of different national and urban settings, where migrant adult learners live as citizens or as non-citizens and how these intersections shape their encounters with LCE programmes and the practices they generate as learners.

Finally, the reported comparative research and the cross-national collaboration that it foments can be useful in instigating self-reflection on the part of the researchers concerning their own assumption about LCE as a pedagogical approach, about LCE as a field of research, as well as on migration as a social process and migrant adult students as co-creators of educational programmes.

7 Outline of the Book

The book is arranged in three parts. All of the chapters in this edited collection reflect work from one comparative case study research project, with the exception of the Foreword by Peter Mayo and the final reflective chapter, 'Reading the migrants' world through emancipatory learner-centred education: Parting reflections on the micro pedagogical contexts' by Carmel Borg. We are grateful for their contributions to the book which frame the research data on adult education within the broader political context surrounding migrants in Europe. The chapters are written to stand on their own, but they also work together as they share a common methodology and conceptual framework. The two chapters in Part 1 inform all the chapters in Part 2; Part 3 synthesises the data presented in Part 2.

Part 1, 'Conceptualisation', provides detail about the context and conceptual framework of the project. In Chapter 1 Gravani and Slade provide an overview of the research project including the research objectives, methodology, design of the case studies, methods and an elaboration on the key elements of learner-centred education from Schweisfurth's (2013) framework – Motivation, Epistemology, Relationships and Techniques. These elements have been used in each case study and this chapter sets the context for the comparative investigation on learner-centred education (LCE) in programmes for adult migrants in Cyprus, Estonia, Malta and Scotland. Chapter 2, by Gravani and Hatzopoulos, explores LCE as a concept. The authors demonstrate the need for research in Adult Education investigating in what ways LCE is being enacted and implemented as a tool for social change across different contexts. The chapter ends by summarising some of the key challenges in thinking about LCE and adult education in the context of migration and migrant subjectivities.

Part 2, 'Contextualisation', presents the data from the two methods – a content analysis of policy documents and an empirical qualitative data from interviews and participant observation.

In Chapter 3, Brown, Gravani, Slade and Jõgi, present a 'Comparative cartography', content analysis work that was done prior to refining the case study design. This research project has grown out the collaboration on the International Master in Adult Education for Social Change (Erasmus Mundus). The comparative cartography mapped the following across the four countries: migration demographics, the political context and legal framework concerning migration, detail about the education sector, and the political context and legal framework concerning adult education. The cartography illuminated differences across the four countries including origins and ethnicities of migrant groups, legal and technocratic jargon, differentiation of types, categories and combinations of legal and irregular immigrants – which, in turn, also shed light on underlying discourses. It was through this comparative exercise that we decided to focus on language classes for migrants as the focus of the research across the four European countries. The cartography also grounds the research in the specifics of the four countries.

Chapters 4 through 7 present the findings on learner-centred education and adult education for migrants from each of the case studies. In Chapter 4 Jõgi and Karu present the Estonian case study. The focus of the Estonian case study was the Welcoming Programme funded by the European Social Fund (ESF), Asylum, Migration, and Integration Fund (AMIF) and the state budget. The target group of the Welcoming Programme are adult new immigrants arriving to live in Estonia from countries of the global South who have lived in Estonia less than five years and who have legitimate grounds for being in Estonia. The Estonian case study demonstrates that language learning and teaching practice are focused on learner-centredness, motivational and cultural aspects of learning. Teaching practice and relationships in the language programme are relevant and suitable for adults as learners. The lessons learned from the analysis of the Estonian case study is that practice targets learner-centredness more clearly than educational policy and there is a need to find possibilities for balancing and finding suitable solutions for expressing those aims in the legal regulations. Moreover, the issues facing adults with a migrant background and the value of LCE education should be more visible in the systematic preparation of adult educators and language teachers for foreigners in Estonia

Scotland is the focus of Chapter 5. In stark contrast to other areas of the UK, the Scottish Government actively encourages migration and welcomes migrants into the country. Migrants are valued and considered important to help mitigate against Scotland's declining population and an aging demographic. Slade and Dickson explore the delivery of English for Speakers of Other Languages' (ESOL) classes to a cohort of migrants living in an area of Glasgow which is densely populated and multi-cultural. The case study revealed that the migrant adult learner is at the core of delivery and the staff value, respect and encourage the learners regardless of cultural background or academic ability The service providers made no claims as to the learner-centredness of their approach to adult education, but the principles underpinned practice at all levels of delivery.

In Chapter 6, Brown reports on the Maltese case study which involved two language programmes formulated, managed, and provided by the state. Like in Scotland, the rationale of these language programmes reflected the broader national legal and policy framework endorsing the right to education for both refugees and migrants, as explicitly guaranteed by state laws such as The Refugees Act; an emphasis on embracing and promoting diversity in state educational policy (MEDE, 2012, 2014); the adoption of learner-centred education, as well as student-centred and cooperative learning in the National Curriculum Framework (NCF) (MEDE, 2012); and the provision of specialised training for adult educators. The Malta case study showed that learner-centred education was used as a tool for enhancing adult education for migrants, albeit with limitations that primarily stemmed from the high content and summative exam-oriented curriculum. The Malta case study also illuminated how adult migrant learners' challenges can be addressed by drawing on migrants' existing knowledge, although the evidence pointed to arbitrary and ad hoc self-developed teacher practices, rather than a formal standard policy. This lack of standardisation, however, allowed for the educator to draw on their knowledge and experience to design and implement engaging ad hoc learner-centred practices.

The case study from Cyprus is detailed in Chapter 7. Gravani, Hatzopoulos, and Papaioannou focused on the Greek language courses offered by state educational institutions. These programmes are open to all non-native Greek speakers, including EU citizens who may be working in Cyprus, but are mainly attended by migrants and may be the only courses in Cyprus where there is a significant participation of adult migrant learners in state-run educational institutions. This case study illustrated a very limited engagement with learner-centred practices as a tool for empowering migrant adult learners. In this respect, the absence of formal, standard policies on adult education for migrants in Cyprus is a crucial factor that precludes organised efforts towards the adoption of such LCE practices.

Part 3, 'Comparative analysis & reflections', consists of two chapters. Chapter 8 focuses on a comparative analysis of the four case studies presented in Part 2. Hatzopoulos, Gravani, Slade, Jõgi and Brown provide a critical interpretation of the data drawing on Schweisfurth's (2013) four conceptual axes of the LCE framework outlined in Chapter 1. The cross-case analysis of the findings revealed significant divergences amongst the four adult language programmes across the four countries in relation to the motivations of adult migrant learners for participating in adult education, the relevance of the curriculum and the extent to which the courses build on the migrant learners knowledges and skills, the utilisation of teaching techniques and methods within the wider framework of fostering dialogic teaching, and ultimately the degree of control that migrant learners do or do not have over their learning. Importantly, the status of adult migrant learners as non-citizens is a critical factor in terms of thinking about relevant and appropriate LCE educational practices. The precariousness of the migrants' residence status, ranging from asylum-seekers to refugees and from legal migrants and to sans-papiers, might significantly affect their motivations to participate in adult learning. These issues can perpetuate hierarchies between educators and learners or between learners, and it can play a deterring role in their capacity to take control of their learning. Engaging with this discussion on citizenship and precarious livelihoods and integrating it into learning activities is a critical step towards empowering migrant learners.

The book ends with a reflection on the overall research project by Carmel Borg, who argues that learning-centred education is not enough. In Chapter 9 he contextualises the project within current events – Black Lives Matter, the Covid-19 pandemic, the impact of individualising neoliberal policies, the rise right in European politics and the migration 'crisis' – and introduces a new concept, Emancipatory Learner-Centred Education (ELCE). ELCE represents a pedagogical ecology where education, perceived as a social act, meets the concept of the student as an independent and autonomous learner, challenging the 'the student as consumer' model. Seen through the lens of ELCE, Borg observes that the four case studies generally respond to the learners' needs on the ground while rarely problematising the ideological stance of the state in relation to the educational plight of migrants. ELCE, as a tool, helps to generate a deep analysis of the situation, seeking to transform education spaces into possibilitarian sites of liberatory practice, where individual needs become communal needs, where marginalised voices become centred voices in all aspects of the curricular experience, and where education for survival is transformed into education for active engagement with the world.

References

Brookfield, S. D. (1986). *Understanding and facilitating adult learning.* Jossey-Bass.
Fejes, A., & Wildemeersch, D. (2015). Editorial: Cartographies of research on adult education and learning. *European Journal for Research on the Education and Learning of Adults, 2*(2), 97–101.
Guo, S. (2013). *Transnational migration and lifelong learning, global issues and perspectives.* Routledge.
Guthrie, G. (2016). The failure of progressive paradigm reversal. *Compare: A Journal of Comparative and International Education, 47*(1), 62–76.
Kliebard, H. M. (1995). *The struggle for the American curriculum.* Routledge.
Knowles, M. S. (1980). *The modern practice of adult education: From pedagogy to andragogy* (2nd ed.). Cambridge Books.
Lattimer, H. (2015). Translating theory into practice: Making meaning of learner centred education frameworks for classroom-based practitioners. *International Journal of Educational Development, 45,* 65–76.
Ozga, J., & Jones, R. (2006). Travelling and embedded policy: The case of knowledge transfer. *Journal of Education Policy, 21*(1), 1–19.

Phillips, D., & Schweisfurth, M. (2014). *Comparative and international education: An introduction to theory, method, and practice.* A&C Black.

Saville, N. (2014). *How have we failed to integrate our migrant population?* Cambridge Assessment. https://www.cambridgeassessment.org.uk/insights/how-have-we-failed-to-integrate-our-migrant-population/

Schweisfurth, M. (2013). *Learner-centred education in international perspective: Whose pedagogy for whose development?* Routledge.

Schweisfurth, M. (2015). Learner-centred pedagogy: Towards a post-2015 agenda for teaching and learning. *International Journal of Educational Development, 40,* 259–266.

Scottish Government. (2014). *Adult learning in Scotland: Statement of ambition.* https://www.education.gov.scot/Documents/adult-learning-statement.pdf

CHAPTER 2

Learner-Centred Education: Debating Conceptual, Theoretical and Empirical Approaches

Maria N. Gravani and Pavlos Hatzopoulos

Abstract

The chapter attempts, first, to make sense of the conceptual confusions around the notion of LCE and its multiple implementations around the world and to suggest a possible way forward towards a cohesive understanding of LCE and its possible applications in the framework of the research study. Second, it documents the urgent need for substantial research in Adult Education investigating in what ways LCE is being enacted and implemented as a tool for social change across different contexts. Finally, it summarises some of the key challenges in thinking about LCE and adult education in the context of migration and migrant subjectivities. It is divided in eight short sections: the first presents an overview of the main theoretical debates around LCE and its associated concepts to better clarify the theoretical approach that is utilised by the research study; the second, briefly discusses the arguments supporting the promotion of LCE as a tool for social change; in the third, fourth, and fifth section, the text reviews some of the key academic studies and analyses on the implementation of LCE programmes and methods in the areas of child education, higher and adult education, respectively. The sixth and seventh sections highlight the existing limitations of the discourse on adult education and migration from both an academic and a policy perspective. Finally, the literature review concludes with a brief discussion of the approach endorsed by the research reported along the lines of a comparative study of LCE in the design and implementation of adult education programmes for migrants.

Keywords

learner-centred education – characteristics – critiques – social change – children's education – higher education – adult education – migration

1 Introduction

This literature review aimed to prepare the ground for the implementation of the case studies that were conducted in the context of the research titled: 'Evaluating Learner-centred Education (LCE) as a tool for social change in Adult Education (AE) programmes for migrants: A European comparative study'. It attempts, first, to make sense of the conceptual confusions around the notion of LCE and its multiple implementations around the world and to suggest a possible way forward towards a cohesive understanding of LCE and its possible applications in the framework of the research study. Second, it documents the urgent need for substantial research in Adult Education investigating in what ways LCE is being enacted and implemented as a tool for social change across different contexts. Finally, it summarises some of the key challenges in thinking about LCE and adult education in the context of migration and migrant subjectivities.

To organise this discussion, the text is divided in twelve short sections. Sections 2 to 5 present an overview of the main theoretical debates around learner-centred education and its associated concepts to better clarify the theoretical approach that is utilised by the research study. Section 6 briefly discusses the arguments supporting the promotion of LCE as a tool for social change. In Sections 7 to 9, the text reviews some of the key academic studies and analyses the implementation of LCE programmes and methods in the areas of child education, higher education, and adult education, respectively. Sections 10 to 13 highlight the existing limitations of the discourse on adult education and migration from both an academic and a European policy perspective. Finally, the chapter concludes with a brief discussion of the approach endorsed by the research reported along the lines of a comparative study of LCE in the design and implementation of adult education programmes for migrants.

2 LCE Concepts and Critique: The Theoretical Foundations of LCE

Learner-centred education has a long history as an idea, elements of which can even be traced back to ancient Greek philosophy and the teachings of Socrates (Schweisfurth, 2013). His explanatory remarks on the foundations of his method of teaching can be read as similar to these of an LCE advocate:

> I will only ask him, and not teach him, and he will share the inquiry with me; and do you watch and see if you find me telling or explaining

anything to him, instead of eliciting his opinion. (Brandes & Ginnis, 1996, p. 10, cited in Schweisfurth, 2013, p. 13)

The modern origins of LCE can be located to the development of the notion of child-centred education (CCE) which was influenced, in turn, by the works of European philosophers, such as Emile by Jean-Jacques Rousseau. CCE's scope is limited to primarily young learners, whereas LCE attempts to cover a wider array of educational practices. CCE was developed as a concept in the academic works of Johann Heinrich Pestalozzi, Friedrich Froebel, Maria Montessori and, in parallel, in the texts of several organisations such as the New Education Fellowship (NEF), the Froebel Society for the Promotion of the Kindergarten System, the National Froebel Union, and the Montessori Society in the UK (Cunningham, 2001, cited in Schweisfurth, 2013).

Western countries, such as the UK and the US, are considered to be the nests were LCE was nurtured and developed as a concept and articulated, subsequently, as a set of principles to be applied and implemented. In the US, John Dewey regarded as the 'patron saint' of progressivism, attempted to rethink education on the basis of its relationship to democracy, focusing particularly on the ways in which educational practices can be transformed into lived experience of democratic principles and ideals. Along this line of thinking, Dewey advocated for a flexible curriculum, arguing that fixed curricula narrow down the knowledge offered to learners and perpetuate their unawareness of democratic ideals (Dewey, 1916, cited in Schweisfurth, 2013).

In the UK, the child-centred approach to education gained significant attention with the publication of the *Plowden Report: Children and their Primary Schools* (Plowden, 1967), a text stressing that exploration, discovery, pleasure in learning, positive reinforcement and curriculum content when connected to the children's experiences and interests can become critical elements in positively shaping the learning environment. The report advocated, along these lines, curriculum adjustments in the direction of more flexibility in the design and use of educational materials and in the organisation of school programmes. Its recommendations were taken over by relevant educational authorities and policymakers and the report is thought to have contributed significantly to the reform of the educational system in England (Alexander, 2000, cited in Schweisfurth, 2013).

3 Defining LCE and Associated Concepts

According to Schweisfurth (2013), the field of study of LCE encompasses a plethora of associated terms such as 'progressive education', 'problem-based or enquiry-based learning' and 'child-centred learning', which are many times used interchangeably, although they might be linked with slightly different emphases and different target learners (p. 9). In this sense, this section will discuss LCE in the light of these eclectic affinities, recognising also that they are partly responsible for the difficulties in pinning down the conceptual of LCE. In chronological terms, the first of these concepts associated to LCE that gained prominence 'progressive education' as defined by John Dewey (1938) which advocated for:

> ... expression and cultivation of individuality; ... free activity; ... learning through experience; ... acquisition of new skills and techniques as a means of attaining ends which make direct vital appeal; ... making the most of all opportunities of present life; ... acquaintance with a changing world. (p. 223)

Paulo Freire (1972) introduced a problem-based approach to education in opposition to the traditional teacher-centred approach, which resembled, as he argued, the act of depositing money in a bank (Freire named it 'banking education'). In this traditional model of education, which seems to be 'suffering from narration sickness' (Freire, 1972, p. 71), teachers are the possessors of the absolute knowledge which they deposit into passive students. The traditional model serves, according to Freire, the needs and interests, not of the students at it should be, but of the oppressors who are trying to control the masses through fixed and controlled curriculums. Problem-based education is envisaged, instead, as a communicative and dialogic process, through which learners and educators simultaneously teach and are taught by critically reflecting on each other's views and the world around them. 'Students, as they are increasingly posed with problems relating to themselves in the world and with the world, will feel increasingly challenged and obliged to respond to that challenge' (Freire, 1972, p. 81).

Problem-centred teaching and learning approaches and practices were also promoted by the work of Malcolm Knowles (1980) as one of the five principles that underlie adult education, in the sense that adults, as learners, prefer problem-centred activities which would eventually assist them in realising the practical applications of what they have just learned. One of these principles introduced by Knowles concerned the self-directed educational needs of adults. The self-directed learning of adults was the kind of learning that was part of their everyday lives and the kind of learning whose organisation and systematisation came from the learners themselves rather than from a teacher or a fixed curriculum (Merriam, 2001). The concept of self-directed learning (SDL) was initially introduced by Tough (1967, 1971) who built on the work of Houle (1961) and was further developed by Knowles (1975, 1980). Knowles (1975) defined self-directed learning as:

a process in which individuals take the initiative, with or without the help of others, in diagnosing their learning needs, formulating learning goals, identifying human and material resources for learning, choosing and implementing appropriate learning strategies and evaluating learning outcomes (p. 18). The goal of the self-directed approach to education is to constitute learners, who can assume responsibility for their learning (Brockett & Hiemstra, 1991), who can critically reflect on themselves and the world (a process which suggests '… a prerequisite for autonomy in self-directed learning' Mezirow, 1985, p. 27), who can become socially active and who can engage in learning with expected emancipatory outcomes (Merriam, 2001). SDL is associated, as well, with the concept of deep learning, stipulating that the acquisition of knowledge suggests a continuous process of understanding as opposed to the concept of surface learning where learners passively accept knowledge and are only encouraged to reproduce it when necessary (Biggs, 1993). Robert Dearden (1975) also raised the question of learner autonomy in relation to self-directed learning. According to Dearden, 'a person is autonomous to the degree … that what he [sic] thinks and does, at least in important areas of his life, are determined by himself' (p. 343). Dearden's work on autonomy and education has many connotations with the approaches on 'self-directed learning' and 'child-centred learning', as both are constructed on the basis of the respect for the vulnerability and individuality of children or learners, although he seems more cautious in endorsing with their agenda on social change, as this is constructed on the basis of covert value judgements.

Drawing on these rich theoretical traditions, Schweisfurth (2013) proposes a working definition of LCE that was adopted in the reported study and presented in Chapter 1 of this book. She stresses, however, that her proposition should not be treated as the definitive elucidation of the concept and is intended more as an effort to pin down the often-elusive theoretical discourses around learner-centred education. She also argues that this definition might be of practical use, only if accompanied by a clear set of characteristics of LCE, which we further discuss below.

4   The Characteristics of LCE

LCE is not teacher-centred. 'Teachers are only of value because of learners: they serve no purpose without them' (Schweisfurth, 2013, p. 10). In a teacher-centred (TCE) learning environment, the teacher is in total control of the curriculum content, the pedagogical approach, the procedure, and the pace of learning and also the educational activities that will take place in the classroom (Schweisfurth, 2013). The expression often used to describe this method of teaching is 'chalk and talk': the teacher being the one who talks most, if not all, of the time, lecturing students and transmitting the knowledge that the fixed curriculum requires. On the contrary, in an LCE classroom, learners are given more responsibility and control over their learning, not only in relation to the content of the curriculum, but also in respect of their autonomy in findings new ways to learn. Meaningful interactions that promote collaboration amongst the learners and also between them and the teacher are essential elements of an LCE classroom, along with the emphasis and the value placed on the learners' personal interests, experiences and needs (Schweisfurth, 2013).

The content of a LCE curriculum is less tight and thus leaves room for a wide variety of activities to be employed during the learning process. This, though, does not suggest that an LCE curriculum is free from ideology, but that it is differentiated from the state's official narratives and the dominant discourses on the proper content educational content (Schweisfurth, 2013).

Another important aspect of LCE pertains to the construction of social relationships. Schweisfurth (2013) suggests that in analogy to the continuum that extends from less learner-centred to more learner-centred education, relationships between educators and learners can similarly be mapped in a continuum that ranges from authoritarian to democratic. The relationships between educator and learners directly shape the degree of control that learners have over their learning. The existence of democratic relationships between educator and learners, however, does not automatically guarantee the development of freedom of action in the learning environment (Davies et al., 2001, cited in Schweisfurth, 2013). In an LCE environment, learners are intrinsically motivated to engage in anything that is part of the learning process so that teachers do not need to constantly struggle for maintaining order (Schweisfurth, 2013).

Schweisfurth (2013) summarises, finally, some teaching and learning activities, such as group discussion, project- and problem-based learning, and scaffolding which have been associated with LCE as a technique group discussions and projects, problem-based learning and assisted learning always in terms of the needs of the learners. Adding to this approach, Small (2011, cited in Schweisfurth, 2013) has created a Teacher's Checklist to mark a learning environment where LCE is successfully implemented and practiced. This checklist suggests, among others, that in an LCE environment, learners are actively engaged in an experiential learning process; tasks, activities and projects are related to the learners' life experiences and interests; the curriculum content to be learned is approached in parallel with the learners' prior knowledge; links between the new knowledge acquired and practical applications are directly drawn; creativity plays a major role and all concepts are connected to each other, thus weaving the web of meaningful and relevant knowledge; higher-order thinking, critical and analytical thinking and problem-solving skills are developed and enhanced; learners feel free to question and discuss anything; there is a wide range of activities employed; curriculum is modified to accommodate learners' different needs and interests.

5 Critiques of Learner-Centred Education

A principal point of critique raised against learner-centred education (LCE) is the semantic confusion and/or contestability associated with the concept itself. Several authors have pointed out that LCE has not been particularly well defined and as a result the concept is often associated with confusion or misunderstanding (e.g., Guthrie, 2016; Lattimer, 2015; Kliebard, 1995). Although these types of arguments on conceptual shortcomings cannot be ignored altogether, they point towards the need for alternative ways of thinking on the dynamic character of pedagogical approaches and beyond unhelpful 'polarisations' of pedagogy into learner- and teacher-centred variants (Barrett, 2007; Schweisfurth, 2011).

There are two other main lines of criticism of LCE; those texts that attempt to politicise the concept and offer a subsequent analysis of its political underpinnings and these that raise the issue of universal applicability and discuss problems of implementation of LCE programmes in different social, cultural, and economic contexts.

Tabulawa's (2003) argument on the inherent association of LCE with neoliberal ideology and the globalisation of capitalism, particularly in relation to its implementation in post-colonial educational systems through Western financing has been quite influential. Starting from the observation that pedagogy is not value neutral and analysing how LCE has been implicated in the politics of international aid in sub-Saharan Africa, Tabulawa (2003) claims that:

> ... learner-centred pedagogy is a political artefact, an ideology, a worldview about how society should be organised. Because it is inherently ideological, justification of the pedagogy on educational grounds is questionable ... [T]he interest of aid agencies in the pedagogy is part of a wider design on the part of aid institutions to facilitate the penetration of capitalist ideology in periphery states, this being done under the

guise of democratisation. The hidden agenda ... is to alter the 'modes of thought' and practices of periphery states so that they look at reality in the same way(s) as those in core states. This process is being accelerated by the current wave of globalisation, which is a conservative neo-liberal ideology. (p. 10)

As Chisholm and Leyendecker (2008) have argued, however, this approach to the complex histories of the inception and implementation of LCE programmes in African states in the 1990s and 2000s is somewhat simplistic. They urge, instead, for a more nuanced understanding of LCE's role in the context of recent educational reforms in Sub-Saharan Africa, one that goes beyond its demonised representation as a tool of an imposed western neoliberal agenda. Their account recognises, thus, the influence of international pressures and the role of international organisations and NGOs in promoting the adoption of LCE by African countries, but is, at the same, more attuned to the role played by local histories, the local desires for improved schooling, the local divergences in the implementation of LCE-based educational reforms, the attractiveness of the social goals that have been attributed to LCE, and so on.

The existing divergences in the implementation of LCE in real-life educational contexts and the problems faced by implementing actors and agencies, is another other principal theme raised by critical texts. Schweisfurth (2013) recognises, for instance, the persistence of critical issues that need to be addressed by all LCE programme designers, mentioning questions such as:
– What the appropriate number of students in each class would be?
– Are teachers capable of successfully implementing LCE?
– Are there the appropriate resources at the learning environments which are to host LCE?
– Is the government capable of encouraging and eventually implementing LCE through policy?
– Are there specialised professionals who would supervise these implementation processes?

Going beyond these issues, which are somewhat limited in scope – however important and pertinent they are – it is perhaps even more crucial to insist on the necessity of additional research and further thinking about the implementation of LCE. Challenging the notion of LCE as a global educational strategy, Thomson (2013), for example, suggests that cultural translation is a precondition for the effective transfer of educational policies across different contexts. Along these lines, a more varying, diversified approach to the concept of LCE is necessary, an approach that does treat LCE as a monolithic body of knowledge and associated practices, but that acknowledges its dynamic, and even hybrid character, in that it interacts and merges with local educational practices under specific cultural and economic conditions.

6 LCE as a Tool of Social Change: The Three Narratives

Schweisfurth's approach underlines the inherent connection between the desire to adopt and implement LCE reforms and the vision of education as a field that can effect social change and promote democratic ideals. They key question, in this regard, is precisely the following: 'Whose pedagogy for whose development?', and with the concept of social change in mind, it could be rephrased as 'whose pedagogy for what type of social change?' In this light, it is useful at this point to examine more closely the main arguments that support the implementation of LCE programmes in different contexts.

Schweisfurth (2013) provides a helpful insight into the arguments that are used in the literature for justifying the choice of adopting LCE reforms. She organises this broad range of arguments in three different categories, or as she terms them, three different narratives: the cognitive, the emancipatory and the preparatory (Schweisfurth, 2013). The cognitive narrative rests on the argument that learners, be it children or adults, learn better when they can have some kind of control over their learning in the sense of adapting the curriculum, when possible, in a way that would be more appealing to them. The emancipatory narrative views LCE as a means of empowering learners to resist control from those in power who limit and construct education in ways that serve their interests. Lastly, the preparatory narrative approaches LCE as a tool for preparing learners for a highly turbulent future life. Drawing from postmodern theories, this perspective denounces fixed and essentialised knowledge and advocates for more 'flexible and personal forms of learning, and skills for metacognition and research' (Schweisfurth, 2013, p. 21).

The emancipatory narrative seems to resonate more closely to the notion of adopting LCE as an educational policy that can effect social change. Along these lines, the work of Paulo Freire and John Dewey seems to fit well in the framework of the emancipatory narrative (Schweisfurth, 2013; Heaney, 1996). One should be careful, not to make assertive, as there are usually significant overlaps among the three narratives. The focus of the emancipatory narrative lies mainly on understanding which pedagogies support or obstruct, democratic freedoms and subjugated knowledge. Heaney (1996) argues that 'adult education' emerged in the US in the light of hopes and aspirations for deepening democracy; with analysts and policymakers supporting a new type of education that can undermine formal schooling, by placing the creation of a democratic social order at the centre of the learning process.

Freire (1972) argued that the emancipatory approach to education will raise the learners' consciousness and fuel their fight against oppression, by inviting them to critically reflect on themselves, on their oppressors and on the world around them. Other critical works point out that schooling itself is a means for perpetuating inequalities and for preparing students for specific roles who are determined for them without them (Bowles & Gintis, 1976, cited in Schweisfurth, 2013). These arguments view schooling and education practices as constituting learners as passive recipients of knowledge which is transmitted by the educator, who is the sole possessor of it, describing a fixed, static reality, namely practices that resemble the action of making a deposit in a bank (Freire, 1972). These kinds of practices contribute to reproducing the subordination of the oppressed, as they prevent them from being awaken through education. An alternative practice of education that can subvert the traditional model, should, accordingly, envisage the relation between educators and learners as democratic and equitable. In this respect, the learning process will not be taking place by educators for students or by educators about students, but by educators in collaboration with students through creative and meaningful dialogue between the two groups (Freire, 1972).

7   LCE and Childrens' Education

As already mentioned, most of the literature concerning LCE takes issue with school classroom contexts and children teaching and learning. Evidence from research on children's education mainly reveals implementation failures of LCE programmes, which are then attributed to a range of factors: the lack of trust in policy proposals, incomprehensible policy discourse which makes it difficult for the teachers to truly understand LCE and which may then result in the lack of motivation of teachers and learners, and finally the insufficient of teacher training on LCE approaches (Schweisfurth, 2013; Harden et al., 1984).

Reviewing the evidence from a broad range of studies, Schweisfurth (2013) has reflected on some key lessons learnt from failures of implementing LCE programmes. First, educational policy remains primarily a reflection of the state's interest. As such its adoption of LCE and the implementation of educational programmes are usually adjusted to fit with the state's interests. Second, there is limited and non-generalisable evidence that LCE can generate benefits in certain contexts and conjunctures. The importance of cultural context cannot be disregarded in the sense that the global discourse of policy may sometimes be inappropriate or unfitting to certain cultural dynamics. Third, LCE as an approach involves many variables which, as mentioned above, are usually articulated within a global discourse. In this sense, due to different cultural contexts, policymakers, stakeholders, and educators, opt for some, and not all, of LCE's elements. Countries with intense social, cultural, and economic instability are the most likely to face LCE implementation difficulties, even though LCE may be simultaneously viewed in these unstable contexts as a lifeboat. Fourth, policymakers, stakeholders, educators, and learners often do not properly understand, or are not motivated enough to engage with the discourse on LCE, a phenomenon that significantly contributes to its implementation failure. Finally, as many studies suggest, LCE discourse and implementation efforts need to be consistent in all kinds of context, not only to strengthen educators and learners understanding and motivation but also to contribute to its much-desired implementation success (Schweisfurth, 2011; Thompson, 2013; Mtika & Gates, 2010).

8   LCE and Higher Education

Schweisfurth's work (2013) mainly focuses on how LCE has become a travelling educational policy in different contexts and the ways in which it has been implemented in the non-Western world with the expectation of reaping socio-economic benefits. In this light, her discussion touches also upon the theme of LCE and higher education, mainly in the form of reviewing the lives and work of overseas students who have come to study in western universities, encountering in this context LCE teaching and learning practices.

The evidence she draws on come from some studies that she participated in (Gu, 2007; Gu et al., 2010; Schweisfurth & Gu, 2009) and can provide a substantial insight regarding the experiences and views of international students who studied in UK universities. According to the findings from these studies, 'stress and cognitive dissonance' (Schweisfurth, 2013, p. 118) were the initial feelings of international university students who came from countries with mainly teacher-centred educational approaches. These studies revealed that the main concern of overseas university students, having attended some classes in the receiving country, was not that they would have to work and communicate in another language, but the 'adjustment to a learning environment that was more active and dialogic' (Schweisfurth, 2013, p. 118). In time, however, students not only felt less and less anxious, but they were also intrigued and motivated by the new learning practices, labelling academic achievement as their greatest experience and acquisition through their studies. Specifically, many students seemed to have altered their learning styles considerably, transferring their knowledge to their home countries with 'the vast majority' feeling 'permanently different from those around them at home, as a consequence of their studies' (Schweisfurth, 2013, p. 120).

There are other academic studies that have taken issue with LCE, or associated approaches, to different aspects or disciplines of the higher education system. Spencer and Jordan (1999) have discussed, for example, self-directed learning as a more effective approach in the field of medical education. Chastonay et al. (1996) also regards self-directed learning as the most efficacious approach to medical education in the sense that students learn through experience which thus assists them to connect new skills and knowledge both into their personal lives and experiences and into their professional skillset, which is the outcome desired after all. In the UK, the education committee of the GMC (General Medical Council) has suggested a shift in the approaches which were used for teaching undergraduate medical students (General Medical Council, 1993), consequently proposing more learner-centred and problem-based teaching and learning activities which would get the students acquainted with adult education principles and thus equip them better to serve the multifaceted needs of the community they are working in (Spencer & Jordan, 1999). The Medical Schools of Manchester, Glasgow, and Liverpool have adopted a completely learner-centred and problem-based curriculum, while the Medical Schools of St Bartholomew's, St George's, Birmingham, and Newcastle have introduced some learner-centred and problem-based activities into their generally traditional teacher-centred curriculum (Spencer & Jordan, 1999). In general, there are 150 Medicals Schools across the globe that have adopted learner-centred curricula. Nevertheless, there is no empirical evidence to prove that doctors, who have been educated and trained in a learner-centred curriculum, eventually become better, or even worse, doctors than others (Spencer & Jordan, 1999). Due to proven implementation difficulties, Woodward (1996) suggests that even a mixed method approach with a combination of traditional teacher-centred along with problem-based activities should be encouraged, especially if this can have a consistent evidence basis. He concludes that, despite the fact that teaching and learning approaches that promote and develop self-directed and problem-based learning are more likely to eventually be proven to be more effective, further research and evaluation on approaches should be conducted before they are implemented since there is no proof that one approach nurtures better doctors than the other (Woodward, 1996).

Pedley and Arber (1997) conducted a qualitative study on nursing university students in the UK to evaluate a student-centred module of learning. They conducted participant observation of one university module for nine months and subsequently provided a questionnaire to 135 students with fixed-choice and open-ended questions. The evidence that emerged from this study showed that the learners found significant benefits in SDL, such as autonomy, freedom of choice and responsibility over their learning. These conclusions, nevertheless, cannot be easily applied to other settings since there are many variables affecting the university programme investigated by Pedley and Arber.

Another study, by Liu et al. (2006), investigated the extent to which educators in a southwestern university in the US are incorporating LCE in their daily practice. Liu et al. observed that most instructors generally opted for more teacher-centred practices, a conclusion which are is confirmed by many other studies of the university system (Dupin-Bryant, 2004; Spoon & Schell, 1998; Conti, 2004, cited in Liu et al., 2006). Liu et al. (2006) also argued that the period of teaching in the US as well as the content of the subject taught were the main factors that influenced the instructors' option of more or less learner-centred approaches. Instructors who have taught longer in the US used more learner-centred approaches, maybe because of the growing interest in these approaches in developed countries like the UK and the US. The same applied to the instructors of language courses, maybe because language teachers think of themselves mainly as facilitators of knowledge in contrast to other courses where teachers may think of themselves as the sole possessors of knowledge. The explanation of why university teachers usually employed teacher-centred practices may lie in Harden's (1984) view that LCE, SDL and problem-based learning approaches are often implemented without being fully understood. In this sense, a teacher's professed adherence to LCE principles may suggest a wish list rather than a concrete activity (Liu et al., 2006).

Finally, Emes and Cleveland-Innes (2003) have provided useful reflection on how to think on the dynamics of LCE and higher education in the light of the contemporary transformations of the university. From the 1990s onwards, universities at a global scale have begun to adopt business-like strategies to adapt to highly rapid developments in communication and technology, with the purpose of becoming more competitive in the globalised market of higher education. The new strategies employed by universities have regularly included the move from traditional learning methods and processes to innovative approaches that can encourage active learning and student's increased participation in the learning process. To accomplish this task, the notion of a learner-centred curriculum has been proposed (Emes & Cleveland-Innes, 2003), a term denoting that learners should become active participants in the curriculum design and thus develop competences that contribute to their educational attainment. These competences include critical thinking, creative thinking, problem analysis, effective communication skills, abstract reasoning, insight in the generation of knowledge, assessment skills and so on (Emes & Cleveland-Innes, 2003).

9   LCE and Adult Education

Learner-centred approaches have primarily been investigated by the existing literature in the context of educational programmes targeting young learners and implemented within school classrooms. Still, some of the key figures in the formation of LCE, like Paulo Freire, strived to develop an emancipator vision of adult education, based on the notion that adult learners can be empowered through education to engage critically and dialogically with existing power relations in their world and to discover how to participate in its transformation (Mayo, 1999; Coben, 2013).

Based on these principles, initiatives such as the adult literacy projects that were introduced by the Workers' Party (PT) local government in Sao Paulo during the 1980s and supervised by Freire himself, may had a local reach, but gained a global influence. Based on this experience and drawing from Freire's work, the non-governmental organisation (NGO), Action Aid, initiated the 'Reflect' programme as an innovative approach to adult learning and social change.[1] Utilised by over 500 organisations in over 70 countries worldwide, these projects utilises a series of participatory methods for linking the literacy acquisition process with individual and community empowerment-strengthening the capacity of millions of people, particularly women, to secure their basic rights (Riddell, 2001).

Discussing the achievements of these initiatives, and mentioning other successful grassroots adult education projects, Schweisfurth (2013) argues that adult learning environments can constitute a more fertile environment for the implementation of LCE. To further support her argument, Schweisfurth discusses the similarities of the influential concept of andragogy as the pedagogy of adult education, as developed by Malcolm Knowles, to LCE. Knowles introduced the notion of andragogy, as 'the art and science of teaching adults' (1980, p. 43). He further developed this definition of andragogy with five principles that should underlie adult teaching and learning practices: an adult learner is self-directed (1) and reflects on the learning process his or her own life experiences (2); an adult's learning needs are interwoven with the social context he or she is living in (3) and this is why adult learners prefer problem-centred education, the usefulness and practicality of which should be clearly obvious (4); finally, adult learners are intrinsically rather than extrinsically motivated (5), which implies that their will to learn emanates as a personal autonomous choice (Knowles, 1980).

Schweisfurth (2013) concludes her discussion on LCE and adult education by highlighting some of the key lessons learnt from the successful implementation of LCE programmes. In sort, one positive factor has to do with the tendency of adult programmes to instigate educational practices that are cultural significant and appropriate to participants. Another aspect involves the observation that adult learners tend to adapt well to the adoption of new pedagogies and to respond creatively to the challenges that these new methods pose in relation to transforming their understanding of what learning process should be like and what it should do. Finally, a positive role is played by the fluidity of the curriculum and the dialogic process between educators and learners through which it is constructed, enabled by the will of adult learners to take responsibility for their learning.

10   Migration and Adult Education

The existing literature on adult education and migration is far from extensive. In a schematic categorisation, one can discern between studies that endorse the main axes of the existing framework of adult education provision for migrants in Europe and elsewhere, intending to examine its performance or limitations and other critical texts that aim to highlight the processes, subjectivities, social relations that are neglected, silenced, or undervalued by the contemporary adult education programmes for migrants. In both cases, existing studies treat pedagogy as a marginal theme, which is rarely addressed and, as a result, LCE does not play a significant role in the contemporary debates on adult education and migration.

In the European context, the dominant framework of adult education and migration rests on three principal propositions: (1) Adult education as policy and practice is inherently linked to the politics of integration of migrants in European societies; (2) Adult education programmes are designed on the basis of the primary need for migrants to learn the host country's language; and (3) Migrants form a targeted social group, especially because they are deemed to suffer from low educational attainment and low participation rates.

Several policy reports or academic analyses tend to explore statistical evidence from varied sources to discuss aspects of the above propositions. For instance, Eurydice report on Adult Education and Training in Europe (2015) indicates, based on Eurostat data, that on average foreign-born participants in adult education programmes suffer more from low educational achievement than the wider adult population, while it stresses that these differences are far more acute in southern European states (Greece, Spain, Italy, Malta, Portugal and France) (p. 19). A similar conclusion is drawn by the OECD's international survey of adult skills (PIAAC)[2]; the survey test results, covering more than 40 countries, show that foreign-born participants have significantly lower proficiency scorers in literacy and numeracy than those born in the countries of residence (OECD, 2019). Other reports highlight the limited migrant access to adult education programmes and the social, economic, and cultural barriers that sustain it, or the low participation rates and high drop-out rates by migrants in adult language courses across European countries, while they might also suggest strategies or measures for reversing this trend, such as ICT-based learning (Desjardins et al., 2006; European Commission, 2011).

In the same context, there are few academic analyses that make usually similar observations based on focused case studies or other qualitative research. Indicatively, the problem of the accessibility of adult education programmes to migrants is tackled by a case study on 'adult education centres in Northern Greece' pursued by Papastamatis and Panitsidou (2009) and another case study on adult language education in Catalonia conducted by Pujolar (2010). A supplementary concern of other academic studies is the investigation of the intersections between adult education programmes of migrants and the politics of integration at the European, regional, national, or local level. In this regard, observations regarding issues of accessibility, the training curriculum, and the educational achievement of adult migrant learners are discussed in relation to the challenge they pose for enhancing social inclusion, civic participation and labour market integration (e.g. Buiskool et al., 2009; Arnesen & Lundahl, 2006).

Critical works on migration and adult education attempt to undermine the foundational assumptions of the above framework, by bringing to light the power relations and social processes that it silences. One theme that is neglected by the mainstream discourse on adult education and migration is gender. Cuban (2010) criticises this omission, which forces, as she argues, adult women migrant learners to become invisible to adult education systems. As a result, adult education programmes rarely meet the needs of migrant women, contributing effectively to the reproduction of gender inequalities in the education system and the labour market. Another neglected dimension, taken over by some authors is the existence of multiple discrimination faced by migrants within education systems and in the wider social system (e.g., Pisani, 2012; Stange & Lundberg, 2014). Along these lines, the dominant discourse on adult education and migration does not acknowledge, nor it attempts to redress, the status of (at least some) migrant learners as non-citizens, as subject who do not enjoy 'the right to have rights' (Martin, 2003).

11 European Policies on Adult Education and Migration

The field of education is still considered as a politically sensitive area in the context of stimulating further European integration. The education systems of European states are characterised, as a result, by a significant degree of autonomy and varying disparities in their organisation, orientation and professed goals (Ballas et al., 2012). Lifelong learning has been one of the main concepts that has served as a point of reference of efforts for aligning EU policies on education and training in the late 1990s–early 2000s (Pépin, 2007). These efforts were also reflected in the proliferation of new policy concepts such as the 'European Area of Lifelong Learning' that were promulgated by the European Commission at the time (EC, 2001). Following this shift, adult education gradually formed a focal policy area in the framework of European cooperation on education; new public programmes were initiated to shape this field, accompanied by the introduction of specific policy targets in relation to access and educational outcomes, as well as the introduction of monitoring mechanisms and measuring regimes for coming to grips with developments in adult education.

The latest major EU policy document for the promotion of adult education is the 'Council Resolution on a renewed European agenda for adult learning', adopted in December 2011. This agenda is inherently associated with the broader economic and social strategy of the European Union (the ten-year spanning Europe 2020) which sets specific targets for education, particularly due to its perceived vital contribution in raising employability and reducing poverty (EC, 2011). The emphasis of the current EU strategy on adult learning is placed on concepts such as 'adaptation to change' (especially in relation to contemporary transformations in the labour market), the 'up-skilling' and 're-skilling' of labour, and the development of the 'skills' and '(key) competences' of learners. 'social inclusion' and 'participation' are also incorporated relatively high on the agenda, remaining, however, in a position of externality to the educational process itself; essentially excluded, in other words, from considerations on how adult learning is organised and structured.

12 Migration in the EU Agenda on Adult Learning

The European agenda on adult education addresses migration as a social process, and migrants living within the EU. Migrants living in EU states are designated as one of the currently, low-skilled social groups that need to be specifically targeted by proposed adult learning initiatives, along with other groups that lag behind, such as early school leavers, young people not in education, employment or training (NEETs), as well as people with disabilities and older adults. Adult learning is also considered as a vital field of action for strengthening social inclusion and active participation for groups that are deemed to be disadvantaged and at risk of poverty and social exclusion, and here, migrants are specifically mentioned again along with the Roma and so-called 'other disadvantaged groups' (EC, 2011).

In terms of specific policy measures, the agenda raises the importance of 'improving access' to adult learning programmes for migrants as well as for Roma and other disadvantaged groups, while a final specific reference is made for the significance of providing adult learning opportunities for refugees and people seeking asylum, especially concerning host country-language learning courses.

13 Pedagogy in the EU Agenda on Adult Learning

The European agenda on adult learning is essentially silent on the question of pedagogy, in general, and is seemingly neutral to the promotion of particular pedagogical approaches. In the whole text of the 'Renewed European agenda for adult learning', there is merely one fleeting reference to pedagogy as a vital element of the educational process, in the form of stating the need of developing 'new pedagogies and creative learning environments' in the field of adult education. These 'new pedagogies' are not further specified in this text; they are, merely, conceived as inherently connected to the acquisition of transversal key competence, the enhancement of the role of cultural organisations, civil society, and sporting organisations in the provision of non-formal and informal adult learning programmes, and the better use of Information and Communication Technologies (ICT) in these programmes.

14 Conclusion: A Comparative Study on LCE and Migrant Education

The discussion so far has shown that we are deprived of research in the area of Adult Education investigating in what ways LCE is being enacted and implemented, while no comparative research has been done on the extent to which LCE is used in adult education as a tool for social change across different contexts.

It has also highlighted the global emergence of LCE as a 'travelling policy' (Ozga & Jones, 2006) widely promoted by international agencies and national governments and local innovators. This development strengthens the need for employing a comparative perspective in the study of travelling policies and global orthodoxies like LCE (Phillips & Schweisfurth, 2014).

For one thing, the comparative approach is crucial, first for exploring the complex global, regional, national and local dynamics that account for varying implementations (or non-implementations) of LCE at different settings, for appreciating the thin or wide differences in practices of implementation, and for assessing the successes, failures and needs for improvement of diverse LCE programmes. Even more, the project's primary focus on migration and migrants pushes further for the adoption of a comparative approach, as it can be useful in unravelling the convergences and divergences of different national and urban settings, where migrant adult learners live as citizens or as non-citizens and how do these intersect with their encounters with LCE programmes and the practices they generate as learners.

Finally, the proposed comparative research and the cross-national collaboration that it foments can be useful in instigating self-reflection on the part of the researchers concerning their own assumption about LCE as a pedagogical approach, about LCE as a field of research, as well as on migration as a social process and migrant adult students as co-creators of educational programmes.

Notes

1 See the official website of the programme for an overview of all past and present projects around the world: https://www.eldis.org/document/A13011 (accessed July 16, 2020).
2 See http://www.oecd.org/skills/piaac (accessed July 16, 2020) on more information and data of the PIAAC survey. The highest differences in literacy skills between the two groups are observed in Sweden and Finland, with the Netherlands, Norway, Denmark, the Flemish Community of Belgium, and Germany following suit.

References

Arnesen, A. L., & Lundahl, L. (2006). Still social and democratic? Inclusive education policies in the Nordic welfare states. *Scandinavian Journal of Educational Research, 50*(3), 285–300.

Ballas, D., Lupton, R., Kavroudakis, D., Hennig, B., Yiagopoulou, V., Dale, R., & Dorling, D. (2012). *Mind the gap: Education inequality across EU regions.* NESSE Network of Experts. http://www.nesse.fr/nesse/activities/reports/activities/reports/mind-the-gap-1

Barrett, A. (2007). Beyond the polarization of pedagogy: Models of classroom practices in Tansanian primary school. *Comparative Education, 43*(2), 273–294.

Baynham, M., Roberts, C., Cooke, M., Simpson, J., Ananiadou, K., Callaghan, J., McGoldrick, J., & Wallace, C. (2007). *Effective teaching and learning ESOL*. National Research and Development Centre for Adult Literacy and Numeracy. http://dera.ioe.ac.uk/22304/1/doc_3341.pdf

Biggs, J. (1993). What do inventories of students' learning-process really measure? A theoretical review and clarification. *British Journal of Educational Psychology, 63*(1), 3–19.

Boud, D., & Feletti, G. (1991). *The challenge of problem-based learning*. Kogan Page.

Brockett, R. B., & Hiemstra, R. (1991). *Self-direction in adult learning: Perspectives on theory research, and practice*. Routledge.

Buiskool, B. J., Lakerveld, J. V., & Broek, S. (2009). Educators at work in two sectors of adult and vocational education: An overview of two European research projects. *European Journal of Education, 44*(2), 145–162.

Chastonay, P., Brenner, E., Peel, S., & Guilbert, J.-J. (1996). The need for more efficacy and relevance in medical education. *Medical Education, 30*(4), 235–238.

Chisholm, L., & Leyendecker, R. (2008). Curriculum reform in post-1990 sub-Saharan Africa. *International Journal of Educational Development, 28*, 195–205.

Coben, D. (2013). *Radical heroes: Gramsci, Freire and the politics of adult education*. Routledge.

Confessore, S. J., & Kops, W. J. (1998). Self-directed learning and the learning organization: Examining the connection between the individual and the learning environment. *Human Resource Development Quarterly, 9*(4), 365–375.

Cuban, S. (2010). Examining the feminisation of migration. *Gender and Education, 22*(2), 177–191.

Dearden, R. (1975). Autonomy and education. In R. Dearden, P. Hirst, & R. Peters (Eds.), *Education and the development of reason* (pp. 333–345). Routledge and Kegan Paul.

Desjardins, R., Rubenson, K., & Milana, M. (2006). *Unequal chances to participate in adult learning: International perspectives*. UNESCO, International Institute for Educational Planning. https://files.eric.ed.gov/fulltext/ED499629.pdf

Dewey, J. (1916). *Democracy and education*. MacMillan.

Dewey, J. (1938). *Experience and education*. Collier.

Emes, C., & Cleveland-Innes, M. (2003). A journey toward learner-centered curriculum. *The Canadian Journal of Higher Education, 33*(3), 47–69. https://www.researchgate.net/publication/268422617_A_Journey_Toward_Learner-Centered_Curriculum

European Commission. (2001). *Making a European area of lifelong learning a reality* (Communication from the Commission, 21.11.01 COM (2001) 678 final). Author. http://aei.pitt.edu/42878/1/com2001_0678.pdf

European Commission. (2011). *Language learning by adult migrants: Policy challenges and ICT responses*. http://languageforwork.ecml.at/Portals/48/documents/lfw-web_item-16_eu_lang-learn-migrants-ict.pdf

European Commission/EACEA/Eurydice. (2015). *Adult education and training in Europe: Widening access to learning opportunities.* https://op.europa.eu/en/publication-detail/-/publication/aaeac7ed-7bad-11e5-9fae-01aa75ed71a1/language-en

European Women's Lobby. (2007). *Equal rights, equal voices: Migrant women in the European Union.* https://www.womenlobby.org/IMG/pdf/1817_BR_en_MP01LR.pdf

Freire, P. (1972). *Pedagogy of the oppressed.* Penguin.

Gerber, R., Lankshear, C., Larsson, S., & Svensson, L. (1995). Self-directed learning in a work context. *Education + Training, 37*(8), 26–32. http://www.emeraldinsight.com/doi/pdfplus/10.1108/00400919510096952

Gu, Q. (2007). *Teacher development: The role of knowledge and context.* Bloomsbury.

Gu, Q., Schweisfurth, M., & Day, C. (2010). Learning and growing in a 'foreign' context: Intercultural experiences of international students. *Compare: A Journal of Comparative Education, 40*(1), 7–23. https://doi.org/10.1080/03057920903115983

Guthrie, G. (2011). *The progressive fallacy in developing countries: In favour of formalism.* Springer.

Harden, R. M., Sowden, S., & Dunn, W. R. (1984). Educational strategies in curriculum development: The SPICES model. *Medical Education, 18*(4), 284–297. http://onlinelibrary.wiley.com/doi/10.1111/j.1365-2923.1984.tb01024.x/full

Heaney, T. (1996). *Adult education for social change: From center stage to the wings and back again.* ERIC Publications. http://eric.ed.gov/?id=ED396190

Houle, C. O. (1961). *The inquiring mind.* University of Wisconsin Press.

Jackson, S. (2010). Learning through social spaces: Migrant women and lifelong learning in post-colonial London. *International Journal of Lifelong Education, 29*(2), 237–253. http://www.tandfonline.com/doi/abs/10.1080/02601371003616657

Kliebard, H. (1995). *The struggle for the American curriculum, 1893–1958* (2nd ed.). Routledge.

Knowles, M. S. (1975). *Self-directed learning: A guide for learners and teachers.* Follett Publishing.

Knowles, M. S. (1980). *The modern practice of adult education: From pedagogy to androgogy* (2nd ed.). Cambridge Books.

Lattimer, H. (2015). Translating theory into practice: Making meaning of learner centred education frameworks for classroom-based practitioners. *International Journal of Educational Development, 45*, 65–76.

Liu, R., Qiao, X., & Liu, Y. (2006). A paradigm shift of learner-centered teaching style: Reality or illusion? *Arizona Working Papers in SLAT, 13*, 77–91. https://journals.uair.arizona.edu/index.php/AZSLAT/article/view/21276

Martin, P. (2003). *Bordering on control: Combating irregular migration in North America and Europe.* International Organization for Migration. https://publications.iom.int/system/files/pdf/mrs_13_2003.pdf

Mayo, P. (1999). *Gramsci, Freire and adult education: Possibilities for transformative action.* Zed Books.

Merriam, S. B. (2001). Andragogy and self-directed learning: Pillars of adult learning theory. *New Directions for Adult and Continuing Education, 89*, 3–14.

Mezirow, J. (1985). A critical theory of self-directed learning. In S. Brookfield (Ed.), *Self-directed learning: From theory to practice. New directions for continuing education* (Vol. 25, pp. 17–30). http://onlinelibrary.wiley.com/doi/10.1002/ace.36719852504/pdf

Milburn, F. (1996). Migrants and minorities in Europe: Implications for adult education and training policy. *International Journal of Lifelong Education, 15*(3), 167–176. http://www.tandfonline.com/doi/abs/10.1080/0260137960150303

Mtika, P., & Gates, P. (2010). Developing learner-centred education among secondary trainee teachers in Malawi: The dilemma of appropriation and application. *International Journal for Educational Development, 30*, 396–404. https://doi.org/10.1046/j.1365-2648.1997.1997025405.x

Norman, G. R. (1988). Problem-solving skills, solving problems and problem-based learning. *Medical Education, 22*(4), 279–286. http://onlinelibrary.wiley.com/doi/10.1111/j.1365-2923.1988.tb00754.x/pdf

OECD. (2019). *Technical report of the survey of adult skills (PIAAC)* (3rd ed.). Author. https://www.oecd.org/skills/piaac/publications/PIAAC_Technical_Report_2019.pdf

O'Shea, E. (2003). Self-directed learning in nurse education: A review of the literature. *Journal of Advanced Nursing, 43*(1), 62–70. http://onlinelibrary.wiley.com/doi/10.1046/j.1365-2648.2003.02673.x/pdf

Ozga, J., & Jones, R. (2006). Travelling and embedded policy: The case of knowledge transfer. *Journal of Education Policy, 21*(1), 1–17.

Papastamatis, A., & Panitsides, E. (2009). The aspect of 'accessibility' in the light of European lifelong learning strategies. *International Journal of Lifelong Education, 28*(4), 335–351. https://doi.org/10.1080/02601370902799143

Pedley, G. E., & Arber, A. (1997). Nursing students' response to self-directed learning: An evaluation of a learning process applying Jarvis' framework. *Journal of Advanced Nursing, 25*, 405–411. https://doi.org/10.1046/j.1365-2648.1997.1997025405.x

Pépin, L. (2007). The history of EU cooperation in the field of education and training: How lifelong learning became a strategic objective. *European Journal of Education, 42*(1), 121–132.

Phillips, D., & Schweisfurth, M. (2014). *Comparative and international education: An introduction to theory, method, and practice*. A&C Black.

Pisani, M. (2012). Addressing the 'citizenship assumption' in critical pedagogy: Exploring the case of rejected female sub-Saharan African asylum seekers in Malta. *Power and Education, 4*(2), 185–195. https://doi.org/10.2304/power.2012.4.2.185

Plowden, M. (1967). *Plowden report: Children and their primary schools: A report of the central advisory council for education (England)*. HMSO. http://www.educationengland.org.uk/documents/plowden/

Pujolar, J. (2010). Immigration and language education in Catalonia: Between national and social agendas. *Linguistics and Education, 21*(3), 229–243. doi:10.1016/j.linged.2009.10.004

Riddell, A. (2001). *A review of 13 evaluations of REFLECT*. ActionAid. https://www.actionaid.org.uk/sites/default/files/doc_lib/192_1_evaluation.pdf

Schweisfurth, M. (2011). Learner-centred education in developing country contexts: From solution to problem? *International Journal of Educational Development, 31*, 425–432. http://www.sciencedirect.com/science/article/pii/S0738059311000472

Schweisfurth, M. (2013). *Learner-centred education in international perspective: Whose pedagogy for whose development?* Routledge.

Schweisfurth, M., & Gu, Q. (2009). Exploring the experiences of international students in UK higher education: Possibilities and limits of interculturality in university life. *Intercultural Education, 20*(2), 463–473. http://www.tandfonline.com/doi/abs/10.1080/14675980903371332#.VlWqy3YrLIU

Senge, P. M. (1990). *The fifth discipline: The art and practice of the learning organization*. Doubleday.

Spencer, J. A., & Jordan, R. K. (1999). Learner centred approaches in medical education. *British Medical Journal, 318*(7193), 1280–1283. http://www.ncbi.nlm.nih.gov/pmc/articles/PMC1115656/

Strange, M., & Lundberg, A. (2014). Education as hospitality. *Peace Review: A Journal of Social Justice, 26*, 201–208.

Tabulawa, R. (2003). International aid agencies, learner-centred pedagogy and political democratisation: A critique. *Comparative Education, 39*(1), 7–26. http://www.tandfonline.com/doi/abs/10.1080/03050060302559#.VlHPS3YrLIU

Thompson, P. (2013). Learner-centred education and 'cultural translation'. *International Journal of Educational Development, 33*, 48–58. http://www.sciencedirect.com/science/article/pii/S0738059312000284

Tough, A. (1967). *Learning without a teacher*. Ontario Institute for Studies in Education.

Tough, A. (1971). *The adult's learning projects: A fresh approach to theory and practice in adult learning*. Ontario Institute for Studies in Education.

Woodward, C. A. (1996). Problem-based learning in medical education: Developing a research agenda. *Advances in Health Science Education: Theory and Practice, 1*(1), 83–94. http://link.springer.com/article/10.1007/BF00596231

PART 2
Contextualisation

∴

CHAPTER 3

Comparative Cartography of Adult Education for Migrants in Cyprus, Estonia, Malta and Scotland

Maria Brown, Maria N. Gravani, Bonnie Slade and Larissa Jõgi

Abstract

This chapter's discussion critically reviews legislative and policy practices in Cyprus, Scotland, Malta and Estonia related to the provision of adult migrant education. The cartography maps several commonalities – such as diverse immigrant cohorts, state expenditure on education, adult education provision by public, private and civil society entities, and language programmes of comparable level; as well as differences – such as the origins and ethnicities of migrant groups, differences in the legal and technocratic jargon. Additionally, the four countries featured diverse policy responses to adult education for migrants, ranging from inclusive visible policy to non-existent – a key finding also because it was not aligned with geographical location. On the other hand, the comparative analysis illuminates the absence of a salient placeholder across the four countries – namely, a concrete policy on adult education for migrants. This chapter also flags the unavailability of data (or of reliable data) in all the four countries on participation rates of migrants in adult education programmes, suggesting the case studies informing the book's broader discussion unfolded in a relative policy vacuum.

Keywords

adult teaching and learning – charting/mapping policies and practices – educational policy – migrant education – policy analysis – policy vacuum

1 Introduction

This comparative cartography contextualises the case studies conducted for the research project, 'Evaluating learner-centred education (LCE) as a tool for social change in adult education (AE) programmes for migrants: A European comparative study'. Using a comparative approach, five themes steered the analysis of engagement with migration and migrants in the four participating countries, namely – (1) salient demographics of migration in each country; (2) the political context and legal framework concerning migration in each country; (3) resources and human capacity deployed in the education sector of each country; (4) the political context and legal framework concerning adult education in each country; and (5) the criteria guiding the sampling of the adult (migrant) learning programmes featuring in the case studies. This chapter's discussion is organised in line with these five themes.

2   Migration Demographics

During the execution of the research project informing this book, the overall share of non-nationals stood below 20% in the respective resident populations across the four countries. Cyprus, Malta and Scotland featured positive net migration, with higher immigrant (than emigrant) influxes (Eurostat, 2019a; National Records of Scotland [NRS], 2019). Cyprus had the highest relative share of non-nationals (Statistical Service, 2018) followed by Estonia, Malta and Scotland respectively (Eurostat, 2019a). Despite being the only one of the four countries with a negative net migration (Statistics Estonia (ES), 2019), Estonia had the highest relative share of non-nationals with non-EU citizenship. Indeed, this was the case for most non-nationals residing in Estonia (Eurostat, 2019a).

A closer demographic scrutiny revealed that, at the time of the project Cyprus has been experiencing positive net migration since 1983, save for the period 2012–2015. Cyprus received 21,306 long-term immigrants comprising Cypriots and foreigners arriving for settlement or for temporary employment for 1 year or more, compared to 17,391 immigrants in 2016 (Statistical Service, 2018). At the time of the study, the five most common EU countries of birth outside Cyprus were the United Kingdom (UK), Romania, Bulgaria, Greece, and Poland; whilst the five most common non-EU countries of birth outside of Cyprus but residents in Cyprus were Georgia, Russia, Philippines, Sri Lanka, and Vietnam (Statistical Service, 2011).

In Scotland, the number of immigrants exceeded the number of emigrants by 20,900 between mid-2017 and mid-2018. Of these, 10,000 immigrated to Scotland from the rest of the UK, whilst 10,900 from overseas. These figures marked a decrease in immigration since the June 2016 Brexit referendum, primarily because of decreased immigration from non-UK countries and increased emigration. Notwithstanding, migration is considered to be the driver of Scotland's growth in population. More than half of the people moving to Scotland were aged 16 to 34 years in the year to mid-2018, which, on average is a younger cohort than the general population (NRS, 2019).

Emigration also emerged to be a highly significant phenomenon in Estonia. At the time of the study, population was predicted to be 8% smaller by 2040 (ES, 2019) due to emigration, but this was revised in the 2019 projection due to increase in immigration by about 1,500 persons per year (ES, 2019). On a much bigger scale, immigration is also on a steady increase in Malta where immigrants from different parts of the world reach Maltese shores by means of regular and irregular channels. The smallest and most densely populated EU Member State has shifted to 'a recipient of migrants since the turn of the millennium' (Miljanic Brinkworth, 2016, p. 103). Over the years the percentage of foreign nationals has increased exponentially (NSO, as cited in Environment & Resources Authority (ERA), 2018, p. 19). Skilled and qualified migration, both incoming and outgoing, increased with Malta's EU membership yielding influxes from Eastern Europe and elsewhere, as well as transnational networks of Maltese working in EU institutions (International Organization for Migration (IOM), 2018). During 2016 Malta received 17,100 immigrants (Eurostat, 2018a) placing Malta second in the EU28 with 38.1 immigrants per 1000 inhabitants – more than eight times the EU average of 4.6.

Heterogeneity in push and pull factors, as well as income and status of immigrants based in each of the case studies could be inferred from immigrants' origins, which also features commonalities and differences across the four case studies. By way of example, the case studies found significant migration from the UK (England, Northern Ireland and Wales) to Scotland, Malta and Cyprus; whilst all the four countries were found to be receiving immigrants from Eastern European countries including Poland, Serbia, Bulgaria and Ukraine. Unsurprisingly, geo-politics played a strong role in the immigrant population and related ethnic diversities of the four case studies, as exemplified by the both the Cypriot case (receiving migrants from Greece), and Estonia (receiving migrants from Belarus, Russia, and Ukraine). In Malta, 'boat arrivals' mostly of Sub-Saharan asylum seekers and migrants between 2002 and 2013 declined substantially over the last few years (IOM, 2018). There is concern about 'volume and unpredictability of the arrivals, as well as the possible lack of social integration of mainly undocumented immigrants' (Miljanic Brinkworth, 2016, p. 103). Responses include resettlement, counter-trafficking projects, relocation and assisted voluntary return, and reintegration (AVRR) programmes (IOM, 2018).

3   Migration: Political Context and Legal Framework

The *Amsterdam Treaty* transferred competences on immigration and asylum matters to common jurisdiction. Notwithstanding, common control of immigration flows was unequivocally rejected by both the Amsterdam and Lisbon Treaty for reasons rooted in the political terrain and in the difficulty of finding a common immigration (economic) model. The fact that immigration policy is assigned to national governments is rooted in the complexity of this politically sensitive issue (Mistri & Orcalli, 2015). Comparative research on post-war immigration politics and policy became a stable research stream only 30 years ago and barely took off until the 1990s. The increased interest of scholars has followed the increase in the importance of immigration issues. Recent research highlights the consequences of ethnic diversity on support for redistributive social policies and the possible contradictions of a popularly supported liberal immigration policy among other issues that characterise the politics of migration (Freeman, Foner, & Bertossi, 2011).

In the light of the above, it is worth noting that in 2016, when the research study was ongoing, around 995,000 persons acquired citizenship of a Member State of the EU, an increase from the 841,000 recorded in 2015 and the 889,000 recorded in 2014. Of the total number of persons obtaining the citizenship of one of the EU Member States in 2016, 12% were former citizens of another EU Member State, while the majority were non-EU citizens or stateless (Eurostat, 2018b). From the four case studies, only Scotland – as part of the United Kingdom – featured among the main EU member states granting citizenships – to Indians (41.7%), Pakistanis (32.9%), Nigerians (18.8%), Filipinos (11.4%) and Chinese (11.4%) (Eurostat, 2018b).

An analysis of legal status in the four countries revealed that, at the time of the study, migrants with refugee status populated the four countries. 'Alien', 'asylum seeker' 'refugee' and 'temporary protection' are terms, which, at the time of the study, featured in the legislation of the four countries (Refugee Law, 2000; Riigikogu, 2013, 2019; Scottish Government, 2018). Discursively speaking, it is noteworthy that such legal terms imply coming from the outside, thus underlining more what happened up till the point of arrival to the host country, rather than looking at the present or looking ahead. Scotland's Convention of Scottish Local Authorities (COSLA, 2015) adds another discursive layer to this using the term 'forced migration' that underlines that absence of, or limited, agency from the migrant's end.

Conversely, in Cyprus, Estonia and Malta 'economic immigrant' or 'economic migrant' are not terms of legislative classification but used to describe people who move from one state to another looking for better job prospects and igher standards of living. This illuminates discursive gaps in the three countries between the legislative and the non-legislative spheres, where the latter is more situated in the present, short-term, medium-term and, possibly, long-term future. Consideration of economic immigration at legal and policy level was found to be exclusive to Scotland. Thus, in COSLA (2015) migrants are broadly defined as either economic migrants (people from the EU and its accession states who come to the UK with the aim of working, studying or setting up a business; or people from outside the EU who come to the UK through the Points Based System with the aim of working, studying or setting up a business.

Comparative analysis also illuminated the use of the term 'relocation', which was found to be exclusive to Estonia. Relocation involves admission of a person from another member state of the European Union who has been granted international protection; whilst 'newly relocated alien' refers to a migrant who has legally lived in Estonia for a period shorter than five years and who has been granted a temporary residence permit on the basis of Aliens Act or Act on Granting International Protection to Aliens (Riigikogu, 2019).

Terminology wise, Estonia also stood out for its legislation's attention to 'resettlement'. This refers to admission of a person from a third country who has been granted international protection (Riigikogu, 2013). In practical terms, resettlement concerns persons who have been granted the status of a refugee by the United Nations High Commissioner for Refugees (UNHCR) but have not reached the EU. On a lesser degree, Scotland's COSLA (2015) also refers to resettlement in discussing forced migration.

Another distinct aspect emerging from comparative analysis was how Maltese laws explicitly address minor members of the subjectivities under study. Subsidiary legislation Reception of Asylum Seekers Regulations (Laws of Malta, 2001) explains that the term 'unaccompanied minors' equates to:

> ... persons below the age of eighteen who arrive in Malta unaccompanied by an adult responsible for them whether by law or by custom, and for as long as they are not effectively taken into the care of such a person; it includes minors who are left unaccompanied after they have entered Malta. (p. 2)

4   Education: Resources and Human Capacity

The four countries featured a comparable state expenditure on general education, ranging between 4.8% to 6.8% of the gross domestic product as well as public, private and civil society provision of adult education programmes. At the time of the study, one state stream funded adult education in Cyrpus, Malta and Estonia. However, in Scotland in 2016–2017, a number of fundings streams could be identified: the Advanced Learning and Science Directorate was responsible for the delivery of further and higher education in Scotland (£4.8m), the Scottish Funding Council provided for Scottish colleges and universities (£1,742m) and the Higher Educational Student Support (£854.3m) (Scottish Government, 2017, p. 48). In terms of budgeting for adult education, research made it possible to identify documented rising expenditure in Estonia between 2016 (€8,672,240) and 2019 (€9,025,836). In Malta the state provides financial support to various entities including the Centre for Development, Research and Training (CDRT), the Ministry for Home Affairs and National Security of Malta (MHAS) and more. It also funds and co-funds scholarships. At the time of the study, the Directorate for Lifelong Learning and Early School Leavers (DLL & ESL)[1] spent around €770,000 in salaries of adult educators and about €341,000 in staff office salaries.[2] Meanwhile, although no official data on expenditure on adult education was available, the Statistical Service of Cyprus (2018) at the time described that 83% of the total budget funded ongoing and capital expenditure for university (including remuneration of teaching and managing staff, research expenditure, funding and scholarships, buildings, furniture, etc.), 8% funded non-university, 5% funded Universities and 4% funded post-secondary education.

As regards human resources, the Statistical Service of Cyprus (2018) recorded 1,888 teachers in post-secondary, vocational education and training (VET) and higher education. However, the research also identified additional teachers teaching in adult education programmes offered by other providers and which are not formally and quantitatively recorded. In Estonia, as to 2015/2016 there were about 2,205 teachers working in vocational education (out of a total cohort of 14,409 teachers working in the Estonian education system). Estonia lacked exact statistical data on the number of teachers employed in higher and adult education. In Scotland, the Higher Education Statistical Agency (HESA, 2016) reported a greater number of academic staff in higher education when compared to reports by the General Teaching Council (Scotland), namely: approximately 10% of the United Kingdom's higher education teachers were based in Scottish Colleges and Universities with 19,250 academic staff contracted in Scotland's Higher Education sector. In Malta, adult educators were estimated to reach 2,195 including 313 part-timers with DLL & ESL, 31 full-timers 37 part-timers at the Malta College of arts, Science & Technology (MCAST), approximately 40 full-timers and 30 part-timers at the Institute for Tourism Studies (ITS) and 823 full-timers and 921 part-timers at the University of Malta (UM).[3] Notwithstanding, none of the four cases studies featured data that explicitly specifies the number of educators teaching adult migrants and related numbers of adult migrant students (per teacher).

5   Adult Education: Political Context and Legal Framework

The EU agenda on adult learning establishes a policy framework of minimum convergence and standards, striving to push for a common ground in the midst of accented differentiations amongst the existing policy approaches of member states (Milana, 2012; Rasmussen, 2014). From this perspective, the limited engagement of the EU agenda on adult education with migrant learners and the challenges posed by migration purposely avoids to tackle some of the more sensitive and contested political issues; primarily, it does not engage with what has been termed as the 'integration debate' (Ager & Strang, 2008) and with the policy discourse on 'intercultural education'.

At policy level, a review of Scotland's New Scots: refugee integration strategy 2018 to 2022 (Local Government and Communities Directorate, 2018) testified to the country's policy commitment to overcome barriers to migrants' participation in adult learning; whilst Malta's National Lifelong Learning Strategy 2020 (Ministry of Education and Employment (MEDE), 2014) considers increased participation of migrants and provision of special programmes targeting migrants amongst its aims. Towards the end of the study under scrutiny, Malta started implementing the Integration = Belonging: Migrant Integration Strategy & Action Plan (Vision, 2020) (Human Rights and Integration Directorate, 2017) to frame integration programmes designed and implemented by the Integration Unit in collaboration with the recognised or licensed institutions and organisations that consider the diversity of the candidates' population.

Conversely, at the time of the study, Cyprus and Estonia lacked targeted policy address to adult migrant learners. At the time of the study, adult education policy in Estonia was directed by social, economic, and political change in the EU and the need to consider EU directives, European policies, and trends in the European educational area. Creating the preconditions for adults to continue their studies and acquire formal education and expanding the access to non-formal training and raising its quality standards also featured with the objectives of the country's adult education programme, The Estonian Lifelong Learning Strategy 2020, together with developing vocational education system and creation of cooperation forms to implement the vision of lifelong learning in adult education. Notwithstanding, identified contradictions in lifelong learning and adult education in Estonia included lowest motivation to participate in adult education among those with lower levels of education, among older adults and among non-Estonian speaking nationalities. Moreover, literature flagged unequal learning opportunities due to regional, social, and economic factors and inequality between various vocational and professional groups (Jõgi, 2012).

Meanwhile, the monocultural, ethnocentric approach to adult education in Cyprus lacked multilingual and intercultural pedagogies, despite the growing presence and growing heterogeneity of a non-native adult population. Fleeting references to the adoption of an intercultural model of education did not bridge the 'striking gap between policy rhetoric and adult educational practice' (Gravani, Hatzopoulos, & Chinas, 2019, p. 14). Contradictions in decisions and reforms, delays, as well as lack of data and information exchange were sourced at lack of policy coordination yielding negative impact on the diverse educational needs of adult migrant learners (Gravani, Hatzopoulos, & Chinas, 2019).

6   Adult (Migrant) Learning Programmes

At the level of practice, none of the countries exclude immigrants from education provision. However, there are clear differences. Scotland and Malta approach migrant learning in a more specialised way through citizenship language and cultural integration programmes such as I Belong (Malta) (Human Rights and Integration Directorate, 2017) and specialised academic programmes for migrants ranging from basic English conversation to degree programmes (Scotland) (Slade & Dickson, 2020). On the other hand, Cyprus and Estonia featured absence of special provisions for adult migrants and limited educational programmes, with the exception of language learning programmes in Cyprus delivered at Adult Education Centres. Greek language for foreigners programmes are open to all non-native Greek speakers, including EU citizens who may be working in Cyprus, but are mainly attended by migrants.

At the time of the study, Malta and Estonia faced challenges to increase rates in further and higher education. In 2018 Estonia had the highest rate of 20–34-year olds not in education, employment or training (NEETs) among the four countries (19.6% – higher than the EU28 average of 16.5%) (Eurostat, 2019b). Cyprus followed with 17.4%, the UK with 13.6% (to infer Scotland's) and Malta with 10.1% (Eurostat, 2019b). In this light, it is notable that the study identified that the adult education programmes of Estonia and Malta explicitly targeted bringing back the adults who discontinued their studies. Furthermore, at the time of the study, the four countries lacked data on participation of migrants in adult education programmes. Analytic review of the language programmes accessible to migrant populations in the four countries showed these were of comparable level.

7 Conclusion

The comparative cartography laid out in this chapter mapped main adult migrant education principles, policies and practices in the four countries that contextualised the case studies – Cyprus, Scotland, Malta and Estonia – in the broader political and legislative contexts of migration and education. As expected, when considering the geopolitical spread of the sampled case studies, the cartography illuminated differences across the four countries at the time of the study. These included the origins and ethnicities of migrant groups, differences in the legal and technocratic jargon, differentiation of types, categories, and combinations of legal and irregular immigrants – which, in turn, also shed light on underlying discourses. The four countries had varied responses to adult education for migrants' policy, ranging from inclusive visible policy to non-existent – a key finding also because it was not aligned with geographical location. By way of example, policymaking for integration of adult migrants in Malta overlapped more with policymaking in Scotland, rather than with policymaking in sister-Mediterranean island of Cyprus.

The cartography also mapped several commonalities among the four countries, such as diverse immigrant cohorts, state expenditure on (general) education ranging between 4.8% and 6.8% of the countries' GDPs, adult education provision by public, private and civil society entities and language programmes of comparable level. The identified programmes ranged from community-based, private provision and state funded.

Remarkably, the comparative analysis illuminated the absence of a salient placeholder across the four countries – namely, a concrete policy on adult education for migrants. Aside from this headline finding this chapter also flagged the unavailability of data (or of reliable data) in all the four countries on participation rates of migrants in adult education programmes. This infers that the case studies unfolded in a targeted policy vacuum. One of the issues explored in this research project is the impact of this policy vacuum on the curriculum and pedagogy of the language programmes under study in the four countries. This discussion unfolds in the chapters that follow.

Notes

1 At the time of writing, this Directorate had changed its name to Directorate for Research, Lifelong Learning and Employability.
2 Information obtained through email communication dated November 28, 2016 with DLL & ESL, MEDE (Malta).
3 Information obtained through email communication dated November 28, 2016 with DLL & ESL, MEDE (Malta).

References

Convention of Scottish Local Authorities (COSLA). (2015). *Migration policy toolkit: An online guide to welcoming, integrating and engaging migrant communities in Scotland.* http://www.migrationscotland.org.uk/migration

Eurostat. (2019a). *Share of non-nationals in the resident population.* https://ec.europa.eu/eurostat/statistics-explained/index.php?title=File:Share_of_nonnationals_in_the_resident_population,_1_January_2018_(%25).png

Eurostat. (2019b). *Young people (aged 20–34) neither in employment nor in education and training, 2018.* https://ec.europa.eu/eurostat/statistics-explained/index.php/Statistics_on_young_people_neither_in_employment_nor_in_education_or_training#Young_people_neither_in_employment_nor_in_education_or_training

Eurostat. (2018a). *Migration and migrant population statistics.* https://ec.europa.eu/eurostat/statistics-explained/index.php/Migration_and_migrant_population_statistics

Eurostat. (2018b). *Acquisition of citizenship in the EU/EU member states granted citizenship to almost 1 million persons in 2016.* https://ec.europa.eu/eurostat/documents/2995521/8791096/3-09042018-AP-EN.pdf/658455fa-c5b1-4583-9f98-ec3f0f3ec5f9

Freeman, G., Foner, N., & Bertossi, C. (2011). Comparative analysis of immigration politics: A retrospective. *American Behavioral Scientist, 55*(12), 1541–1560.

Gravani, M. N., Hatzopoulos, P., & Chinas, C. (2019). Adult education and migration in Cyprus: A critical analysis. *Journal of Adult and Continuing Education.* https://doi.org/10.1177/1477971419832896

Higher Education Statistical Agency. (2016). *Higher education staff data.* https://www.hesa.ac.uk/data-and-analysis/staff

Human Rights and Integration Directorate. (2017). *Integration = belonging: Migrant integration strategy & action plan (Vision 2020).* https://meae.gov.mt/en/Documents/migrant%20integration-EN.pdf

International Organization for Migration (IOM). (2018). *Malta.* https://www.iom.int/countries/malta

Jõgi, L. (2012). Understanding lifelong learning and adult education policy in Estonia: Tendencies and contradictions. *Journal of Adult and Continuing Education, 18*(2), 44–60.

Laws of Malta. (2001). *Refugees Act (Chapter 420).* Malta: Ministry for Justice, Culture and Local Government. http://justiceservices.gov.mt/DownloadDocument.aspx?app=lom&itemid=8886

Miljanic Brinkworth, M. (2016). Demography. In M. Briguglio & M. Brown (Eds.), *Sociology of the Maltese Islands* (pp. 99–112). Miller Publishing.

Ministry for Education and Employment. (MEDE). (2016). *Malta national lifelong learning strategy 2020.* https://lifelonglearning.gov.mt/dbfile.aspx?id=37

Ministry of Education and Research (Estonia). (2018). *The Estonian lifelong learning strategy 2020.* https://www.hm.ee/sites/default/files/estonian_lifelong_strategy.pdf

Ministry of Finance of the Republic of Estonia. (2013). *State budget strategy 2014–2017.* https://www.rahandusministeerium.ee/et/system/files_force/document_files/res_2014-2017_20-06-2013_en_vol2.pdf?download=1

Mistri, M., & Orcalli, G. (2015). The European Union's immigration policy: A stalled form of the strategy of conflict? *International Economics and Economic Policy, 12*(2), 239–256.

National Records of Scotland (NRS). (2019). *Population by country of birth and nationality, 2018.* https://www.nrscotland.gov.uk/files//statistics/population-estimates/pop-cob-18/pop-cob-nat-18-publication.pdf

Refugee Law. (2000). *Refugee law* [of Cyprus]. http://www.refworld.org/docid/4a71aac22.html

Riigikogu. (2013). *Act on granting international protection to aliens.* https://www.riigiteataja.ee/en/eli/530102013009/consolide

Riigikogu. (2019). *Aliens act.* https://www.riigiteataja.ee/en/eli/ee/501112017003/consolide/current

Slade, B. L., & Dickson, N. (2020). Adult education and migration in Scotland: Policies and practices for inclusion. *Journal of Adult and Continuing Education.* https://doi.org/10.1177/1477971419896589

Scottish Government. (2017). *Draft budget 2018–2019.* https://www.gov.scot/publications/scotlands-budget-draft-budget-2017-18/pages/9/

Scottish Government. (2018). *New Scots: Refugee integration strategy 2018 to 2022.* https://www.gov.scot/publications/new-scots-refugee-integration-strategy-2018-2022/

Statistical Service. (2011). *Population – Country of birth, nationality, nationality, language, religion, national/religious group.* https://www.mof.gov.cy/mof/cystat/statistics.nsf/All/80E605E7C0057264C2257AD90053F58D/$file/POP_CEN_11-POP_FOREIGN_LANG_RELIG-EL-220419.xls?OpenElement

Statistical Service of Cyprus. (2018). http://www.mof.gov.cy/mof/cystat/statistics.nsf/populationcondition_21main_en/populationcondition_21main_en?OpenForm&sub=1&sel=2

Statistics Estonia (ES). (2019). *Population projection shows population decrease is slowing down.* https://www.stat.ee/news-release-2019-077

CHAPTER 4

Learner-Centred Education and Adult Education for Migrants in Estonia

Larissa Jõgi and Katrin Karu

Abstract

Informed and structural migration policy requires an attractive social and economic environment and appropriate educational programmes. This chapter is based on a case study and focuses on the analysis of the implementation of the module "Language training course", which is part of the Welcoming adaptation programme (WP), which involves three components – society study, socio-economic integration, and essential language learning. The target groups of the WP are adult migrants arriving in Estonia. In the chapter we describe the case, present the case context, and discuss motivational components of language learning. As a process, adult and language learning is based on social interaction and personal motivation. Motivation for language learning relates to the value component of motivation, which include personal interest, interest in tasks, conscious and self-attributed motives. We analyse the extent to which adult migrant learners were intrinsically motivated to be involved successfully in the Estonian language learning and education process. Data collection was based on semi-structured interviews and observation. Empirical data was analysed using content and thematic analysis. Learner-Centred Education, as a concept has been applied as a framework for analysing data. Analysis showed that learners were motivated to learn Estonian language due to several external and internal factors: supportive engagement, dialogue and relationships, the teaching-learning process, personal and communicative needs. Findings from the case study indicate several positive advantages of the Welcoming programme, which offers for adult migrants in Estonia supportive service and learning possibilities simultaneously.

Keywords

case study – Estonia – Welcoming Programme – learner-centred education – adults learning – language learning

1 Introduction

The focus of this chapter is on the analysis of the implementation of the module 'Language training course', which is part of the Welcoming Programme[1] (WP) for migrants, started in Estonia in 2014 and initially provided by the non-state organisation Expat Relocation Estonia OÜ. Since 2015 the company Expat Relocation Estonia OÜ has been providing the Welcoming Programme. The company was established in 2013 and its main activity is the provision of various support services to foreign specialists who migrate to Estonia. Its purpose is to strengthen the network of supporting persons and increase the state's capacity and readiness to provide necessary assistance to the target group to help them cope with living in Estonia and integrating into Estonian society. The chapter provides an introduction, description of the case study, an analysis of the case study and conclusion.

The legal basis of the Welcoming Programme and implementation of the 'Language training course' for adults with a migrant background is based on legal acts, the broader national policy, an institutional framework and cooperation between programme coordinator and language teachers. Estonia has granted international protection since 1997 when it joined the UN 1951 Refugee Convention and its 1967 Protocol. Estonia has a rather well-developed legal system which is well adapted for resolving immigration related issues (Loogma et al., 2012, p. 219). The clear legal framework creates opportunities for adults with a migrant background to adapt in the new society. The asylum policy in Estonia has been implemented since 1997, when the Refugee Act came into force. The Refugee Act expired in 2005 when the Act on Granting International Protection to Aliens was passed. This Act regulates the bases for granting international protection to an 'alien', the legal bases for his or her temporary stay and their social rights. Aliens Act, passed in 2009, regulates the bases for the entry of aliens into Estonia, their temporary stay, residence, and employment in Estonia and their legal responsibilities.

The number of applications for international protection submitted to Estonia is relatively small compared to the other EU member states but has been growing over the years. In 2017 there were 196,344 foreigners living in Estonia, including EU and Non-EU Nationals (Minifact about Estonia, 2017). According to the Integration measure[2] the majority of non-Estonian permanent residents live in Tallinn (43%), followed by Virumaa (35%) and the smallest number of non-Estonians reside in South Estonia (3%). The prevailing migration type is family migration (39%), followed by labour migration (37%), study migration (21%), enterprise migration (3%) and permits issued on the basis of legal income (1%). The experience of piloting and implementation of the adaptation programme, as well as Estonian statistical data, show that almost 70% of the migrant population choose the capital Tallinn and the surrounding Harju county. In the period 2009–2014 the greatest number of people settled in Tallinn (n = 9901), Tartu city/rural municipality (n = 1593), Narva (n = 850), Kohtla-Järve (n = 367) and Maardu (n = 258). The reasons for the preferred choice of the capital and its surrounding area are better job and study opportunities. Ida-Virumaa is an option for language reasons as it has the largest number of Russian-speaking residents.

2 Case Context: Adult Education, Policy Framework and Migrant Population in Estonia

Integration of people with a migrant background and educational policy falls under the responsibility of different state institutions. The aim of integration is to ensure adequate opportunities for the successful coping, well-being, and educational possibilities to all inhabitants of Estonia regardless of their ethnicity and native language. The main state institutions involved in the issues of migration and international protection in Estonia are: The Ministry of the Interior; Police and Border Guard; Ministry of Education and Research; Ministry of Culture; Ministry of Social Affairs and Estonian Unemployment Insurance Fund; Ministry of Foreign Affairs; and the Ministry of Justice (Migration and Asylum Policy, Annual Report, 2015).

The Ministry of Education and Research coordinates the general organisation of adult education in Estonia. The Ministry of Social Affairs together with the public-law institution Estonian Unemployment Insurance Fund are responsible for the training of the unemployed and jobseekers. An open, informed, and structural migration policy requires an attractive social and economic environment, an appropriate adaptation programme and a support network and leadership role in creating a friendly environment image and communication (Lüüs, 2014). The integration indicators compiled at the request of the Ministry of Culture reflect the educational attainment, labour force participation, socio-economic status and living conditions of population groups with different domestic languages, citizenship and origin. The above-mentioned indicators could facilitate assessing the level of integration (Statistical Yearbook of Estonia, 2015). The goal is to implement an approach towards learning that supports each learner's individual and social development, learning skills, creativity and entrepreneurship in work at all levels and types of education (LLLS, 2020). The key objectives of the implementation of the Integration measure are to create opportunities for providing information, providing language courses, supporting the emergence of social competencies and shaping attitudes. Knowledge of the Estonian language is a prerequisite for receiving a long-term residence permit and applying for Estonian citizenship but is clearly also important for other aspects of integration, such as accessing education and employment as well as civil, cultural and social integration ('Integration of refugees ...', 2016). Learning opportunities should be available to all members of society, particularly those with lower competitiveness in the labour market. This includes young mothers, the elderly, those who do not speak Estonian, people without secondary education, the unemployed, the disabled, new immigrants, so that they can acquire a qualification and maximise their potential in their working life as well as in their family life. Estonian Lifelong Learning Strategy (LLLS, 2020) sets out the strategic visions, goals for developing learning opportunities and equal participation in learning and integration possibilities for all as well as defining the roles of teachers in society. The general goal of Lifelong Learning Strategy 2020 is to provide all people in Estonia with learning opportunities that are tailored to their needs and capabilities throughout their lifespan, to maximise opportunities for dignified self-actualisation within society, in their work and in their family life. The strategic goal is equal opportunities and increased participation in lifelong learning, which relates to the creation of opportunities for people with lower competitiveness to participate in learning.

3   Case Description

The focus of the Estonian case study is the Welcoming Programme[3] (WP) and Language training module which is a part of this programme. WP started as an adaptation programme with the implementation of its module 'Language training' in 2014 in Tallinn (Figure 4.1). The Welcoming Programme was developed for:

1. foreign nationals who have been granted temporary residence permit in Estonia either on the basis of the Aliens Act (AA) or the Act on Granting International Protection to Aliens (AGIPA);
2. citizens of the European Union who have acquired the temporary right of residence in Estonia on the basis stipulated in the Citizen of the European Union Act (EUA);
3. family members of citizens of the European Union who have been granted the temporary right of residence in Estonia on the basis stipulated in the Citizen of the European Union Act.

The Welcoming Programme is funded by the European Social Fund (ESF), Asylum, Migration, and Integration Fund (AMIF) and the state budget. The target

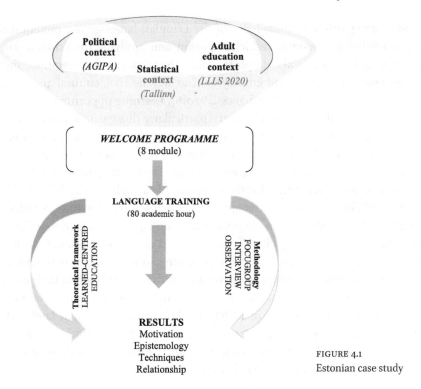

FIGURE 4.1
Estonian case study

group of the Welcoming Programme are adult new immigrants arriving to live in Estonia from countries of the global South who have lived in Estonia less than five years and who have legitimate grounds for being in Estonia. The conditions for participation and the procedure of enrolling persons in the Welcoming Programme is established by 13.08.2014 regulation number 34 'Welcoming programme'.

The Welcoming Programme consists of three informative and interactive training modules (Figure 2): (1) the *basic module* provides primary information for settling in Estonia and gives an overview of the functioning principles of the Estonian state, society, culture and people, rights and obligations of residents, and public services; (2) the *thematic modules* give an overview of working and entrepreneurship, family life, studying and research and consists of the following units: working and entrepreneurship, studying, research, family life, children and young people, and international protection; and (3) the *language training course module* at A1 level is based on a language training course programme and is offered in English and Russian in Tallinn and Tartu as well as in Narva, if there is interest. The language course lasts for approximately 80 academic hours. Participants can choose between morning or evening classes.

All the training modules include vital practical examples that help new arrivals to better understand the material in the modules and use the acquired knowledge in their daily lives. Study in all modules is carried out in the form of lectures, conversations, watching films and discussions as well as in the form of practical activities and tours. The modules guide and support in finding key information for understanding Estonian culture, valuing mutual communication, cooperation and establishing contacts. They take place in a comfortable, open, and diverse learning environment. All the modules offered are tuition-free. Teaching methods and training days are structured according to the specifics of adult learning. The result of the modules is that the new immigrants acquire knowledge and skills which help them adapt and integrate into Estonian society.

In addition, there is an e-assistance platform[4] and a web-based self-learning portal Keeleklikk,[5] which includes a free online Estonian course for beginners based on English or Russian, which is suitable for individual study to reach level A2. The course consists of 16 comprehensive language learning units which include a total of 200 animations, over 100 videos explaining grammar, and roughly 1200 exercises. It is unclear how many migrants have used this, or if they are aware of it ('Integration of refugees ...', 2016).

3.1 Language Training Module

Learning to speak Estonian makes it easier to deal with various day-to-day activities and is an advantage in socialising as well as coping with everyday life and job seeking. The programme for the language training module as a part of the Welcome Programme was designed for new immigrants from the language module aims to give basic knowledge of Estonian at level A1. New arrivals who have successfully completed the language module will be able to use everyday expressions and simple phrases, introduce themselves and others, ask simple questions and understand short messages.

3.2 Structure and Content of the Language Training Programme

The language training programme is designed and structured around themes/subtopics and consists of 80 academic hours – 60 contact hours and 20 independent work hours and is based on either English or Russian. The programme runs for approximately two months. Commitment requires attending a three-hour lesson, doing weekly homework and sitting an exam. The choice of topics is based on the learner's needs. Special/individual needs are important for choosing the topics and teaching methods. The language lessons usually take place two days per week and there are options to take a morning class or an evening class. On the last day of the language module, the participants take a written test, and the teacher conducts an oral conversation test with them. The written test corresponds to the A1 level and consists of simple questions. In the conversation, the participant needs to talk about oneself, ask questions and answer simple, clearly posed questions according to the language level.

3.3   Teaching Content and Methods

The language module provides basic language skills to cover specific primary communication needs. There are eleven topics in the language module: polite expressions, getting acquainted, introducing oneself and one's companions, numbers and the clock, countries, nations and languages, food, and beverages, eating habits, café conversations, arranging a meeting, 'my day' and hobbies, my family, asking for and giving directions, and feeling well/unwell.

Language courses take place in a secure and motivating environment which encourages the learners to participate. Teachers use active learning techniques that involve the learners. Every lesson day includes exercises in pairs and/or groups that provide an opportunity for independent language use. The basic level language acquisition contains exercises directing the participants to contact people speaking Estonian as their native language, participate in situations with Estonian conversation, and apply their skills in practice and monitor their language. In addition, audio visual materials and games are used in the language course.

3.4   Teaching and Learning Materials

Before the language classes or on the first day, every participant receives a folder with learning materials, including references to additional materials (glossaries, textbooks, online materials). The cultural background of learners is also integrated into different topics and tasks. The completion of the language course is based on the learner's self-assessment. At the end of the course the learners can test their skills and knowledge themselves by using a written test in accordance with level A1. Learners confirm their participation in the course with a signature. The final result does not determine the acquisition of a certificate. The final results of the examination are collected and submitted to the Ministry of the Interior.

3.5   Language Teachers

The teacher's role is to support a learner to manage their own learning, to cope with changes in their surroundings independently and to take responsibility for their own development and learning. The teacher is a person who creates connections and shapes value judgements, whose task is to develop critical and creative thinking, as well as analytical and entrepreneurial skills, teamwork skills and written and oral communication skills. To give 'weaker' learners, the ability to cope and to challenge the 'stronger' learners at the same time, teachers and teams of supporting specialists need to approach each learner individually.

There is wholehearted cooperation between the developers, coordinators, and teachers on the Welcoming Programme. The programme was developed with input from teachers with previous experience in language teaching, teaching adults and counselling. The purpose of the programme developers is to support the motivation of the teachers to feel like they are programme owners. Estonian language teachers, who teach on the programme, should be experts in teaching the Estonian language to foreigners and they all should have experience in teaching adults. Twice a year workshops are delivered to language teachers for adults with a migrant background to support their professional competence.

6 Case Analysis. Learner-Centred Education Practice in Adult Education Programmes for Migrants

6.1 *Sampling*

The targeted sample for data collection is formed by two adult learners with a migrant background, one teacher and one policymaker. The learners were both men of the same age: learner 1 was 37 years old, from South-Africa, and had lived in Estonia for 3 years; learner 2 was 37 years old, from Pakistan, with two years in Estonia. The language teacher was 41 years old from Estonia, a university lecturer of practical Estonian. She has 17 years of experience as a language teacher and has been teaching Estonian in the Welcoming Programme since 2015. The policymaker, aged 39, coordinator and adult educator, is a member of the board of Expat Relocation Estonia OÜ and one of the developers of the Welcoming programme. He has been involved in the programme for 4 years since 2015.

6.2 *Data Collection*

Data collection was based on semi-structured interviews and observation. Four semi-structured interviews and observations were conducted during March-September 2017 by two researchers. Interviews were held with two adult learners (learner 1 and learners 2), one teacher and one policymaker. Interviews were recorded and transcribed by the two researchers. It should be noted that interviews with the learners were run in the English language which is not their native language. The observation took place before the final exam in the last language lesson with 14 learners and lasted for 1,5 hours. An observation guide was used for observation and two protocols were produced based on observation notes written by the two researchers. Selective observation was used for finding evidence and examples of the types of teaching practice and processes (Flick, 2006, p. 221). According to the observation guidelines, special attention was paid to space, objects, actors, interactions, dialogues, and time.

6.3 Data Analysis

Empirical data was analysed by using content and thematic analysis (Miles & Huberman, 1994, p. 10). The qualitative data underwent a 'selective process' (Miles & Huberman, 1994, p. 55) to filter data relevant to the research objectives of the research study. Content analysis was used to reduce data to essential content; to explain, clarify and annotate data (Mayring, 2000). We used hybrid (inductive and deductive) coding (Evans, 2002, p. 157). The process of creating codes started with initial inductive coding and was based on predetermined codes, which refer to the main concepts from Learner-centred Education/LCE (Schweisfurth, 2013a, p. 146). Predetermined (deductive) codes had four categories: *motivation, epistemology, techniques, relationships,* which are based on components of LCE practice (Schweisfurth, 2013, p. 11).

7 Findings and Discussion

Below we present the results from data analysis based on four components of the LCE (Schweisfurth, 2013b, p. 11) and discuss empirical findings.

UNESCO's five pillars of learning: learning to know, learning to do, learning to live together, learning to be, learning to transform oneself and society is the conceptualisation of learning, which provide an expansive approach to adults learning (Boucouvalas & Lawrence, 2010). The learning process as an andragogical process consisting of eight elements: preparing the learners; considering the physical and psychological climate setting; involving the learners in planning for their learning; involving the learners in diagnosing their own need for learning; involving the learners in formulating their own learning objectives; involving the learners in designing learning plans; helping the learners carry out their learning plans; and involving the learners in evaluating their own learning outcomes (Knowles et al., 2005, p. 295).

7.1 Motivation

In this section of our chapter, we analyse the extent to which adult migrant learners were intrinsically motivated to be involved successfully in the language learning and education process at the time and in the context of the programmes of the Estonian case study. Analysis showed that learners were motivated to learn the Estonian language due to communicative and practical needs and several external and internal factors related to supportive engagement and the teaching-learning process, relationships, open-respectful atmosphere, respectful contacts, interactive communication, teacher's personality and competency, personal and communicative needs.

Language learning in a formal context is contextual, social, and situational and is affected by cultural differences (Dörnyei, 2003). As a process, language learning is based on social interaction and personal motivation. The general basis of motivation are motives, needs and values which influence intrinsic and extrinsic motivation. Motivation is always contextual. Knowles (1990) stated that adults need to know why they should learn something before they will engage themselves in learning it, emphasising that '... real or simulated experiences in which the learners discover for themselves the gaps between where they are now and where they want to be' (p. 37) stimulate self-awareness and the need to know (cited in Boucouvalas & Lawrence, 2010). External and internal factors are two main factors, which have an impact on developing motivation for language learning and development of intrinsic or extrinsic motivation. External factors include communicative needs, the existence of a clear target, as well as practical needs from everyday life. Adults are driven to learn new skills or understand new concepts based on the ever-changing demands of work and life, so timing the learning to correspond with the tasks at hand is at the heart of this principle of adult learning (Boucouvalas & Lawrence, 2010).

7.2 *Extrinsic Motivation*

Extrinsic motivation relates to the role of teacher, communication with other learners and engagement in the learning process. The findings from the analysed data and the observation allows us to say that learners were involved in the learning process through respectful contacts and communication with the teacher and other learners. There is clear evidence that language training was a fully supportive and engaging teaching-learning process, in which the teaching approaches, the tools and tasks she used in the language class and the teacher's personality affected the learners' motivation:

> The teacher was respective, positive and calm. The learners were actively involved and motivated. She always asked if we understood the lesson. (Learner 1)

The previous experience of implementation of the language learning programme in language courses in Estonia (Tallinn) shows partly unclear motivation and a drop-out rate attributed to time and family problems (Rannut, 2009,

p. 54). The language course under observation did not have any dropouts. However, the students pointed out that work created difficulties for choosing a suitable time to attend the language course.

7.3   Intrinsic Motivation

Internal factors include desire and willingness to learn the language, interest in the language and learner's activity. 'While adults are responsive to some external motivators (better jobs, promotions, higher salaries, and the like), the most potent motivators are internal pressures (the desire for increased job satisfaction, self-esteem, quality of life, and the like)' (Knowles, 1990, p. 63). A specially arranged room for interactive communication and an open-respectful atmosphere are important factors for intrinsic motivation. The teacher expressed that it was important to her to create a safe environment in the classroom:

> In my case, and generally in this programme, it is typical that the learner is welcome. Because it is a WELCOME programme, so they have to feel welcome, well and safe, that the teacher knows the names and shows interest in the students. (Teacher)

7.4   Motives for Learning

According to previous research there are three factors which might impact motivation: expectancy component, affective component, and a value component (McClelland, Koestner, & Weinberger, 1989; Pintrich & de Groot, 1990, pp. 33–34). The results of our data analysis show that motivation for language learning relates to the value component of motivation (Pintrich & de Groot, 1990, p. 34), which includes personal interest, interest in tasks, conscious and self-attributed motives organised around personal needs and related to specific goals. Learners are motivated to learn Estonian as they are required to find a job, communicate, and interact with local people, to adapt and integrate into Estonian society and live a 'normal' life. One learner said:

> I attended this course because if you live here, you must communicate with local people, you must know the language. If you avoid speaking Estonian and only use English, it is not good for your career. Another reason – I have no experience of learning other languages. I know the languages that are being spoken in my country. Not the international language. Except the English language. (Learner 1)

Knowles (1990) proposed that adults become more independent when they mature, therefore increasing their desire to direct their own learning. The motivation to learn Estonian also stems from the need to communicate with relatives who do not speak English. The learner's motivation needs to be supported throughout the language learning process. As Dörnyei (2014) has highlighted, it is important to find motivation strategies that focus on the learner's experience. This approach was expressed by the Welcome Programme Coordinator:

> We encourage the learners to speak about their experience ... If you have a foreigner, who is a bit afraid, being in a strange environment, and then comes a teacher, then he listens to them – but if he sees someone like himself who has overcome the same problem and found a solution, then he believes this. (Policymaker: coordinator)

Learners understand that such a language level (A1) does not allow them to find work because of regulations for language requirements but they feel the need to be able to speak Estonian very well; they realise that the language skills are important in conversations with local people, when looking for a job, making a career or acting as an investigator. One learner indicated that they appreciated the limits of the WP:

> To understand basic conversation and sentences, vocabulary. I wanted to be able to participate in conversations with people. If I want to ask for some kind of help and people can help me. It is very good at A1 level – you know the basics. I would very much like to go to the next course – A2. It is very important – to study. (Learner 1)

7.5 *The Role of the Teacher in the Motivational Process*

Teachers can 'inspire a lifelong commitment to the subject matter' through a motivating teaching style and open and dialogical communication (Dörnyei, 2007, p. 719). To support learners' motivation, to develop social and language skills, the language teacher used various ways in class to encourage interest in the language and in the learning process. The learners who participated in the language training programme were different in their language knowledge and skills. They did not only have different background and life experience, but also different motives for participation in the language learning class. We noticed during the observation that the teacher focused on learners and their learning by giving them possibilities to feel free, open and to communicate actively with each other in class in various forms. The language teacher lived and studied several years in Hungary and she is an experienced foreign language learner. Drawing on her experience, she understood that foreign language learning is emotionally demanding, learners need a lot of practice, and that feelings also play an important role in the learning process especially at the beginning of the language course:

> I wrote the language learning module for the Welcome programme. It was easy to relate to this programme. I like international groups, they are very tolerant. And this is important for language learning. I have been in adult education for the whole time I've taught Estonian, and that is 16–17 years already. I think this is my explanation, why I want to do this. I would like to make this language course as genuinely communicative as possible ... I want them to feel well and to have fun too. (Teacher)

Based on the analysed data from the interview with the teacher and notes from the observation, we assume that the role and personal motivation of the language teacher in supporting motivation of adult learners was significant because of her personal motivation to be a language teacher for migrant adults, her enthusiasm and openness, the nature of interactions with the learners, and her ability to create an open atmosphere of trust in the class. She enabled learners to feel and experience an open and emotional atmosphere, enjoy the dialogue and small progress in tasks and active participation. Based on the results from the data analysis, we can assume that the teacher's previous experience as a foreign language learner, also her professional experience as an adult educator as well as her role in supporting learners' motivation is important and relates to her motives and values: conscious teaching goals, an aspiration to support adult learners with a migrant background and commitment to work as an adult educator and language teacher.

7.6 *Epistemology*

In this section of the chapter, we discuss the extent to which the adult education programme for migrants under study is characterised by a 'fixed knowledge' and curriculum, or whether knowledge is fluid and the content is negotiable with migrant learners. By viewing this programme from a social constructivist approach to teaching (which emphasises the social context for learning) and learning-centred education perspective (Schweisfurth, 2013a), we assume that the programme is grounded in a particular cultural and language context with concrete epistemology, teaching approaches and values. Learning challenges build on learners' existing knowledge and experience (Schweisfurth, 2013a). At the beginning of programme, the learners' background and needs are determined, and the programme and teaching are adapted to these.

> In the first part of the language course we ask people to introduce themselves, to introduce their background – where they came from, what is

> their personal and professional background and profile, we ask them to describe what they expect. (Policymaker: coordinator)

The programme was developed by an experienced language teacher. The results of the analysis of the empirical data based on interviews with the coordinator and the teacher demonstrate that the programme follows the requirements for A1 level and the topics set by the Aliens Act.[6] However, the choice of what exactly and how to teach each concrete topic remains for the organisers and the language teacher to decide. That is why the programme, created with their cooperation, is flexible and enables the teacher to take into consideration the learners' needs in an Estonian context and is carried out with the application of learner-centred principles.

> The programme is based on the A1 level requirements and the learners' primary needs, the need for basic communication when migrants arrive to Estonia. The starting topics are connected with immediate needs. For example, arranging meetings, negotiations, visiting the doctor, enlarging vocabulary and learning the basics of Estonian grammar. (Teacher)

Based on the analysed data from the observation and interviews, we can say that the language training programme and the language course are designed and delivered according to the real needs of adult migrant learners and take into account their experience, skills, interests and expectations.

> I am focusing on the immediate needs, the need for primary communication, I rely on their experience. (Teacher)
> If we wanted to add anything else, maybe from our own lives, this could be included somehow, what we wanted to know or learn more. The teacher made learning easy for us. She always asked about our experiences. A lot of discussions. (Learner 1)

7.7 Knowledge and Skills for Future

The general aim of the language course is to support the integration of adults with a migrant background into Estonian society. Therefore, during the language course the language teacher supports the acquisition of knowledge and skills that can help and support the learners to cope with their lives. The findings show that the language programme is relevant to migrants' future knowledge and skills.

> If they have participated in the programme and the language course, it shows that they integrate better and participate in Estonian society. (Policymaker: coordinator)

In the teaching process an individual approach was used. For instance, learners were encouraged to train the skills that may be necessary in their everyday life (for example, writing a CV to apply for a job, writing an email). The language course supported the learners' acquisition of vocabulary and encouraged them to use it. However, the learners realise that they need to continue learning the language to better manage situations.

> This course helped me a lot, but the most serious problem I found – I need a good vocabulary … language is a skill. I can understand a little bit. I can listen when Estonians speak, and I can understand about 10%. I could understand whether somebody was friendly or not. (Learner 2)

7.8   *Learning and Teaching Challenges*

Language learning is influenced positively if learners have previous language learning experience. The more languages they have learnt before, the easier it is to study Estonian. Moreover, knowing the Latin alphabet or knowledge and skills of English or the Russian language might support the learning process. As the language teacher's experience shows, it is easier for Finnish people to study Estonian as these are related languages, however, being in a group with people from other countries, is not an obstacle for their learning. The difficulties in language learning are created more by the lack of writing skills using Latin letters, insufficient or non-existent knowledge of the course's basic language and a low education level manifesting itself in the lack of general learning skills.

> Some students don't have the habit of writing, that's the choice when I have to think what to do as a teacher … I had one student who knew almost no English, then I had another Spanish-speaking student, and I used an interpreter and tried to communicate with him using my little knowledge of Spanish. (Teacher)

> We have had students with limited language skills and students who have no skills in the use of the Latin alphabet (e.g., Israel, Asia). These students had difficulties as one needs language skills for the programme. (Policy-maker: coordinator)

7.9   *Relevance*

The observed language course was designed by the language teacher and based on the prior experience and language learning needs of adult learners and on everyday life situations. The course was generally flexible and interactive, with a clear focus on open communication between learners, discussion in pairs and small groups. During the course, the teacher used methods and tasks that supported learners' activity, and cooperation between learners, helped to solve real problems and supported coping with different communication situations. 'Curriculum is based on skills and attitude outcomes as well as content. These should include skills of critical and creative thinking (bearing in mind that culture-based communication conventions are likely to make the 'flavour' of this very different in different places)' (Schweisfurth, 2013a, p. 6). The content and implementation of the programme was based on the cooperation between learners and teacher, as well as the teacher and coordinators of the Welcoming Programme.

7.10 Feedback on the Course

The learners gave their feedback at the end of the course and it was sent to the Ministry of Interior. Based on the learners' feedback, several changes were made to the study materials. Overall satisfaction with the language learning course was very positive. Estonian language learning is supported further; the learners are informed about various options for language learning after completing the language course. In conclusion to this section, we can summarise that the language course programme is tailored to the requirements of A1 level. The course supports the acquisition of vocabulary of the Estonian language and improves self-expression skills. The course also introduces cultural traditions of Estonian society.

7.11 Techniques

To assess the degree of responsibility for learning taken by learners we examine the techniques and activities that the teacher used in the classroom, Language learning in the context of learner-centred education is seen as an activity which involves learners as human beings, not 'simply' as language learners. The pedagogical approach used by teacher gives learners, and demands from them, a relatively high level of active control over the content and the process of learning. What is learnt, and how, are therefore shaped by learners' needs, capacities, and interests (Schweisfurth, 2013a, p. 20). Teachers who are aware of their roles can – and do – take many practical measures in their work to adapt the programme to meet the needs of learners (Churchill, 1994, p. 138). Teaching methods need therefore to be chosen not only based on what seems theoretically plausible, but also in the light of the experience, personality, and expectations of the students involved (Tudor, 1993; Thompson, 2013). There is evidence of using a learner-centred approach and open dialogue in terms of two-way communication between the teacher and the learner or learner/s and learner/s.

> At the first meeting, I ask what they know about the language, if there's any factual knowledge. I also ask for a phrase that they already know or heard. Then I play the game and we learn all names together in that time. This is important. And then I introduce the Estonian language, its peculiarities, main phrases. And so 3 hours are over. (Teacher)

7.12 Teaching Practice

Teaching is based on active and interactive principles, on previous learners' and language learning experiences, considering their needs, expectations and interest. According to our observation learner involvement and activity are important in the class. The learners were encouraged to share their knowledge and experience. There are three approaches to teaching practices, which are based on dialogue and activity and which support learner-centred learning: (a) social/interactive/dialogue-based (e.g., discussion, asking and answering questions, group work, pair work), (b) emotional/activating (e.g., games, jokes, sociometry) and (c) situational (e.g., enhanced lecture, case-study, role-plays, practical exercises).

> It's all one big dialogue. You are listening, answering questions, discussing. (Policymaker: coordinator)
> We had dialogues, sometimes discussions in groups, often moved around in the classroom. (Learner 1)

The teaching process involves asking and answering questions to promote the dialogue between the students and immediate use of the learned vocabulary.

> We had a dialogue in Estonian. I thought it would be too difficult, but it wasn't ... She always answered, even when I asked very complex questions. I often asked, how to complete this sentence in the past tense, or something else. She always tried to answer, especially when it was related to this topic. (Learner 2)

The learning process enables the learners to solve different tasks in various real-life situations and acquire practical skills to cope with everyday life and work circumstances doing such topical tasks as asking for and giving directions.

> We do tasks in a practical way, for example, when we are learning giving directions, we stick the town roads on the floor, use pictures and actually act asking for and giving directions .... (Teacher)

In the teaching process such materials as videos, poetry, songs, writing e-mail, reading, and translating were used, including a presentation about different countries.

> Usually the teacher uses videos, poetry, songs and writing emails. Information and technological resources, course materials and tasks are used also …. When the lesson was new, dialogues were started by the teacher. If the subject wasn't new, she usually asked the students to start the dialogue. (Learner 2)

An important place in the learning process was taken by independent work in the e-learning environment www.keeleklikk.ee in addition to traditional course materials. The independent work is valued as it directs the learners to make their own choices, which, in its turn, supports the formation of an independent learner and gives responsibility for the process to the learner. It is possible to implement a learner-centred approach in teaching practice if the goal of the teaching is related to creating learning space with possibilities for dialogue and training concrete skills. The goal in the current case was a safe, comfortable and learner-friendly environment. The atmosphere during the observed lesson was positive, open and safe. Mutual respect between the teacher and the learners was obvious. The observers were also involved in the learning process.

7.13 *Flexibility*

Andragogical elements in teaching are empathy, trust, and accommodation. The analysed data reveals that the programme coordinator, the teacher, and the learners value flexibility in the study process, which is seen in the different students' studying tempos, expectations and needs.

> The expectations are different, sometimes he or she said that I came to find out something else, the other said that I am interested in a specific aspect of company taxation or how I will find a job. We ask about and take into consideration the learners' wishes for the language course. (Policymaker: coordinator)

The teacher took into consideration the students' individual needs and, if it was necessary, introduced changes and offered alternatives.

> Mostly we followed the plan. There wasn't any need to change the curriculum or plan – because the course was very well organised. It was easy

> for everyone. The teacher kept the course simple for everybody – change wasn't needed. I think if somebody had asked to change something, she would have agreed in that case. The learning process was very good. I couldn't have learnt more. (Learner 2)

The teacher also understands the problem that learning Estonian can cause a certain resistance on the part of the students if it is too difficult to learn. One possibility to overcome the resistance is to offer alternative exercises to the learners making it clear for them that they are responsible for the choice.

> I see what problems they encounter. If I explain the Estonian language – learners have to be given a period of adaptation, because it is difficult to acquire and there may be some resistance .... I always give choices. (Teacher)

The teacher is faced with the challenges of teaching and supporting language learning when the learners lack knowledge of the Latin alphabet; if there are insufficient learning skills or a lack of English or Russian language skills, which form the language basis of the course, then specially designed tasks and approaches are used.

7.14   Relationships
In this section we discuss the relationships between the teacher and the learners in the context of the language course. The key question is to assess these relationships along a continuum that ranges from authoritarian to democratic, which reflects the amount of control that migrant learners do or do not have over their learning.

7.15   Learning Atmosphere and Respect
The literature in adult education has placed a great deal of emphasis on the importance of establishing a climate for learning (Knowles, 1990) and establishing an adult learner-teacher relationship with the learner at the 'centre' (Chappell et al., 2003; Tennant & Pogson, 2002, p. 171). Malcolm Knowles suggests that adults learn more if they feel supported. They are more open to learning if they are respected and learn more from those they trust, a climate of openness is essential (1990, p. 127). In the context of the language course the relationship between the teacher and the learners developed in a supportive and open atmosphere as Schweisfurth states (2013a, p. 6) it reflects mutual respect between teachers and learners and gives value to mutual communication, cooperation and establishment of contacts, therefore it is important to create

a friendly atmosphere of trust for learning. The aim of the language course is to create a positive and dialogue-based environment. It is also one of the main tasks related to creating an atmosphere, where learners feel safe and respected. Issues and topics that could lead to conflicts are consciously avoided.

> It's important that you have to be nice and safe, it's important how to create an atmosphere. The learner must feel well, safe and secure. (Teacher)

As the programme coordinator assumed that *trust and relationship are important always in all modules of the Welcoming programme*, the atmosphere during the observed lesson was positive, open, and safe. Mutual respect between the teacher and the learners was obvious.

> Learning atmosphere was friendly, it was fun … we were able to share our experiences and thoughts, we had common coffee breaks and we talked to everyone …. Everybody felt free, you could say anything. (Learner 1)

The aim of the language course is also to support interaction and group processes to form a collaborative learning group and to support dialogue based relations between learners.

> The teacher knew and noticed every student. We used to sit in a circle, also in a group. Usually, the teacher asked us to find a dialogue partner in the group. After this we started to have a conversation. (Learner 2)

The learners created their own closed group on Facebook for interaction and communication with each other. Joint free time events were organised during which Estonian was used to practice the language. The teacher was also invited. The relations between the learners and the teacher were positive and open. The learners had good relations, which supported collaborative learning. Learning with the group was reported as a meaningful and useful experience for participants.

7.16 *Assessment*
Assessment follows up these principles by testing skills and by allowing for individual differences (Schweisfurth, 2013a). During the course the formative assessment was informal and at the end of the course more formal formative assessment took place. The language exam consists of an oral and written part. The aim of the assessment is not to check the results, but to support self-assessment and self-confidence of learners in using the Estonian language

in different situations. The final formative assessment is based on the final exam/test, which is conducted in pairs and based on a dialogue between two learners. After completing the exam/test, the results are discussed in the class with the teacher.

During the language course, students do tasks and tests that are discussed in several ways: with the teacher and in collaboration with other learners (pair discussion, a discussion in the small groups, self-check). The assessment in the process takes place in the form of giving feedback and discussion of tasks and homework assignments. Learners, who participated in at least 50% of the language course, get the certificate confirming attendance.

8 Conclusion

The peculiarity of the Estonian case is that the language study course is a part of the Welcoming programme focusing on needs of language learning and coping of adult migrants from countries of the global South. The programme offers necessary supportive services for settling and language learning is carried out simultaneously with other measures aiding the migrants to enter the labour market. The adaptation programme involves three components – society study, socio-economic integration, and essential language learning. All legal regulations in education are applicable to adults with a migrant background (Lifelong Learning Strategy, 2020). The right to education is equally guaranteed for all residents, regardless of ethnic, religious or citizenship background.

There is evidence that the main components of the LCE are implemented in the context of learner-centred teaching. There is concrete evidence that the language course for adults with a migrant background encourages collaboration, dialogue and motivates cooperation between learners by giving them possibilities to control their own learning process in a dialogue (in pairs, groups and with the teacher) during and at the end of the language course.

The language learning programme (80 hours) was designed by the team (coordinators of the Welcoming programme and language teachers with experience in teaching adults). The programme is based on A1 level and has structured content with concrete topics. The aim of the language course is to create a positive and dialogue-based environment for language learning. It is also one of the main tasks, which is related to creating an atmosphere where learners feel safe and respected. The language course programme is flexible and supports developing and improving the knowledge and skills of adults with a migrant background, helps them to manage better in their social integration and cope with real life experience in Estonia. The language study group is differentiated according to the language on which the course is based – which can be either Russian or Estonian. In the case under observation the basis language was English. The cultural background and previous experience of the learners was considered and constituted the basis for the language learning and teaching methods. The programme implements interactive and dialogue-based techniques and values the importance of independent work. This directs learners to make their own choices and supports the formation of an independent learner as well as giving responsibility for their language studies. The room and its setting, learning-teaching environment, study materials and online materials are relevant for teaching adults and their learning.

Learners are motivated to learn Estonian language due to communicative and practical needs and several external and internal factors, which are related to supportive engagement and teaching-learning process, relationships, open-respectful atmosphere, respectful contacts, interactive communication, teacher's personality and competency, personal and communicative needs. There are three approaches to teaching practices based on dialogue, activity and which support learner-centred learning: (a) social/interactive/dialogue based, (b) emotional/activating and (c) situational. The teacher used flexible approaches and suitable interactive techniques, individual approaches, and methods, which were relevant for adult learners.

The Welcoming programme (WP) and the language learning course as a part of WP creates a safe and supportive opportunity which facilitates coping with life and language learning in Estonia, which is necessary for adults with different cultural backgrounds, arriving to Estonia from outside the EU. The Estonian case study reflects that language learning and teaching practice are clearly aimed, focusing on learner-centredness, motivational and cultural aspects of learning. Teaching practice and relationships in the language programme are relevant and suitable for adults as learners.

> We did not have any examples to follow, we created both the form and the content in cooperation with the workers from the Ministry of Interior. An immensely interesting process. I think this programme could be an example for other EU countries to follow. As the pilot period of the current programme is ending, I am happy and sure that the programme must continue. The management of the Ministry of the Interior, who have visited our courses, holds the same view. It is considered to be a necessary and well-done thing. We will participate in the state tender for the next period of 3 years and will make our own suggestions to our offer. Concerning the content, needs and organisation of the programme, all went well, though some changes are necessary. I think that the programme

has found its place and is ready for development in the following period. (Policymaker: coordinator)

We did not find in our analysis any tensions in discourses of learners, teacher, and policymaker. Firstly, all legal regulations in education in Estonia are applicable to adults with a migrant background. Secondly, the main components of the LCE are implemented in the context of learner-centred teaching during the language course. Thirdly, the language course programme is flexible and supports developing and improving knowledge and skills, helps to manage better social integration and cope with real life experience. Finally, the case study indicates several positive advantages of the Welcoming programme, which offers supportive service and learning possibilities simultaneously.

The lessons learned from the analysis of the Estonian case study is that practice targets learner-centredness more clearly than educational policy and there is a need to find possibilities for balancing and finding suitable solutions for expressing those aims in the legal regulations. Moreover, the issues of adults with a migrant background and specifically the value of LCE education should become a far more visible part in concrete regulations and of the systematic preparation of adult educators and language teacher for foreigners in Estonia.

9 Limitations of the Methods

One main limitation in this case study is observation as method for collecting data, which does not guarantee reliability for data collection. The validity of research concerns the interpretation of observation (Silverman, 2004, p. 289). Another problem with this method is that not all phenomena, related with research questions can be observed (Flick, 2006, p. 226). We are fully aware that our data and interpretations are based only on one observed situation.

Notes

1 See Welcoming Programme, Your guide to settling in Estonia, https://www.tallinn.ee/eng/Uudis-Welcoming-programme.-Your-guide-to-settlingin-Estonia
2 https://www.kul.ee/en/activities/cultural-diversity/integration-measure
3 The information on the homepage https://settleinestonia.ee was used to explain the Welcoming programme.
4 www-teenus.blogspot.com
5 https://www.keeleklikk.ee/et/welcome
6 https://www.riigiteataja.ee/en/eli/525062015003/consolide

References

Boucouvalas, M., & Lawrence, R. L. (2010). Adult learning. In C. Kasworm, A. Rose, & J. Ross-Gordon (Eds.), *Handbook of adult and continuing education* (pp. 35–49). Sage.

Chappell, C., Hawke, G., Rhodes, C., & Solomon, N. (2003). *High level review of training packages phase 1 report*. ANTA. https://pdfs.semanticscholar.org/678c/da2ab367b5b15d2a5b112432865db49e2375.pdf

Churchill, S. (1994). Teachers as facilitators of cultural development: New roles and responsibilities. In L. Dubbeldam et al. (Eds.), *International yearbook of education, Vol. XLIV – Development, culture and education* (pp. 133–157). UNESCO.

Dörnyei, Z. (2003). *Attitudes, orientations, and motivations in language learning: Advances in theory, research and applications*. http://www.zoltandornyei.co.uk/uploads/2003-dornyei-ll(s).pdf

Dörnyei, Z. (2005). *The psychology of the language learner: Individual differences in second language acquisition*. Lawrence Erlbaum Associates.

Dörnyei, Z. (2007). Creating a motivating classroom environment. In J. Cummins & C. Davison (Eds.), *International handbook of English language teaching* (2nd ed., pp. 719–731). Springer.

Dörnyei, Z. (2014). Motivation in second language learning. In M. Celce-Murcia, D. M. Brinton, & M. A. Snow (Eds.), *Teaching English as a second or foreign language* (4th ed., pp. 518–531). National Geographic Learning/Cengage Learning.

Evans, W. (2002). Computer environments for content analysis: Reconceptualising the role of humans and computers. In O. V. Burton (Ed.), *Computing in the social sciences and humanities* (pp. 67–86). University of Illinois Press.

Flick, U. (2006). *An introduction to qualitative research*. Sage Publications.

Integration measure. (n.d.). Ministry of Culture. https://www.kul.ee/en/activities/cultural-diversity/integration

Knowles, M. S. (1990). Fostering competence in self-directed learning. In R. M. Smith (Ed.), *Learning to learn across the life span* (pp. 123–136). Jossey-Bass.

Kriger, T., & Tammaru, T. (2011). *Uusimmigrantide kohanemine Eestis*. http://www.kul.ee/sites/kulminn/files/intmon_2011_pt_8.pdf

Loogma, K., Sau-Ek, K., & Loogma, L. (2012). Country report: Estonia. In A. Nonchev & N. Tagarov (Eds.), *Integrating refugee and asylum-seeking children in the educational systems of EU Member States* (pp. 215–232). Centre for the Study of Democracy.

Lüüs, B. (2014). *Siseministeeriumi tegevused ESF-i meetmes „Võimaluste loomine Eestis elavate ning ühiskonda vähelõimunud püsielanike aktiivse hõive ja ühiskondliku aktiivsuse suurendamiseks ja hilisema lõimumise toetamiseks"*. Migratsiooni- ja piirivalvepoliitika osakond.

Mayring, P. (2000). Qualitative content analysis. *Forum Qualitative Sozialforschung/ Forum: Qualitative Social Research, 1*(2), art. 20. http://nbn-resolving.de/ urn:nbn:de:0114-fqs0002204

McClelland, D., Koestner, R., & Weinberger, J. (1989). How do self-attributed and implicit motives differ? *Psychological Review, 96,* 690–702.

Miles, M. B., & Huberman, A. M. (1994). *Qualitative data analysis: An expanded sourcebook* (2nd ed.). Sage Publications.

Patton, M. (2002). *Qualitative research and evaluation methods.* Sage Publications.

Pintrich, P. R., & De Groot, E. V. (1990). Motivational and self-regulated learning components of classroom academic performance. *Journal of Educational Psychology, 82,* 33–40.

Rannut, M., & Rannut, Ü. (2004). Uusimmigrantide kohanemine sihtkultuuris. In Ü. Rannut (Ed.), *Uusimmigrandid meie ühiskonnas ja haridussüsteemis. Käsiraamat eesti õppekeelega kooli õpetajatele, koolijuhtidele ja haridusametnikele* (pp. 102–124). Ilo.

Rannut, Ü. (2009). *Käsiraamat kolmandate riikide kodanike lõimimiseks.* Eestis.

Schweisfurth, M. (2013a). Learner-Centred education in international perspectives. *Journal of International and Comparative Education, 2*(1), 1–8.

Schweisfurth, M. (2013b). *Learner-centred education in international perspectives: Whose pedagogy for those development?* Routledge.

Silverman, D. (2004). *Qualitative research. theory, method and practice.* Sage publications.

Statistics Estonia. (2017). *Minifacts about Estonia.* Ofset OÜ. https://www.stat.ee/sites/default/files/2020-07/Minifacts_about_Estonia_2017.pdf

Tennant, M., & Pogson, R. (2002). *Learning and change in the adult years: A developmental perspective.* Jossey-Bass.

Thompson, P. (2013). Learner-centred education and 'cultural translation'. *International Journal of Educational Development, 33,* 48–58.

Tudor, I. (1993). Learner-centeredness in language teaching: Finding the right balance. *System, 20*(1), 31–44.

CHAPTER 5

Learner-Centred Education and Adult Education for Migrants in Glasgow

Bonnie Slade and Nicola Dickson

Abstract

Slade and Dickson explore the delivery of English for Speakers of Other Languages' (ESOL) classes to a cohort of migrants living in an area of Glasgow which is densely populated and multi-cultural. In stark contrast to other areas of the UK, the Scottish Government actively encourages migration; migrants are valued and considered important to help mitigate against Scotland's declining population and an aging demographic. The case study revealed that the migrant adult learner is at the core of delivery, and the staff value, respect and encourage the learners regardless of cultural background or academic ability. The community-based adult educators made no claims as to the learner-centredness of their approach to adult education, but these principles underpinned practice at all levels of delivery.

Keywords

community-based adult education – Scotland – ESOL classes – learner-centred education – migration

1   Introduction

There are a host of Government programmes designed to support migrant populations and enable them to 'work, to join family, or to study' in Scotland (Scottish Government, 2018, p. 6). In stark contrast to other areas of the UK, the Scottish Government actively encourages migration into the country. Here, migrants are valued and considered important to help mitigate against Scotland's declining population and an aging demographic (National Records of Scotland, 2018). The Scottish Government advocates that adult learning and education (ALE) should be life-long, life-wide and learner-centred and accessible for all, regardless of status (Slade & Dickson, 2020). Migrants coming to

Scotland tend to be are young and economically active, and 'have the potential to compliment the stock of human capital in the host country' (Scottish Government, 2016, p. 7). The Scottish Government provides adult learning and education (ALE) opportunities through public sector agencies for migrants to improve their English language skills and to integrate. English for Speakers of Other Languages' (ESOL classes) are a critical component to this provision, as they 'enable participation and integration to Scottish life through work, study, family and local community' (Scottish Government, 2017, p. 54). This chapter explores the delivery of ESOL classes to a cohort of migrants living in an area of Glasgow which is densely populated and multi-cultural. A case study from the area is presented using Schweisfurth's 'learner-centred education' (LCE) framework (2013), in which LCE is defined as 'a pedagogical approach which gives learners, and demands from them, a relatively high level of active control over the content and process of learning. What is learnt, and how, are therefore shaped by learners' needs, capacities and interests' (p. 20). In this chapter we consider the application of four elements of LCE (motivation, epistemology, techniques and relationships) in relation to the learning needs of a diverse group of migrants accessing an ESOL class in this small geographical area of Scotland.

2 ESOL Provision

The area of Glasgow selected for this study hosts a culturally diverse community. The area has historically attracted large numbers of migrants and 'probably has the most ethnically diverse population in Scotland' (COSLA, 2015, p. 12). The population continues to diversify and grow, and due to immigration between 2001 and 2010, the community grew by almost 15%. Scottish Government agencies meet the many challenges of this diverse and densely populated area by providing statutory services which target the needs of the migrant population. They strive to offer community-based, flexible adult learning opportunities for English speakers of all abilities. In 2017, our research team explored the provision of 'English for Speakers of Other Languages' (ESOL) classes for adult migrants in this community. We identified an ESOL centre which catered for the diverse needs of the adult migrants in the area and conducted 5 interviews with the Programme Coordinator, an 'English for Speakers of Other Languages' (ESOL) Tutor and three adult learners. In addition, we observed two taught ESOL sessions and ate a hot meal with migrant learners and their families in the centre's public space, where a conversation café took place following the taught classes.

3   The Centre and the Provision for Adult Migrant Groups

The Scottish Government speaks of the need for Learner-centred Education (LCE) in their 'Statement of Ambition' (2014) policy document and recommends that education providers consider the diverse needs and interests of the adult learner. The Programme Coordinator was aware of the ALE policy but stressed that the service had developed organically and responsively, transforming over time to meet the changing needs of the population served. Originally designed as an employability service for migrant adults, it was recognised that English language training was a primary requirement for all migrant groups, as written and spoken language skills were intrinsically linked to employability and integration:

> The needs and demand for this service is through absolute necessity. We first started doing English language training when this programme was an employability programme. First, we thought we'd teach people English, then we realised we needed to teach many people to simply read and write. We didn't digest the Scottish policy documents when we began …. I think the fundamental thing is that you need a level of English to work here and there are so few jobs they need everything they can. (Programme Coordinator)

There were a diverse range of migrant groups in the area. When visiting the centre, the research team met individuals from varied ethnic backgrounds, including those from Romania, Pakistan, Afghanistan and Czechoslovakia accessing the learning facility. We observed large family groups at the centre. The staff reported that it was not unusual to have three generations of the same family (grandmother, mother, and daughter) attend any one ESOL session. It was estimated that approximately 300 people a year engaged with the service, with many attending on a weekly basis. The remarkable diversity of the migrant population was highlighted by the Programme Coordinator, who commented, 'we've done social surveys where we're found there are 32 languages and 52 nationalities just in 13 housing blocks. So that's the kind of thing we are dealing with. It's very unusual in Scotland but it is the most diverse community in Scotland'.

3.1   *The Centre Offering: ESOL Classes, a Free Lunch and Creche Facilities*
In addition to weekly English language classes, the centre offered a free lunch in the form of a conversation café in the public space. This provision offered

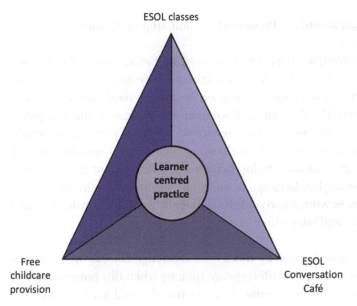

FIGURE 5.1   The service delivery, with learner-centred practice at the core

an opportunity for informal learning, as outlined in the Scottish Government's policy on migration. Migrants were invited to attend one of two streams of formal English classes (basic and advanced) in the morning, then receive a free hot meal and practice their conversational English over lunch. Free childcare was also available to parents of pre-school age children during the ESOL class and lunchtime meal. Figure 5.1 illustrates the offering of the case study organisation, in which we observed a form of holistic practice, with learner-centred adult learning at the core.

In the following section we detail the ways in which this holistic practice shaped the delivery of the ESOL provision and how this, along with the three core deliverables, appeared to benefit the migrant groups accessing the centre. The centre's offering is considered in relation to the four elements of LCE (motivation, epistemology, techniques and relationships).

4   Motivations

4.1   *Speaking English, Attending the Conversation Café and Utilising the Crèche*

A primary motivation for migrants accessing the centre was to learn English. The centre staff identified that irrespective of background, the migrant groups all shared the need to be able to communicate effectively in written and spoken

English. In interview, the Programme Coordinator summarised: 'people may come from traumatic circumstances. Some come from non-traumatic circumstances, or they may be highly skilled workers from their home countries, but they have that commonality of needing to communicate in English'.

The conversation café was recognised as an additional draw for many migrant families. The staff recognised that the provision of hot food was an important component to the service delivery: 'the idea of the ESOL café is people can come here and learn, they can forget about their kids and the other things and just concentrate on learning' (Programme Coordinator). Staff and adult learners commented that the hot meal was a key draw for the migrant groups. One adult learner described the importance of the café to some of the migrant learners who did not have access to hot food in their shared accommodation. She also spoke of the welcoming and hospitable atmosphere in the café, and the encouragement from staff to mix and converse. This provision, she said, was of great value:

> We come to the table. Talking, laughing maybe. I'm very happy. I sit down and I like it. There's some cooking, (it's) good …. Sometimes people no eat in the house. Here the children go in the school and get the meal. Some lady not cook. Not understand how. (Adult learner from basic ESOL stream, originally from Romania)

The crèche provision was also considered to be central to the service, particularly for the women who cared for their young families. This was an additional extra provided by the centre, as typically Scottish ALE providers do not provide a crèche. In Scotland, childcare is expensive and limited in availability. In interview, both staff and service users recognised that the crèche was a useful tool to involve parents and young families into the service:

> The crèche is important. About two thirds of our learners are women and many of them come and leave their children in the crèche. (Childcare is) a real barrier and it's so expensive. It's not possible to do this in the college or more formal setting. We need to support people where they are at. (Programme Coordinator)

In interview, the female adult learners spoke of the importance of the crèche facility for access to the ESOL sessions and identified the free childcare as a key motivator to their attendance. The provision allowed them to attend lessons, practice their English and meet other migrants in the community, without the distraction of their caring responsibilities. One adult learner described the freedom the childcare had allowed her as a parent and as an adult learner. She reflected on the difference the centre had made to her perceived confidence and place in the community, and how important it was to encourage other women to come and take advantage of the free childcare provision:

> My family, they say why you go school. I say I go for my life. I go for my mum, my father and for my children. For myself. To understand more. It's no good being at the home and do some cooking. I go and look people in the face. I go and see people and I learn new things. I tell my friends this and they say maybe I'll come with you. I say come! Anytime they can come. I tell them come. This person has three children; she come three times. I say come and you'll understand English. She come! (Adult learner from basic ESOL stream, originally from Romania)

4.2   The Social Aspect of the Service Delivery

The need to promote and sustain opportunities for the migrants to mix socially was identified as a key component to the service provision. The research team observed staff engaging with a range of adult learners, from early teenage learners to older adults, and encouraging them to access the centre to meet, talk, and congregate. The staff acknowledged that the opportunities for socialising were key to the service provision. The Programme Coordinator highlighted: 'some may come for the café. Others because they have a good relationship with the Tutors, or they need some one-to-one support. If particular families are difficult to find, they know they'll be here and so they come to find them. People's motivations are so varied'. In interview, the Tutor recognised the importance of providing opportunities for socialising for the migrant groups. She gave the example of twin brothers who accessed the centre because they could play the piano in the community café following their language class:

> Some people come because they feel they want it, some come for just socialising. For example, we have 18-year-old twins who used to come simply because we allowed them to play the piano. They were so musical, they came to class, and then they played the piano. They weren't allowed the piano unless they came to class. This was a real incentive for them to come every week. This is why they came here. And they were here all the time. (Tutor)

4.3   Gendered Learning

When observing the sessions, the research team saw that large numbers of female learners were in both the café and the taught classes in comparison to low numbers of males. The staff reported that there had been a dramatic change in the numbers of men accessing the centre since the emphasis shifted from an employability programme to an English language programme. The Tutor and Programme Coordinator commented that in previous years, many Romanian men attended the centre. This was due to an economic draw; In 2016, it was a prerequisite to speak and understand English to sell a magazine to help the homeless. In 2017, the magazine owners changed their policy and English speaking was no longer a requirement. Following this shift, the number of men accessing the centre noticeably dropped. The Tutor detailed how this policy change resulted in a dramatic decrease in the number of male learners:

> When the other Tutor came back she was shocked and says where have all the Romanian men gone? I used to have full classes of them … what turned out is the job centre said that for them to sell 'The Big Issue' they had to have a stamp saying they were learning English, so they would come every week. This is no longer the case and if there is no requirement, they will not come. (Tutor)

Gendered motivations impacted on the uptake of services available at the centre. The staff recognised that in some migrant cultures, traditional gender roles were expected. The Programme Coordinator said that for some Roma communities for example, low-paid employment can be seen to be of greater value for men than ad hoc learning opportunities. For this migrant group, men were more likely to pursue economic opportunities than prioritise adult learning: 'education is recognised as valuable but it's not as essential as paid work. So, if you have the option to learn or go and work in the car wash, you're going to the car wash every time. They don't see the merit' (Programme Coordinator).

The research team were unable to formally speak to the men accessing the centre but interviewed three female adult migrants and spoke about their motivations. In both the basic and more advanced classes, the female adult learners stated that their primary motivation was to learn (or improve on) their written and spoken English to assist their children in their schooling. They saw language acquisition as important for their family's integration into Scottish society. They argued that English proficiency would improve their position in relation to the jobs market in the future, but this was not their current primary focus:

> … At this time, I need my English for my kids. I can't do it properly yet. Maybe the kid's homework, I will be a help for them. I'm not thinking about the future or the jobs now. (Adult learner from advanced ESOL stream, originally from Pakistan)

... I help with work at home with my boy. I look and say you do this one, this one. I help. We have a small notebook and I help with homework. (Adult learner from basic ESOL stream, originally from Romania)

In the next section we consider the nature of knowledge in the epistemology of the service delivery, including the accessibility of the provision, the perceived relevance of the curriculum and the ways in which learning is assessed.

5 Epistemology

The Learner-centred Educator should build on the existing knowledge of the adult learner. The staff identified that this was a key issue with service provision as the migrants accessing the centre were from varied academic backgrounds and had differing abilities and knowledge bases.

5.1 *Accessibility of the Provision*

The centre staff streamed their adult learners by their English ability and classroom experience. The first stream catered for migrants who had rudimentary spoken English and required simple reading and writing classes. The second stream was for more advanced English speakers with a higher level of English literacy. The Programme Coordinator explained their approach: 'we have two classes to develop literacy. There are people there who can barely hold a pen right up to the people ready to learn and understanding the phonics'.

Both streams of ESOL provision were organised to be as accessible as possible for the migrant learners. There was no booking system and no need to enrol on the programme to access the sessions. Where possible, the migrants were pre-assessed before joining a class to determine which learning stream best met their requirements. However, time constraints and the large numbers of people accessing the centre meant that the teaching staff sometimes had to be responsive, and place learners in a class without assessment. This led to occasions where adult learners were moved from one stream to the other during the taught session. There was in-built flexibility to do so, as the teaching staff recognised that their priority was to accommodate many skills sets in the classroom. The Tutor described: '... sometimes we have to make the decision to shift people because suddenly you get 20 plus Romanians turning up suddenly. You have to sometimes organise the classes. You cannot plan. You have to move people around'.

The research team witnessed this adaption during the observed session, when a large migrant family entered the second half of an ESOL class. The Tutor skilfully accommodated the new arrivals and welcomed three generations of learners from the same Roma family into the session. On reflecting on this in interview, the Tutor spoke of the challenge of ensuring her learners were working with materials which are appropriate to their learning needs. She identified the importance of bringing people together with similar competencies to engage in learning, commenting: 'people who re-educated need differentiated materials. They are not here in the first stage for very long. It would slow them down and intimidate others' (Tutor).

The centre staff did not know how many migrants would attend any one session, and as people were welcomed to join at any point during the 2-hour lesson, the Tutors sometimes had to manage very large class sizes. In interview, the adult learners stated that this flexible provision and sometimes larger class sizes did not adversely impact on their learning experience: 'the difference of a big or a small class, it doesn't matter. Today is a very big class. It doesn't matter. I like a big class, you get to meet other people. What matters is what the Tutor (is) telling us' (Adult learner from advanced ESOL stream, originally from Pakistan).

To assist with the numbers of learners and different skill sets, the centre was well supported by volunteers who joined the classes and offered one-to-one support for the less able learners. This helped the wide range of literacy in the class. During observation, we noted that the first stream class had three volunteers on hand to support the learners. The Tutor directed the volunteers to work one-to-one with the more novice English speakers while she supported the rest of the group. The adult learners reported that the class experience was a good one and were not affected by the complex organisational issues. One adult learner positively reflected: 'the class is nice organised from the teacher. In other classes the helper is here as well. It is nicely organised, a good experience' (Adult learner from advanced ESOL stream, originally from Pakistan).

5.2 Relevance of the Curriculum

To live well in Scotland, it is understood that migrants have to understand and speak English. The adult migrant learners wanted to improve their English language skills, as these were critical for their (and their families) integration. One adult learner said: 'we are here to learn English. In the community we are going to the doctor, we are going to the hospital, teachers. But we can't speak properly. We need to speak English. We are trying but it is hard. So, we are just trying to speak. Everybody needs better English!' (Adult learner from advanced ESOL stream, originally from Pakistan).

The ESOL programme's curriculum was tailored to meet the perceived information needs and interests of the migrants. There was no fixed content, with the staff preferring to offer a fluid, responsive and tailored approach to learning. The Programme Coordinator stated that the curriculum had been developed to reflect the 'real life' experiences of living in Glasgow:

> We try and relate the curriculum back to real life, like learning about transport, health provision, local services. We certainly historically have worked with the NHS, employability services. We are better letting people know about how the school system works than building a sandcastle at the seaside.

5.3 Meeting the Information Needs of the Migrant

In interview, the Tutor spoke of her commitment to build and maintain communications with the migrant learners to help them to thrive. She understood that adult learners could become demotivated if they did not progress with their English. However, as many of the migrants accessing the centre were only exposed to English speaking once a week in the ESOL class and café, learning English could be a long and frustrating process:

> This class is very, very difficult. People come and they go. You could see, they came in halfway in the lesson .... People who are beginners who don't have literacy, it takes ages. It takes ages to learn. They lose motivation very quickly and feel they are stupid, that they can't learn. (Tutor)

The staff worked closely with different migrant groups to explore their information needs. The Tutor tailored the curriculum to ensure relevant information was conveyed through the classes. In interview, the example was given by the Programme Coordinator and Tutor of many migrants struggling with the concept of a date of birth, as this was neither required nor recorded in their home countries. In Britain, the date of birth is essential as it is used to identify and link a person to their health and social security records. The migrants told the staff they were confused by this pre-requisite and had encountering many problems with the National Health Service (NHS) and doctor's surgery. The staff adapted their lesson plans to work with learners and help them understand the need for a date of birth. They coached the migrants to know how to communicate their birth date. With this information, the migrants were better equipped to use the services in Glasgow, as the Tutor elaborated:

> ... there are things like are important, like health (and) making appointments. Telling your date of birth, which some people don't know because it's never been recorded. (Or) if you've never been to school you may know but can't say. We have to deliver a session to help the NHS, to help them to get people to communicate their date of birth. So, we focus on this, to get it into their heads that it's very important to know.

In interview, an adult learner described how her self-perception had changed because of her visits to the centre. Through adult learning, her self-belief and the perception of her abilities had transformed. She had a new confidence and was able to reflect on her role in the family and her identity as a mother and wife. She argued that this was a great positive and that other women from her community could also benefit by broadening their horizons through learning:

> I like to understand more from the life. Not just cooking, cleaning in the house, it is no position. Yes, clean and cook a little for the children, but need more from life. Some lady from Romania, they have six or seven children, ten children some lady! And I say put the children in the school. That be you free and you come in the school and I help you. (Adult learner from basic ESOL stream, originally from Romania)

5.4 Assessing Learning

No formal assessment was used to measure the migrant's learning. The drop-in nature of the class and the transient way in which the migrants accessed the centre meant it was not possible to formally assess the extent of the migrants' learning. In class we observed the Tutor using simple tests to check the information was being conveyed and the migrants understood the course content. In interview, the adult learners stated that they did not expect to be examined or assessed in their learning, as this was as an informal, once weekly provision: 'no, I don't think we come here regularly. We only come here when we can, it is not three days a week. There are no exams, I don't think so' (Adult learner from advanced ESOL stream, originally from Pakistan).

Staff encouraged the adult learners to progress to the local college if they were ready to gain a qualification for their English. The college courses were appropriate for those hoping to secure employment; they involve continual assessment and are able to grant certificates. For many migrants accessing the centre however, a commitment to a college education was not feasible. For example, two of the adult learners interviewed had previously held college places but had to withdraw due to their family commitments:

> I come here I have some problems. My husband has the heart attack and I'm caring for this baby. I say to the teacher I'm sorry I have some problems and I have this baby. The college say okay, you go to this place (The centre). They gave me a letter. Go together with this letter and go. So, I meet (the Tutor) and I show her the letter and she says, 'say it'. And I begin and start my reading and writing. (Adult learner from basic ESOL stream, originally from Romania)

The lack of childcare provision in the colleges was perceived to be an additional barrier. In interview an adult learner said that she would like to attend college as this would give her more opportunities to learn English in the week, rather than just via a weekly session. However, due to her childcare constraints she could not attend until her three young children are school age:

> ... when they 10 weeks ago tell me about college here I say do they have the crèche at the college? I say to her please you take the request for me that the college start with the crèche and I'll be there. (Adult learner from advanced ESOL stream, originally from Pakistan)

Another more advanced learner spoke of preparing to return to formal education but being unable to access formal provision due to the long waiting lists for English classes: 'I enjoy going to college but feel not well and so stop it. So now I reapply, but no spacey [sic]. I reapply many times but I'm just on the waiting list. One day only at community class'. (Adult learner from advanced ESOL stream, originally from Pakistan).

Many migrants stay therefore, unassessed, at the centre and work to improve their English at a level and pace appropriate to them. Rather than formal assessment, the Programme Coordinator spoke of how the participants can still progress by volunteering in the classes and assisting other migrant learners in their English literacy and development. This is how progression can be best measured and understood:

> I think we see the value in everyone, and we don't turn learners away. But we also want to see people progress, we don't want them to become stagnant .... We like to see the progression in the people who use our services. People might come to us and go on to volunteer with the service, to go onto become sessional workers. (Programme Coordinator)

In the following section, some of the techniques used in the classroom to engage with the migrant learners are explored.

6   Techniques

Lessons were designed and taught in a creative and engaging manner, building on the knowledge of the diverse group of learners. Flexibility was a necessity in this vibrant environment. The centre staff attempted to make the ESOL sessions as accessible as possible and tailor the content to the interests of the adult learners. A mix of 'frontal, chalk and talk' to independent group work and inquiry, as highlighted in the LCE continuum was observed in the classroom setting (Schweisfurth, 2013, p. 11).

6.1   *Building on the Knowledge of the Learner*

In interview, the adult learners in the more advanced ESOL sessions said that they were satisfied with the teaching style and content of the ESOL sessions. They respected the Tutor's judgement and welcomed the course content. When given the opportunity to comment on the content of the ALE, they were unwilling to critique the teaching in any way. The adult learners stated they had no additional learning needs outside of those on offer. In the more advanced learning stream, an adult learner said that she implicitly trusted the Tutor: 'it is a surprise every time. We take a lesson, last time it was on Edinburgh, one time the library, the job …. The teacher knows what is best for us' (Adult learner from advanced ESOL stream, originally from Pakistan).

The Tutor, who is originally from Poland, stated that her own migrant status helped her understand the many challenges involved in learning the English language. She described the value of knowing certain words or phrases in a different language: 'it's important to use key words they need (or) understand. Like 'is it normal?', 'Stop' and so on … I come from a different culture and I can understand how they can feel! My language is the same, in that I'm not a native English speaker, so I can understand'.

A key question in the literature is how the Learner-centred Educator builds on the existing knowledge of the learner. The Tutor spoke of the difficulty in building on migrant students' knowledge as first they need to establish a shared vocabulary. A common language and mutual understanding were needed to communicate to the wider group. The Tutor's initial focus is to provide the appropriate language tools to allow the adult learners to communicate. From this, they can build. The Tutor argued that until the adult learner has the right words, the building on knowledge outside of language acquisition is problematic:

> It's very difficult to do unless you have the shared experience. Like if it was a lesson about jobs, they can speak about the jobs in the family or what do you do at home? … It has to come from the learners, but you need to give them the vocabulary first. To get them to talk about families and what they do, first I need to give a lesson on jobs and what that involves, stuff like that. Then we have the vocabulary. (Tutor)

In interview an adult learner echoed this sentiment, describing how she now understands the importance of vocabulary and the correct pronunciation of

English words. Through her engagement with the more advanced ESOL class, she can be more clearly understood and communicate more effectively in English: 'I was learning about the jobs. I was saying PlumBer and my teacher says no Plumber, it's said like this, not PlumBer. I also didn't know the difference between employed and unemployed. My teacher told me employed means you have the job, whereas unemployed means you do not have the job' (Adult learner from advanced ESOL stream, originally from Pakistan).

6.2   Teaching Techniques

Key to the teaching practice was the provision of accessible information. The Tutor described a range of techniques she used to communicate and engage her learners. In observation, we saw the Tutor engaging her students through song. She asked the adult learners to sing a phrase and learn the rhythm of the words. They did so with laughter and interest. Afterwards the Tutor explained: 'one of the best techniques is to get them to sing the sentences. It's much easier to sing than to say it' (Tutor). In interview, the Tutor described the many ways in which she worked with her students. She said that using songs, words, and phrases from the migrants' own culture was also particularly effective. These interactions were enjoyable and fun and showed that she is interested in their own language. She explained:

> I've learnt songs for my Romanians, I know some phrases, it's a great icebreaker. I also know some Slovak which is close to Russian and to Polish so …. And Arabic helps very much for people also from Afghanistan they speak Farsi but there are one or two words which are the same. Sometimes if I have one or two learners and one is lost and is asking the other one, I can understand and say in Arabic 'Yes'. This also gives some assurance to them. Especially if I know for example, the meaning of their names. They like this! 'Ah you are called a flower' You know? That's kind of nice. (Tutor)

The research team observed the Tutor using her body movements and exaggerated gestures to engage with the learners. Throughout the class, she was expressive and demonstrative. The learners watched her with interest and are keen to share their attempts at speaking and spelling in English. Each effort was praised with a loud 'Bravo' from the teacher.

The Tutor spoke of the many roles she adopted to develop rapport in class, and the importance of drawing on different personas to engage with the learners. These techniques resulted in successful exchanges in the classroom. She

ADULT EDUCATION FOR MIGRANTS IN GLASGOW

concluded: 'you have to be motherly, you have to be a clown, singer ... entertainer. Also, you have to be strict. People are used to this' (Tutor).

6.3 *Teaching Activities*

The Tutor offered a description of a group activity she used with learners as they try and understand the complexities of the Scottish dialect. Glaswegian is an argot with a heavy accent and liberal use of slang. One activity to counter this was described, whereby common Scottish phrases were offered, and the learners encouraged to try and translate them into the English. She explained: 'for St. Andrew's Day we did Scottish expressions and they had to match them with the English words on the wall. They loved this! Then we got a Scottish person to say the words in Scottish in a very animated way. There is learning, there is always learning' (Tutor).

The Tutor encouraged learning outside of the classroom using mobile technology and educational 'Apps'. However, she identified that the effectiveness of the approach was dependent on the degree of responsibility the migrant learner could take for their own learning. If motivated and engaged, they could use the recommended Apps and progress quickly. The responsibility for learning was be dependent on a number of factors including the support and encouragement to learn at home, as the Tutor described: 'I show them applications on the phone. They do it. For example, we went to the library and I wanted to show them literacy for learning. They all loved it, but not all could use it at home. If they don't have the support, the understanding. They will not use it. This is the problem' (Tutor).

In the final section we consider the importance of classroom relationships in relation to the delivery of the ESOL sessions and the inclusion of the learners. Once again, we see that the holistic, nurturing approach is integral to the delivery.

7 Relationships

The centre staff were inclusive and welcoming, building in opportunities for relationships with both the staff team and the wider migrant community. In relation to LCE and the continuum from 'authoritarian' to 'democratic' teaching relationships, we observed the Tutors to be nurturing and positive, rather than authoritarian in their approach (Schweisfurth, 2013, p. 12). This inclusivity was particularly important when welcoming such a diverse range of migrant groups, where outside of the classroom, tensions were sometimes felt.

7.1 Classroom Relationships

Due to the many nationalities and migrant groups accessing the ESOL provision, the staff reported that sometimes there were some tensions felt between those accessing the centre. In the classroom, however, the staff promoted respect and equality, and the negative attitudes towards different races and cultures were not considered problematic. The staff identified and understood that there were deeply engrained differences between cultures, but the classroom was reserved as a place of tolerance and acceptance:

> I don't treat people any differently and people in the class respect each other, even if they didn't go to school. Here there are no tensions in the class but the way they talk about each other outside! (laughs). It can be very negative but here in class it is very positive. (Tutor)

> When you have the Slovakians, Roma and Pakistani communities you have lots of dynamics there. Sometimes you have gestures, eye-rolling and so on. There is usually always tolerance in the class but individuals bring their own prejudices into the classroom, like anywhere. (Programme Coordinator)

When the teaching process was recognised to be challenging for the staff it was not because of the many migrant groups and their conflicting ideologies, but due to the flexible and inclusive learning environment. For example, when necessary the Tutor allowed pre-school children to be present during the basic ESOL sessions, even though a crèche was provided. In the session which we observed, two young children were on the laps of migrant mothers throughout the class. The Tutor explained in interview that she allowed the women to bring their children in because if she did not, they would have to leave the class and lose the chance to learn English. Therefore, as long as the children were not too disruptive, they were able to stay with their parent. This respectful and accepting approach to the migrant women is another example of the holistic model of practice offered at the centre. An adult learner stated in interview that this was different to other establishments where there was no childcare provision:

> Yes, they bring her to me if she is crying. That's okay. In college, the crèche is not allowed but I'm here and that's why – the crèche is here …. My child is with me and quiet and not crying, then yes, I can have her in class. (Adult learner from advanced ESOL stream, originally from Pakistan)

7.2 Supporting the Vulnerable Adult Learner

The friendly and open relationships between staff and adult learners was apparent to the research team, as observers at both the ESOL classes and café.

Throughout our visits, the staff were welcoming and inclusive. The positive approach of the Tutors was recognised by the Programme Coordinator as key to the project delivery, as it was understood that some of the migrants may have had negative and damaging learning experiences in their pasts. The Tutor spoke of striving to build positive relationships with her students; to show compassion, understanding and respect through her teaching. She recognised that the quality of the experience the migrants had at the centre would impact on them as adult learners. She hoped to motivate them to attend and thrive, not to demotivate individuals and give them a poor experience of adult education. She summarised: 'if you spoil it as a teacher, (or) if they come to you once and you spoil it, she will never come to school again' (Tutor). An Adult Learner, originally from Romania, described the democratic and respectful environment as a surprise, particularly in relation to the Tutor's acceptance of her limited abilities:

> I'm looking and the teacher very nice and looking at all people, asking what country? The teacher the same to them and have respect. I like very much. I say to my teacher, 'sorry I never went to school' and 'I no read this or speak this' and they say 'no problem'. They have the time to do this with you, slowly. (Adult learner from the basic ESOL stream, originally from Romania)

However, relationships could be difficult when a more vulnerable learner developed dependency on a staff member. One adult learner spoke of her disappointment when her Tutor was unavailable for her lesson. She said she had a 'friendship' with the Tutor and did not want to move class or be taught by another teacher: 'It's a problem. I sometimes feel sad. Last month my Tutor not coming. I say no good. I no understand and she not a very good friend to me' (Adult learner from the basic ESOL stream, originally from Romania).

The Tutor was sympathetic to the vulnerabilities of the migrants. She recognised that they have experienced many hardships and be inherent vulnerable. It was understood that many have had traumatic pasts and simply need to feel safe and wanted:

> ... they want to be loved. I had one saying she loved me and sometimes called me her Mum and I said don't call me your Mum, I'm your teacher .... I know this girl, she was trying to get my attention all the time, she was a child with nothing.

The Tutor's solution was to build the relationships, show compassion, understanding and acceptance through her teaching: 'many of the learners have additional problems, loneliness, not being accepted. Many of them their families don't support them. This is the only thing to enjoy and feel loved. This is so important' (Tutor).

7.3   Working in Partnership

There was a feeling of mutual respect between the learners and staff at the centre. The adult learners trusted the Tutors and welcomed their guidance. The relationships were built on equality. In addition to women with young families, the research team observed teenagers accessing the centre. Staff spoke of the need to support these young people, as they needed guidance and tailored information. Working holistically, the staff ensured that the young people were able to access information and were aware of local support services. The Tutor described how her conversations with the young people would lead to deepened understanding of their needs. She gave an example of how she worked with outside agencies to ensure they communicated with the adolescent migrants in a manner which could be understood:

> ... When kids tell me about their drug intake and problems with the police, there is not a lot you can do. We try to get other agencies here, like Rape Crisis, the Police; We had 6 sessions for rights and responsibilities for this country. I asked the police to send their materials so that it was pitched at the right level. I had to make sure they knew the vocabulary so they could follow the information. (Tutor)

The Programme Coordinator invited government representatives in to work with the migrant groups and share information about Scotland's housing policy, health service, benefits and education. They adopted a coordinated approach, worked together in partnership, to serve the complex needs of the migrant population:

> ... We have a family support service for people in six main areas: education, training, health, social connections, English and literacy. Through that work we've got a really good sense of what people are entitled to, their needs and what's out there. We tend to build on the connections we've got from that work. We also work closely with the voluntary sector and local and national providers. (Programme Coordinator)

7.4   Barriers to Learning for Adult Migrants

The staff at the centre recognised that even with the strongest of relationships, the influence the external environment could impact on the adult learners' ability to learn. Some learners seemed to be naturally resilient and regardless of the many challenges in their lives, they were able to attend the classes, learn English and move through the learning streams. Others, however, did not progress as easily and were unable to improve on their English language skills. In many cases, staff recognised, this was not due to a lack of personal motivation. Some migrants lived in chaotic households, where the acquisition of English language was frowned upon or considered a low priority. The Programme Coordinator spoke of delivering more than an English learning programme because of issues faced by migrants outside of the centre:

> ... We would just focus on learning the English language and written word, but if you have to go back to a house where there are eighteen people living there, you've got a landlord that's treating you like dirt and so on, you have to look at everything .... If you have someone with nine kids (or) there's domestic abuse going on, then learning will never be sustainable. We can't do everything to help these people, but we do our best. (Programme Coordinator)

The staff had learnt of the complex home environments of those accessing the centre, with migrant families often living together in one communal space, sometimes with many children in one overcrowded room. The Tutor explained that when in this environment, even the most motivated adult learners could struggle to focus: 'I've seen households where there is no space, where it's buzzing with children. There is a difficulty to just sit down and work'.

It was understood that cultural expectations formed barriers to learning for some of the migrant groups. The perceived value put on adult education was dependent on the perceived role of the individual within the family unit. The example has been given that in some migrant groups, the men are expected to be the primary earners and to prioritise paid employment over learning. In the same vein, women are often expected to adopt caring responsibilities in the home and not leave the house to learn or to secure employment. The Tutor spoke of how she had heard family members say that that a woman's place was in the home, not the classroom:

> [Learning] is not seen well in some houses. One I asked why her Mum stopped coming and she said it's because of her Father ... he is not happy. He wants her to cook (and) if he sees her at home doing something else, it's no good. (Tutor)

As a result of the family environment and cultural expectations, some adult learners were unable to practice their English outside of the once-weekly session at the centre. For these migrants, the process of learning English was slow and frustrating. According to the Tutor this was a common issue amongst her learners and led to slow progress in the basic English class: 'these learners, at least half of them, don't do anything at all. This is their only chance to do any learning when they come here, once a week' (Tutor). When opportunities are limited to learn and practice English, an adult learner's ability to develop language skills is impacted. One adult learner said:

> My daughter and son think it is easy for English, but I think it is very, very hard. In school all the time English, then when my daughter came home, only English. My son speaks in Punjabi. I need to speak English but I only here. (Adult learner from advanced ESOL stream, originally from Pakistan)

8 Conclusions

This is a centre where the holistic needs of the migrant learner are at the core. The staff team work hard to consider the adult learners' motivations, including the provision of free childcare, a hot meal, and an understanding of meeting the migrant populations social needs in order to fight isolation and loneliness. They built on migrants' diverse knowledge base, while maintaining their primary focus of developing spoken and written English language skills. The staff strove to work with the varied groups to ensure that their language skills were sufficient to navigate their host environment. They tailored the curriculum to meet the needs of the migrants by working closely with the differing ethnic groups and in partnership with government agencies, to ensure there was a shared understanding of their information and support needs. The classroom relationships were nurturing, responsive, encouraging, and safe. The service providers made no claims as to the learner-centredness of their approach to adult education, but the LCE principles underpinned practice at all levels of delivery. The centre is a unique offering in the ALE field in terms of the package of support available to Glasgow's migrants and it could be argued that it is an exemplar of learner-centred adult education. The migrant adult learner is at the core of delivery and the staff value, respect and encourage those who access the centre, regardless of cultural background or academic ability.

References

Convention of Scottish Local Authorities (COSLA). (2015). *Migration policy toolkit: An online guide to welcoming, integrating and engaging migrant communities in Scotland.* http://www.migrationscotland.org.uk/migration

National Records for Scotland. (2018). *Scotland's population – The Registrar General's annual review of demographic trends.* https://www.nrscotland.gov.uk/files/statistics/rgar/2017/rgar17.pdf

Schweisfurth, M. (2013). *Learner-centred education in international perspective: Whose pedagogy for whose development?* Routledge.

Scottish Government. (2014). *Adult learning in Scotland: Statement of ambition.* https://www.education.gov.scot/Documents/adult-learning-statement.pdf

Scottish Government. (2015). *Welcoming our learners: Scotland's ESOL strategy 2015–2020.* https://dera.ioe.ac.uk/22892/2/ESOLStrategy2015to2020_tcm4-855848_Redacted.pdf

Scottish Government. (2016). *The impacts of migrants and migration into Scotland.* https://pdfs.semanticscholar.org/e312/82dfed72eacb4fa4c0e425b34858051d8aa1.pdf

Scottish Government. (2017). *New Scots: Integrating refugees in Scotland's communities 2014–2017 final report.* www.gov.scot/publications/new-scots-integrating-refugees-scotlands-communities-2014-2017-final-report-9781786526960/

Scottish Government. (2018). *New Scots: Refugee integration strategy 2018 to 2022.* https://www.gov.scot/publications/new-scots-refugee-integration-strategy-2018-2022/

Slade, B. L., & Dickson, N. (2020). Adult education and migration in Scotland: Policies and practices for inclusion. *Journal of Adult and Continuing Education.* https://doi.org/10.1177/1477971419896589

CHAPTER 6

Learner-Centred Education and Adult Education for Migrants in Malta

Maria Brown

Abstract

This chapter documents salient findings of the case study with stakeholders of state-provided language programmes offered to adult migrants in the EU island state Malta. Qualitative evidence included use of learner-centredness, albeit collaterals of the high content and summative exam-oriented curriculum. Analysis enabled the identification of a paradox, whereby the void resulting from lack of centralised and standardised epistemology and techniques targeting learner-centredness generated a space where the educator drew on his/her knowledge and experience to successfully design and implement ad hoc learner-centred practices. Notwithstanding, this was at the expense of uniform delivery and possibility of centralised and standardised monitoring, quality assurance, appraisal, and evaluation. The paradox was identified because had the latter been implemented, the educator's creative rationale would have, potentially, lost its *raison d'être* or become suppressed. Additionally, limitations to learner-centredness resulted when the explored dimensions of motivation, epistemology and relationships intersected with socio-demographics. Family background and gender impacted motivation; whereas epistemology and relationships were found to be limited for adult migrant learners of non-European/non-Western nationality and ethnicity. The findings make case for a sociologically informed approach to adult migrant education to foster learning spaces that allow educators to practice learner-centredness by drawing on the identities of student cohorts, particularly those with minority backgrounds. Technological and online resources must be capitalised upon to enhance techniques and learners' responsibility for learning. Investment in professional development and enhanced employment conditions and status of the adult educator emerged as significant and required.

Keywords

adult migrant teaching and learning – qualitative case study research – continuous professional development (CPD) with adult educators – educating ethnic minorities – education in EU island states – status of the adult educator

1 Introduction

The Maltese case study involved two language programmes formulated, managed and provided by the (then known as the) Directorate for Research, Lifelong Learning and Innovation (DRLLLI) of the Ministry for Education and Employment (MEDE) (Malta). The rationale of these language programmes reflected the broader national legal and policy framework endorsing the right to education for both refugees and migrants, as explicitly guaranteed by state laws such as The Refugees Act (Laws of Malta, 2001); an emphasis on embracing and promoting diversity in state educational policy (MEDE, 2012, 2014); the adoption of learner-centred education, as well as student-centred and cooperative learning in the National Curriculum Framework (NCF) (MEDE, 2012); and the provision of specialised training for adult educators.[1]

More specifically, the two language programmes under investigation were English as a Foreign Language Level 1 (of 2) (EFL1) and Maltese as a Foreign Language Level 1 (of 2) (MFL1). At the time of the study and as to the time of writing, both programmes were state provided against payment of a nominal fee and run once a year between October and May. Congruent to the broader educational system in Malta that is, generally speaking, highly content-based, the sampled language programmes were highly structured, rich in content and exam-oriented, with a component of creative writing. The required student commitment involved attending three-hour lessons once a week, doing weekly homework and sitting for the exam at the end of the year. Success in the exam granted access to Level 2, although students with basic language competence were registered for the Level 2 course without having to pass through Level 1.

Fieldwork was carried out during May 2017 at the Lifelong Learning Centre located in Msida (Malta) and comprised one (1) structured observation during class time of the EFL1 programme where one teacher (1) and seven (7) students were observed; and four (4) semi-structured one-to-one interviews. The interviewees were one (1) female adult migrant learner studying EFL1; one (1) male adult migrant learner studying MFL1; one (1) female adult educator employed by MEDE as a part-time adult educator teaching EFL 1; and one (1) female policymaker, a former adult educator who, at the time of the study, filled the full time position of Assistant Director at DRLLLI.

During the observation, notes were taken in response to the prompt of the project observation schedule. Interviews were audio recorded and transcribed ad verbatim. The qualitative data underwent a 'selective process' (Miles & Huberman, 1994, p. 55) to filter data relevant to the research objectives of the research study. Content analysis was used to reduce data to essential content; as well as explain, clarify and annotate data (Mayring, 2000). Thematic analysis was used to derive inferential meaning (Miles & Huberman, 1994) to deconstruct and organise data in thematic concepts and categories (LaRossa, 2005). Axial coding was used to link the retrieved themes to one another in a meaningful way (LaRossa, 2005).

2 Motivation

This section will analyse the extent of which adult migrant learners were intrinsically motivated to be involved successfully in the education process at the time and in the context of the programmes of the Maltese case study.

2.1 *The Intrinsic-Extrinsic Continuum*

Generally speaking, adult migrant learners participating in this case study were motivated to learn in response to difficulties experienced due to the diversity in language and culture in European Malta at the time of the study, when compared to their native background:

> I couldn't speak English. I couldn't. I ashamed outside for shopping but now I can go outside. I have a friend, Korean friend. Very happy .... It's very important for communicate [sic]. (Female adult migrant learner, EFL1)

> I mean, some friends suggested that I – because I already knew some words and I had some vocabulary – but I wanted to start from the basics – because I thought it's better to start – to have good fundaments [sic]. (Male adult migrant learner, MFL1)

Motivation was predominantly intrinsic, namely, self-help to enhance one's linguistic competence. This confirmed learners' need to be intrinsically motivated to be involved successfully in the education process (Schweisfurth, 2013, p. 12). Also following Schweisfurth (2013, p. 55), as adults, students were most interested in subjects which had evident relevance to their professional or personal lives. This analysis also corroborates Knowles (1980) since the most potent motivators for adults were the internal pressures. Indeed, students were likely to feel uncommitted to any decision or activity that they felt imposed on them.

Nonetheless, the same data reported above, also testify to instances where internal motivations and external motivations co-existed on a continuum. Indeed, respondents linked the internal motivations to learn (just explained) to external motivations. Particularly, fulfilling the generalised other's expectations concerning linguistic competence, especially peers' expectations who, notably, might not have necessarily been of the same nationality or ethnic background as migrants. Such expectations establish linguistic competence as foundational to effective person-to-person interaction on a short-term basis, and as foundational to integration within the host country on a medium-term and potentially long-term basis:

> I can found [sic] good friend and we have relation with WhatsApp, you know .... Yes, on the mobile, speak, it's very good because the writing is better for me, and the speaking [sic]. (Female adult migrant learner, EFL1)

2.2 The Social Scapes of Motivation

Research participants indicated that perseverance and commitment to the course was significantly affected by how taking the course interrelated to the learners' work-life balance:

> ... a lot of people are here with their children. It's amazing! They bring their children to Malta to attend schools here and so they even start learning Maltese. They have a very hectic life because then they take them for lessons in Arabic, lessons in Russian, because they want to keep in touch with their culture. So, their life is very much full, I would say. (Female adult educator, EFL1)

> It also offered me lessons in the morning, because usually in the afternoon I am busy with trainings, so that was convenient ... we started – I don't know maybe we were between 15 and 20 – but by the end the class diminished .... There were some problems. I mean some people were busy with work. Basically most of the students were women, except me and another guy who's Dutch. Obviously, you know how, the women. There were two women who got pregnant as well .... So basically they stopped coming because of that. I mean, I didn't see them anymore .... There were two or three who I think changed the time of the course and they started going in the evening, because they were busy. So at the end I think we finished from, I don't know – 17, 18 about 7, 8 at the end. (Male adult migrant learner, MFL1)

Notably, the latter participant's testimonial illuminates a perceived gender dimension of work-life balance as an external motivation of learner-centred adult migrant learning and education. Regular attendance and commitment by women were perceived as more challenging. Nonetheless, research data also showed how this could be mitigated by support from the learner's family, which, in the process, was projected as an external motivator:

> My husband when ... see me I stay at home, I am alone, and he told to me, 'It's better going to class. It's better because you can speak English and you can found [sic] friend' .... And he go to Valletta for register school [sic] ... And my husband going and speak to the people and register [sic] ... my husband speak English and a little French [sic]'. (Female adult migrant learner, EFL1)

These data also suggest that this participant's husband's knowledge of foreign languages, and of English in particular (also because English, together with Maltese, is an official language in Malta), was another external motivator, which facilitated his wife's access to the course. In other words, the learner's agency for motivation to learn was affected by the family's cultural capital.

Consequently, the data of the Maltese case study illuminated both internal and external motivations; yet there was no evidence that the former were more relevant than external motivations. Indeed, the data indicated that though supportive family and work-life balance variables may be classified as external motivations, they were highly relevant to adult migrant learners' access and commitment to the language courses under scrutiny.

2.3   A Motivating Educational Milieu

Qualitative observation allowed the identification of initiatives that targeted the enhancement of learners' motivation. Data testifying to such initiatives form part of a broader set of data concerning strategies and resources deployed to enhance the educational milieu: for both the teacher and the learners being observed, from the moments when the teacher made preparations before the start of the lesson, shortly followed by the learners stepping into the classroom and being welcomed by the teacher, till the end of the session. Thus, whilst preparing for the lesson before students' arrival, the teacher played relaxing background music. This music accompanied her first name-based greeting to each student. Other objects in the classroom utilised to enhance interest included educational charts, as well as the day's announcements displayed on the interactive whiteboard for students to familiarise with as they wait for the lesson to start.

Generally speaking, during the lesson, the adult learners were intrinsically motivated, as manifested by their focus on and collaboration in responding to teacher's prompts and invitations to participate. The small class size, comprising seven (7) students, facilitated learner-centred classroom interaction. It was clear that this was also possible because of the teacher's steady but gradual pace, which made it possible to follow the details of the lesson (even for the researcher recording observation notes).

During the actual lesson, the teacher also made use of websites for listening tests, picture hand-outs for the conversation exercises and a listening comprehension comprising an excerpt that she read out accompanied by a list of questions handed out to students. Notably, the listening comprehension's story was about a semi-retired adult working (part-time) on skates at Tesco. Thus, a relatively innovative and amusing story that adults could relate to since the adult protagonist would run around the supermarket in skates, assisting customers. It was especially humorous when they were at the cash and realised they had forgotten to get something and then sought the protagonist's assistance so as not to miss the queue at the cash. Learners' motivation in these circumstances was intrinsic as manifested by their amusement, non-verbal engagement (gestures) and verbal engagement (comments) on how useful it would be to have an assistant on skates at the supermarket. It was evident that, despite the challenges of the listening comprehension, the chosen story was interesting for adult learners to engage with, as well as to compare with their own experiences of the ups and downs of shopping for household needs. At this time and on other occasions, the teacher flavoured the lesson with some humour, to freshen the pace yet brief enough to retain focus; the adult learners responded. This testifies to understanding and ownership of the shared content and knowledge, as well as to learners' having language capabilities developed enough to support sharing humour, despite cultural differences.

In analysis, the teacher was proactive in linking the adults' learning experience of this language programme to the broader context. This was also evident when she was explaining the announcements to the migrant learners. Indeed, the announcements included details of forthcoming programmes applicable to learners, for which she encouraged them to apply. Such data do not only illuminate the teacher's agency and its relevance, but also the learner-centredness inherent to policy and the infrastructure underpinning the provision of language programmes in Malta since adult migrant learners were provided with opportunities to learn the language on a modular basis (e.g. English/Maltese as a Foreign Language 1, English/Maltese as a Foreign Language 2), that allowed learner-centred entry and exit points within a broader programme of continuous lifelong learning.

In conclusion to this section, the general synthesis derived from the Malta case study is that motivated adult migrant learners and teacher populated the language programmes under scrutiny. The motivation was both cause and effect of the educational milieu, which, in turn was the outcome of both structure and agency. Although the policies and infrastructure were foundational to the learner-centredness characterising the researched learning and educational experiences, the qualitative data analysis revealed that the agency of the teacher and the adult migrant learners was a more broadly diffused catalyst of motivation. As one learner pointed out during the introduction of the lesson observed, the adult migrant learners were keen on learning; whilst the data discussed in this section also illuminated the teacher's capacity to develop and implement innovative and learner-centred ad-hoc motivation strategies grounded in continuous lifelong learning.

3   Epistemology

This section discusses the extent of which the adult education programme for migrants under study was characterised by a fixed knowledge and curriculum, whether knowledge was fluid and whether the content was negotiated with migrant learners.

3.1   *Negotiating Curriculum and Content with Learners: Themes and Practices*

Data retrieved from the observation and interviews carried out for the Malta case study include a minority of instances where learners were invited to draw on existing knowledge and their own experiences; such as taking care of children or everyday routine activities like shopping for groceries, thus addressing learners who are also parents or guardians of minors or heads of household:

> Lessons about ... For holiday next time or last time, yes, when you are going for holiday. Or for sale for the home, rent for the home. Where is your home? Where are you living? The subject is very important. Sometimes subject is shopping, and fruit, street, you know. It's very important ... And ... Yes! And about skiing ... what do you do for weekend, and about family [sic]. (Female adult migrant learner, EFL1)

> For example to describe my family, as well, or what I am doing here – my work ... I could talk about myself, my family, my work, the reasons why I like Malta, what I like in Malta ... the first lesson was basically to know about us – about the students, about the teacher, about the place, here, and also a bit about the curriculum, whatever we'll work on ... So, basically we had to say, obviously in English – some things about us – where are we from .... (Male adult migrant learner, MFL1)

Other more educationally oriented instances (retrieved through the observation) included when three (3) students read the coursework submitted the week before and corrected by the teacher, to showcase good practices and ways of improving. It was evident that, on this occasion, the teacher purposely asked the relatively less vociferous Korean student to read her coursework. Together with the other two testimonials, delivered by the student from the Canary Island and the student from Russia, the teacher's culturally inclusive approach stood out: it voiced subaltern adult migrant voices with lack of (relative) proximity to the Anglo-Saxon, European and Westernised cultural paradigms that are deeply rooted the Maltese socio-cultural context. The teacher rewarded diversity of expression with positive and constructive feedback. Another similar instance was when learners were prompted by the teacher to *'use the words that you know'* (*Female adult educator, EFL1*) when attempting spontaneous participation and responses. The teacher also drew on narratives for examples targeting consolidation of learning, albeit the time allocated for some exercises was relatively brief, e.g., three (3) minutes to answer the first round of listening comprehension.

Notwithstanding the above epistemological strengths, the content-driven nature of the courses limited the value attributed to migrants' existing knowledge by the teacher and the other learners; as well as the extent of which learners were asked about their learning needs and expectations. The evidence points to arbitrary and ad hoc self-developed teacher practices, rather than a formal standard policy. In fact, data from learners' interviews suggested this was limited to occasional attempts:

> ... we always try to see what the students need, but in this particular case, when you're teaching EFL 1, you get people with very, very, basic English. (Female adult educator, EFL1)

Researcher:	Did you sometimes choose the subject?
Female adult migrant learner, EFL1:	No.
Researcher:	The teacher gives you the subject.
Female adult migrant learner, EFL1:	Yes, yes, yes. The teacher send email [sic] and before we come to class we searching at home, with the homework [sic].
Researcher:	Yes. Did you sometimes tell the teacher, for example, 'Can we change something?' or, 'Can you explain again?' Or ... You know, like, you put forward suggestions? What does she do?
Female adult migrant learner, EFL1:	Yes, again, again.
Researcher:	Does she repeat?
Female adult migrant learner, EFL1:	Yes, she repeat [sic].

Researcher:	Could you choose, sometimes, the topics that you learn? Were you sometimes given a choice?
Male adult migrant learner, MFL1:	Yes.
Researcher:	For example …?
Male adult migrant learner, MFL1:	For example to describe my family, as well, or what I am doing here – my work.
Researcher:	All right, so you could talk about yourself.
Male adult migrant learner, MFL1:	I could talk about myself, my family, my work, the reasons why I like Malta, what I like in Malta.

Notably, the lack of standardisation might be key to successful implementation although at the expense of uniform and consistent delivery.

3.2 *Negotiating Curriculum and Content with Learners: Citizenship Education*

Moreover, the observation session illuminated how, prior to learning needs, the teacher had to prioritise citizenship education by giving attention to more basic, generic, cultural and life-skills' needs – such as reminding students to take their identity card or passport on the day of the exam. She also reminded learners where personal identification details need to be filled-in on the exam paper. The need to prioritise learners' needs that are not strictly programme-related learning needs is common to other educational contexts in Malta and, consequently, illuminating the need to question if and how more basic, generic, cultural and life-skills' needs are being catered for at some other stage and/or by other parties, particularly for adult migrant learners. A related issue is whether educators of adult migrant learners should be officially equipped and engaged to cater for adult migrant learners' more basic, generic, cultural and life-skills' needs. To date, this is not stated officially as part of their official list of duties (MEDE, 2016). Related implications would include rethinking and revising course organisation and content, as well as the recruitment package of educators of adult migrant learners.

The data retrieved from the Malta case study also show that the curriculum is relevant to migrants' lives and their perceived future needs because it is underpinned by learner-centred pedagogical principles:

> It's not only seniors, so we cater for everyone from 16+. Em, which means that, em, really and truly, we are … We're not only focusing on, for example, learners with disabilities – that's another niche, migrant learners – em, women, early school leavers. We cater, sort of, our offer is open to everyone.

> We are now, and over the past three years since I've been here, realising that you have these different niches and you need the specialisation in that area – at management level. Both myself, and, of course, there is a director – we're not specialist in all of this but what we do is we work with NGOs (non-governmental organisations), and this is where we find the specialisation and these are the people who know their audiences more, and their learners more, em because they, they know the specific needs, including, for example, what timings work for particular groups – as basic as that. From here it's very centralised – this is the Ministry – so because we have … Just for you to know the general background … To cater for, em, 400+ courses – for example, now we've just launched 459 courses in 90 subjects – so that is, sort of, management-wise it's quite huge, em, and centrally you're looking at making sure the machine works …. But, of course, adult learning is not about the numbers, then. It's about the individuals and this is where we have Coordinators and also NGOs who then are working more one-to-one with the specific learner groups. (Female policymaker, Assistant Director at DRLLLI)

The above shows that, from the part of the central management, learner-centredness was manifested not only in principle but also in practice. For example, the Department endorsed resourcing the implementation of the curriculum through outreach with NGOs. Although the interviewed learners did not mention intervention from such NGOs specifically, excerpts from the data they provided testify to an educational milieu where interaction takes place in a language that is accessible to them, and that is also based on skills and attitude outcomes, as well as content:

> The teacher send email and before we come to class we searching at home, with the homework [sic]. (Female adult migrant learner, EFL1)

> Yes, always I speak to my teacher [sic]. I'm very happy I'm here in this class because I can speak …. (Female adult migrant learner, EFL1)

> … they was [sic] times when we listened some songs – Maltese as well – some, how do you say, chit-chat not connected to the lesson, about our life, about what we did today, about what we did last week, or when we go abroad. Some things that are not connected with, but also sometimes to try to reply in Maltese, as much as we could, so it was not boring, but she tried to make it a bit more interesting. (Male adult migrant learner, MFL1)

Notwithstanding, specific learners' expectations are occasionally unmet, particularly as regards use of technological resources:

> I expected that we use a bit more and to have exercises on computer as well, as a student, not only on the board and on the paper. (Male adult migrant learner, MFL1)

3.3 Assessment

As regards assessment used in the sampled language courses, there is evidence that the teachers tested for skills, allowing for individual differences, as opposed to being purely content-driven, success-based and based on rote learning. This analysis is sustained by data showcasing the formative targets and outcomes of assessments, particularly accentuated by the priority given by the teacher on assessing with individualised comments (rather than a mark) and the reflexive response that this assessment technique had on the MFL1 learner interviewed:

> ... we used to get not a mark [sic], we used to get 'Tajjeb' (Good) or Hafna tajjeb (Very good). Most of the time Tajjeb but then the teacher will comment, 'But you have to be attentive on this, this, this ...' ... I look at the paper, basically. I see where I made the mistakes and I try at home to see in which part the mistake is, for example, the number or the article, or the verbs, so I come back to that and I try to revise the part. (Male adult migrant learner, MFL1)

Moreover, relatively early on during the courses, learners were assessed by developing content that drew on their own socio-demographic background:

> I think after one month, after one or two months we start the class, we have subject in the story, in your country. I speak to my teacher about my country [sic] ... Subject we have: 'A walk in the country', 'A party to which I went', and 'Your email for my friend', 'I am in Malta'. [sic] ... I writing, I writing for my teacher. This is homework. Or this one 'Where are you living?' and I writing and my teacher ... [sic]. (Female adult migrant learner, EFL1)

Fieldwork also yielded data that confirm the positive evaluation learners made about teachers' approach and methods of assessment:

> About homework, finished the class, my teacher take the homework, and for next time give to us and correct. I have a lot of for homework. And she checks for me – this is correct, this is not correct, you know. But always we have a question, or we need practice, she help us [sic]. (Female adult migrant learner, EFL1)

The above data concern the continuous formative assessment that is by and large managed by the course teacher. The data depict a different scenario as regards the summative assessment, which comprises an exam that learners sit for at the end of the course. The rationale and execution of the summative exam is far from learner-centred and democratic, not just for students, but also for educators:

> ... when it comes to examining students, it always comes from the top, you know, so you cannot give your input, and, well, I'm sure that they're going to say that if they ask some teachers they do it. They do ask some teachers to set the paper, but if, em, you had to see the papers, which I have here – I mean we'll be working on them during the lesson – you will see that the content is, many times, not appropriate. For example, they gave them a listening comprehension about seals. Seals. What is a seal? How many times do you talk about seals in a classroom where you have foreigners trying to survive in a foreign language? You know? Stuff like that. So, I think sometimes they are insensitive to the needs of the students, you know, and also whoever set the MQF 1 level – I don't know how they did it – I know there's the Malta Qualifications Authority – but it's not Level 1. It's quite advanced, you know. I would say you can take this and give it to Year 6 students, you know, who have been learning English for at least six years, you know. It's not the type of thing where you get a group of people who hardly know the alphabet and you have to get them to that level. That, I would say, would help a lot if the papers were left in the hands of the teachers rather than, you know. For example, with EFL 2, we're lucky that the Malta Qualifications Authority has been too busy to set the standards, you know. So I gave them my own exam, you know, I can assess them – I assess them in listening, in grammar, vocabulary, comprehension, writing, they ... We had a presentation, em – that was my assessment and I'll give them a report at the end. It's much easier when I know what we have done, you know, and what Level 2 is for me, you know, because I mean, I told you, I go by the EFL standards and with Level 2 I was working on pre-intermediate. Now they reached intermediate and they are about to start training for SEC. But at the beginning of the year, next year, I'm going to get people who want to do SEC and whose level of English is really, very low. (Female adult educator, EFL1)

> And basically, we are moving, always towards an exam. I think that is our greatest problem ... courses that have to be exam oriented. You know, so you prepare them for an exam and there's ... What we do is dictated, you know, it's not my choice. They want a qualification, so you try to cater both for what they need and also for sitting an exam. (Female adult educator, EFL1)

In conclusion to this section on epistemology it can be said that, generally speaking, adult migrant learners' direct access to curriculum unfolded through teachers' communicative and pedagogical practices. When, extremely rarely, rote learning was used, it was used to consolidate, as will be elaborated in the next section discussing Techniques. Thus, despite evidence of highly content-driven language programmes, ad-hoc teacher practices allowed for small-scale learner-centredness. The evidence concerning formative continuous assessment designed and implemented by the educators corroborated this analysis. Use of individualised comments on corrected scripts and feedback to individual students during class participation enhanced the assessment epistemology with continuous and formative attributes. Epistemological limitations encountered in the data ranged from the highly content-driven programme of studies that yielded a focus on the summative exam, to accessibility limitations (especially related to limitations of time allocated) for migrant learners whose native cultures and languages differed significantly from the ones being learnt in the host country.

4 Techniques

This section will analyse the techniques and activities that teachers use in the classroom with migrant learners, to assess the degree of responsibility for learning taken by migrant learners.

4.1 'Comforting' Constraints?
Generally speaking, being highly content-based and exam-oriented, the data collected testify to a limited degree of responsibility for learning taken by migrant learners. Primarily, this emerged from the use of 'traditional' techniques such as counting and comparing marks of listening comprehension, as observed during the EFL1 lesson. Nevertheless, data do not show negative evaluation by students:

> ... we revised a lot, and today, our last lesson, basically we didn't do ... She asked whatever problems we have with anything to tell her so we go through it once more. I find it good, very good. (Male adult migrant learner, MFL1)

Even in the case of a minority of data testifying to rote learning, it was evident that, together with drilling, it was used for consolidation. In turn, such techniques reassured both students and educators, more so, given the insecurity felt due to time restraints, particularly by educators:

> [Referring to some learners] ... they come from languages where even the alphabet is different, where there are language peculiarities that, many times, you're not aware of, for example, you get Japanese, Chinese, Eastern European people, Russians. They don't have the article and unless you're aware of that, you know, they keep on writing without using it. And so you must draw their attention to that. (Female adult educator, EFL1)

> You don't have much time for drilling, and drilling is important. And as you go along you realise that you think that you've taught them something but they haven't actually grasped it because there wasn't enough repetition, I would say, or drilling, you know. (Female adult educator, EFL1)

> Some work is very easy because always we practice – 'Excuse me', 'Thank you' ... after months it's very easy for you [sic]. (Female adult migrant learner, EFL1)

However, learners' perceptions emerged as limited by comfort zones, which made them feel safer when they had to take limited responsibility for learning. Data show that some educators also sought comfort zones, although the DLLLI used a pilot strategy and professional development courses (also overseas) to slowly and gently introduce innovative techniques:

> So, introducing something new, like, em, you know, interactive ways of working with adult learners, sometimes, em, we might find resistance, not from everyone, but when they experience ... When you open up opportunities for them as a test, and as something extra, then they are more willing to introduce it in their learning ... And we've sent some of them abroad, eh, as well ... We worked with Norway – because they have Vox and now they're quite strong in adult learning and working with adults – to the UK, and we were working with UCL, yes, so it was quite ... They could really observe, em ... They didn't go to University, they went to the Adult Learning Centres, but, sort of, that was very good. Em, Cyprus, em, because they're obviously similar to us and they also work with two languages ... Macedonia – but that wasn't a training, it was a transnational meeting ... And now we're working with Ireland. So we have, em ... We have someone flying in next week ... Em, that is more on work-based learning ... But, em, they have a lot of work prac-

tices which, sort of, we've been observing and which hopefully will help our educators as well. (Female policymaker, Assistant Director at DRLLLI)

4.2 Digital Capture for Learners' Rapture

The data from the Malta case study show that techniques that successfully captured adult migrants' interest are those that deployed technological resources. The analysis is sustained significantly because data in this regard surfaced both when techniques were enhanced with technological resources, as well as when technological resources were limited or not deployed:

> ... for grammar it's very important you has a YouTube because in my country YouTube close – we don't have YouTube – because we can all subject found in YouTube [sic]. (Female adult migrant learner, EFL1)

> Maybe during the lesson we should have some audio things to listen, or maybe even some parts of some programmes on TV, but maybe, I don't know if it's possible, with translation, because that's how I learnt a lot of Greek in Greece ... I expected to be a bit more modernised ... I mean when you listen something [sic], I think for me, when you listen and even when you see, because maybe there are some actions and the person or the other person explains what the person is doing ... I don't know ... So maybe like that you hear the words and you hear the sentence – because I think most of us we knew the words – but when you connect it we find it a bit difficult, to understand the connection – the word and the noun and the article together, it's a bit different perspective. (Male adult migrant learner, MFL1)

> We don't have listening facilities, so we have to get a ... Because these computers were installed without ... And you can't put in a CD, so that would help as well. (Female adult educator, EFL1)

Moreover, when techniques were enhanced with technological and online resources, learners' responsibility for learning was better catered for:

> I tried to teach them skills, such as how to use Google – for finding, for checking spelling, for vocabulary, for pronunciation, for how to access video clips which they need, how to access online exercises which they can check. So, I try to teach them the skills that they need to know if they are working on their own, you know. (Female adult educator, EFL1)

In this sense, the EFL1 adult educator was targeting the preparation narrative, whereby 'skills developed through inquiry-based self-regulated learning such as flexibility, critical independent thought are believed to support the development and sustaining of an effective knowledge economy' (Schweisfurth, 2013, p. 2).

4.3 Open-Door Dialogue

The data testify to more positive evaluations concerning the component of dialogue in the techniques used for teaching and learning. Data obtained from adult migrant learners taking different language courses corroborate that both EFL1 and MFL1 teachers were constantly supportive and approachable:

> … the teacher was very open to us for any help that we need … she was always there … so if you come a bit before – 10, 15 minutes, 20 minutes, she was always asking us if we have any problems, so we were revising the first twenty minutes, half an hour. We were always doing something that we did before, so maybe to catch up. (Male adult migrant learner, MFL1)

> most of the people there were quite, how do I say, extrovert. They were not afraid to speak up. They were not afraid to ask questions. And I think we had the … I think the teacher was tolerant and she accepted all. (Male adult migrant learner, MFL1)

> … it's very important and good relation with teacher because she understand [sic]. (Female adult migrant learner, EFL1)

It can be concluded that the teachers' approachable disposition undergirded the techniques component of learner-centredness within the Maltese case study. This disposition supported students in feeling safe enough to target the language programmes' learning outcomes, and to grow and progress as learners. Thus, responsibility for learning was experienced by learners within these 'safe' parameters, which, though relevant, were not accompanied by more critically engaged dimensions of responsibility, such as responsibility for curriculum, methodologies, content, and resources. The case study has also shown that technological and online resources were key to enhance learner-centredness in terms of techniques and learners' responsibility for learning.

5 Relationships

This section will analyse the relationships between educators and migrant learners and between migrant learners themselves in the context of the adult education programme under study. The key question is to assess these relationships along a continuum that ranges from authoritarian to democratic, which reflects the amount of control that migrant learners do or do not have over their learning.

5.1 Self-Sought Informal Strategies

The main themes regarding relationships involved teachers' 'open-door' practices; proactive approach and practices whereby teachers do not wait for students to approach them with difficulties but 'chase' students to verify if there is need for further support; as well as the confidence and reassurance that adult migrant learners experience when seeking support and assistance beyond standard lesson times. The common denominator here is that democracy flourished outside the strict work parameters, in the spaces that educators and learners sought creatively and, to a certain extent, informally. In fact, there is evidence that educators and the management team of the lifelong learning centres were willing to go that extra mile, beyond their job description, to consolidate the educational milieu framed by the learning programmes by transforming the learning space into a vivid learning community that also voiced subaltern cultures and discourses. Nevertheless, the evidence also suggests that there were limited occasions when this took places, particularly to avoid jeopardising authenticity with institutionalisation. The downside of this approach is the risk of tokenism:

> We have classes that really gel and they might even at Christmas time go out together. We have Centres – the Gżira one and the Mosta one – em, and the Msida one – that the Coordinator is so, em, is so enthusiastic that they organise parties, for example, and they had an event where all the migrants, so of, brought in some food, and, em, they had songs, and so on at Christmas time ... It's something small and maybe for some it's insignificant ... But, you know what I mean? For the Coordinators, that's not part of their remit. We don't force that because then, again, it would become institutionalised. We encourage it. Maybe we don't encourage it enough. So it varies, but as a structure .... (Female policymaker, Assistant Director at DRLLLI)

5.2 The Relevance of Language Capital, Cultural Capital and Social Capital

Notwithstanding this strong evidence, the democratic component of relationships was limited since the nature of the dialogue did not necessarily translate to dialogue with a critical component or momentum, thus limiting the amount of control that migrant learners had over their learning. The evidence is also informative enough to flag that language limitations of the adult migrant learners hindered following the lesson, let alone articulation of elaborate thought associated with critical dialogue:

> ... some of the students, especially the Filipinos and even the Arabs, they had some problems with English as well ... So I think for them it was a bit more difficult to follow the lesson. (Male adult migrant learner, MFL1)

Notably, these data also show that the limited critical ingredient in the dialogue was not a pervasive experience affecting all students. On the contrary, there was Intersectionality with nationality and ethnicity. Paradoxically, the reflections embedded in the data above (provided by the male adult migrant registered for the MFL1) testify to a critical engagement with the learning experience as he commented on how language limitations intersected with ethnicity in affecting the experience and achievement of the programme's learning outcomes. Indeed, the MFL1 learner was manifesting an emancipation narrative by critically questioning canons of received knowledge and the unequal structures of the society that they support (Schweisfurth, 2013). However, the student's analysis was critically limited as well because it was limited to the ability to 'follow the lesson' rather than the ability (or lack of) taking charge of one's own learning.

There is also evidence highlighting the need for professional development for adult migrant educators to familiarise themselves with the spectrum of cultures that the learning programmes are likely to attract, more so because the lesson time was not enough for educators to gain the exposure, knowledge and skills required to cater for the different learners' backgrounds:

> ... there is always the problem of culture, you know. And culture comes even in the name. You start realising, for example, that [common Scottish] names like Sue, John, mean nothing to them and ... it takes a while even to learn [their names], and you don't have much time – there's the time restriction. (Female adult educator, EFL1)

In a more general sense, the atmosphere and conduct of the programmes reflected mutual respect also between migrants as adult learners:

> (Referring to the atmosphere) ... it's very friendly, supporting, it's accepting. In fact, last Tuesday ... I have this man from Nigeria, who has been here for ten years, and his family is here, and he was telling me that this was the first class where, the first time where he did not have any racial comments, you know. He said, 'Wherever I've been, there has always been a feeling of people not wanting me'. (Female adult educator, EFL1)

> I am tolerant for all religions and anybody can be and believe what they want, so I respect you, you respect me. (Male adult migrant learner, MFL1)

Learners from both sampled programmes communicated beyond the hours and needs of the respective language courses, particularly using social media such as WhatsApp:

> Yes, yes, I friend, eh, all the people, yes … Always in class speaking or with WhatsApp speaking … Yes, yes … I'm very happy I'm here in this class because I can speak … I can found [sic] good friend and we have relation with WhatsApp, you know [sic]. (Female adult migrant learner, EFL1)

> [We communicate] … with email … we have quite a lot communication, during and also in the break, and after on the Facebook chat as well … It helped as well … In English, although some of the students, especially the Filipinos and even the Arabs, they had some problems with English as well … So I think for them it was a bit more difficult to follow the lesson. (Male adult migrant learner, MFL1)

Remarkably, the linguistic barrier was once again identified as the one main impediment to more communication. In the context of this study, communication is being used as an indicator of mutual respect which, in turn, is being associated with control over one's learning and, consequently, to learner-centredness. It follows that language limitations are also limiting the extent of which the mutual respect dimension of learner-centredness can be empirically explored, particularly for some ethnic cohorts of adult migrant learners or adult migrant learners of specific nationalities. In this regard, the data of the Malta case study also show that some non-European nationalities and ethnicities are particularly vulnerable to the explained dynamics.

Moreover, the data concerning informal communication in English language during break and on WhatsApp between adult migrant learners with European/Anglo-Saxon backgrounds corroborates the limitations to learner-centredness experienced by learners from non-European nationalities and ethnicities. This suggests that, in the context of the Malta case study, Eurocentrism limits learner-centred adult migrant education. The pertinent questions are to what extent are policies, educators, and adult migrants themselves sensitised about this? If so, would they be equipped with the broad range of required resources (time, materials, spaces, interest, motivation etc.) to overcome the explained cultural and communicative limitations?

6 Conclusions

The analytic discussion of this chapter verified that in language programmes sampled for the Malta case study learner-centred education was used as a tool for enhancing adult education for migrants, albeit with limitations that primarily stemmed from the high content and summative exam-oriented curriculum. The Malta case study also illuminated how adult migrant learners' challenges can be addressed by drawing on migrants' existing knowledge, although the evidence pointed to arbitrary and ad hoc self-developed teacher practices, rather than a formal standard policy. The evidence retrieved from the sampled language programmes corroborated this analysis by illuminating continuous and formative pedagogies, classroom and assessment practices developed and implemented by the educator.

Consequently, the overarching finding of the Malta case study is that learner-centredness within the sampled language-programmes was characterised by a paradox, arbitrary labelled as the paradox of the proactive learner-centred pedagogy. To explain better, data retrieved from the Malta case study has shown that the void resulting from the educator's experience of a lack of centralised and standardised epistemology and techniques targeting learner-centredness, generated a space where the educator's creativity could draw on his/her knowledge and experience to successfully design and implement ad hoc learner-centred practices. Notwithstanding, this was at the expense of uniform delivery and possibility of centralised and standardised monitoring, quality assurance, appraisal, and evaluation. That said, the paradox is identified because should the latter be implemented, the educator's creative rationale would, potentially, lose its *raison d'être* or be suppressed.

Moreover, the Malta case study has also shown that limitations to learner-centredness resulted when the explored dimensions of motivation, epistemology and relationships intersected with socio-demographics. Motivation was found to be affected by family background, support from family, sex and gender, whereas epistemology and relationships were found to be limited for adult migrant learners of non-European/non-Western nationality and ethnicity.

It follows that, policy and practices targeting learner-centredness in adult migrant education need to target a fine balance that breeds a creative rationale that motivates teachers to adapt and re-invent learner-centredness by understanding the particular student cohorts, particularly those from minority backgrounds. The relevance of a sociologically informed approach to adult migrant education follows. Technological and online resources must be capitalised upon to enhance techniques and learners' responsibility for learning.

Ultimately, further research about and investment in professional development and enhanced employment conditions and status of the adult educator are key.

Note

1 At the time of research continuous professional development was strongly encouraged by the Directorate; however, not compulsory for adult educators. In part this could be hardly demanded considering the unattractive remuneration package, which, in turn, was also impinging on the (low) supply of adult educators.

References

Knowles, M. S. (1980). *The modern practice of adult education: From pedagogy to andragogy* (2nd ed.). Cambridge Books.

LaRossa, R. (2005). Grounded theory methods and qualitative family research. *Journal of Marriage and Family 67*, 837–857.

Laws of Malta. (2001). *Refugees act (Chapter 420)*. Ministry for Justice, Culture and Local Government. http://justiceservices.gov.mt/DownloadDocument.aspx?app=lom&itemid=8886

Mayring, P. (2000). Qualitative content analysis. *Forum Qualitative Sozialforschung/ Forum: Qualitative Social Research, 1*(2), 20.

Miles, M. B., & Huberman, A. M. (1994). *Qualitative data analysis: An expanded sourcebook*. Sage.

Ministry for Education and Employment (MEDE). (2012). *A national curriculum framework for all*. https://education.gov.mt/en/Documents/A%20National%20Curriculum%20Framework%20for%20All%20-%202012.pdf

Ministry for Education and Employment (MEDE). (2014). *Framework for the education strategy for Malta 2014–2024*. http://education.gov.mt/en/strategy/Documents/BOOKLET%20ESM%202014-2024%20ENG%2019-02.pdf

Ministry for Education and Employment (MEDE). (2016). *Position of part-time adult educator within the directorate for lifelong learning and early school leavers*. https://education.gov.mt/en/Documents/Vacancies/Position%20of%20Part-time%20Adult%20Educator%20Rolling%20EN.pdf

Schweisfurth, M. (2013). *Learner-centred education in international perspective: Whose pedagogy for whose development?* Routledge.

CHAPTER 7

Learner-Centred Education and Adult Education for Migrants in Cyprus

Maria N. Gravani, Pavlos Hatzopoulos and Eleni Papaioannou

Abstract

This chapter presents the findings of the case study conducted in Cyprus designed to investigate educational practices in adult education programmes for migrants to assess the extent to which these are learner-centred. It focuses on the Greek language courses offered by state educational institutions, via the so-called Adult Education Centres. These courses are named 'Greek language for foreigners' and are mainly attended by migrants. The chapter critically describes the context of the research, the methodological approach followed, in the collection and analysis of the data, and the analysis of the findings under the four axes identified in the theoretical framework adopted, namely: motivation, epistemology, technique, relationships. The findings of the case study attest to the very limited engagement with learner-centred practices as a tool for empowering migrant adult learners in the Cypriot context. In this respect, the absence of formal, standard policies on adult education for migrants in Cyprus is a crucial factor that precludes organised efforts towards the adoption of such LCE practices.

Keywords

migrants – Cyprus – adult education programmes – learner-centred education – adult education centres – Greek language courses

1   Introduction

This chapter presents the findings of the case study conducted in Cyprus during the spring of 2017, designed to investigate educational practices in adult education programmes for migrants to assess the extent to which these are learner-centred. The research conducted for this case study had to face a number of challenges and shortfalls emanating from the current policies on adult migrants' education in Cyprus. On the one hand, migration and migrant learners are relatively absent as subjects of concern in state policies on adult education. On the other, this lacuna is partially filled by ad-hoc and ephemeral initiatives, which in many cases are EU funded, that aim at promoting migrants' participation in adult learning, offered by NGOs, solidarity groups and other education providers.

To address these dynamics, also considering the research project's focus on official educational practices, the Cyprus research team chose to focus on the Greek language courses offered by state educational institutions, via the so-called Adult Education Centres. These programmes, named 'Greek language for foreigners' are open to all non-native Greek speakers, including EU citizens who may be working in Cyprus, but are mainly attended by migrants. During our preliminary research, we found that these language programmes are possibly the only courses where there is a significant participation of adult migrant learners in state-run educational institutions. The research was conducted in the context of one such 'Greek for Foreigners' course, as it is officially named, which was organised in a district city between November 2016 to May 2017 in one of the state-run Adult Education Centres.

2   Context of the Research

The research took place in Cyprus, a country that is situated in the crossroad between Europe and the Middle East. After its accession in the EU in 2004, Cyprus has experienced increased influxes of immigration and, according to the latest Eurostat statistics (2019) relative to the size of population, Cyprus recorded the third higher rate of immigration after Malta and Luxemburg. This new reality necessitated the compliance of the country with EU directions and regulations on immigration. At the same time, Cyprus – similarly with other small states of the EU periphery – experienced significant social, legislative, and structural challenges (Mainwaring, 2014, 2016). Among these challenges is the provision of successful educational structures to ensure that non-Greek speaking migrants have the opportunities to learn the language of the host country. The EU (Council of Europe, 2017) directs member states towards the development of inclusive language policies and provides tools and recommendations for effective language training.

In Cyprus, most of the educational provisions are controlled by the Ministry of Education and Culture (MoEC). The Cypriot educational system is highly centralised, meaning that all aspects of education, from curriculum to teaching material and teachers' training, is controlled centrally by the respective ministry (Gravani & John, 2005). That being the case, on the island there are three main provisions offering Greek language lessons to adult migrants, all public: the Adult Education Centers (AEC), the Open Schools in various municipalities and the Institutes of Further Education (Gravani & Ioannidou, 2014). The former two offer a non-formal education and the latter a formal one. During the mapping of the field, the researchers found out that most of the migrants are directed to the language lessons offered by the Adult Education Centers.

Adult education in Cyprus is relatively a new field and, as a result, policy texts are not abundant but rather fragmented and scattered in policy texts of different educational levels. As Gravani, Hatzopoulos, and China (2019, p. 2) argue 'adult education for migrants on the island is characterised by a lack of cohesive policies, extensive research and systematised data and statistics'.

3   Methodological Approach

3.1   *Data Collection*

The Cyprus case study adopted a qualitative approach (Denzin & Lincoln, 2005; Patton, 2002) in an effort to come closer to participants' experiences, employing two principal research methods: (a) research interviews with learners, teachers, and policymakers, as well as (b) observation conducted in the class of the Greek language programme under study.

The research team conducted five semi-structured interviews. Among the participants, there were three migrant adult learners who participated in the course: a female asylum seeker from Sudan, a male asylum seeker from Kurdish Iraq, and a female migrant from Lebanon. The interviews also included one educator, a female philology teacher who was employed as the sole instructor of the language course under study and one policymaker, a public employee at the Ministry of Education.

All the research interviews were semi-structured (Charmaz, 2006), following the protocol and guidelines agreed upon by the four research teams participating in the project. They were organised along six principal research questions, related to the issues of motivations for participation, the organisation of the course, teaching practices that are employed in class, the learning climate/atmosphere, and evaluation practices that correspond to the four elements which comprise LCE practice, according to Schweisfurth's (2013, p. 11) approach, namely: techniques, relationships, motivation, epistemology.

In addition to the interviews, in order for the research team to have a first-hand experience on the site under research, participant observation was conducted. The observation was held in May 2017, before, during and after one

90-minute class of a Greek language lesson. The presence of the research team in class was secured through an official authorisation which was granted by the Ministry of Education. During the observation, the research team collected field notes (Emerson, Fretz, & Shaw, 2001) guided by a template to ensure that all relevant data would be collected. The field notes template included seven main categories to which the research team paid particular attention: *space* – the physical place of the classroom; *objects* – the physical things which are present; *actors* – the people involved in the class; *interactions* – events that take place amongst these actors; *dialogues* – what is being said between teachers and learners and also amongst learners during these interactions; *non-verbal communication* – what is shown rather than said in these interactions, and *time* – the sequencing of educational practices that takes place over time.

Participant observation is a useful method for researchers who aim at gaining insights concerning human interaction. During observation, the researcher comes closer to the participants' experiences and she has the opportunity to familiarise herself with the participants, the setting and the process taking place in the given context (Scott, 1996). For the presented research, participant observation provided an opportunity for a more nuanced analysis of the data collected by allowing the research team to focus on concrete educational practices. The inclusion of participant observation as a research tool provided the chance to compare these observations with the discourse of teachers, migrant learners and policymakers articulated in the interviews. The multiple data sources and participants' group ensured data triangulation (Patton, 1999; Seale, 1999) as a means of enhancing the quality of the research. Furthermore, observation had been a tool for the research team to analyse in depth the learner-centred dimensions of the language programme under study and their impact as motors for social change.

3.2 Analysis of Findings

The analysis draws extensively from the data collected from the research interviews and participant observation in the classroom. To ensure anonymity, the chapter uses pseudonyms for all the interviews whose views are directly quoted or paraphrased in the text.

The analysis that will follow in the main body of this chapter is organised along four themes, captured under the chapter headings of (a) Motivations, (b) Epistemology, (c) Techniques and (d) Relationships. The above themes correspond to the four main elements that comprise learner-centred educational practice according to Schweisfurth's conceptualisation (2013). The present case study employs these elements heuristically as a conceptual framework that can help us to unveil the extent to which is learner-centred education used as a tool for enhancing adult teaching and learning in the field of adult education for migrants in Cyprus.

The discussion in the first section focuses on the question of motivations for participating in the Greek language course for both learners and educators. It argues that adult migrant learners and educators participating in the course are not intrinsically motivated to be involved successfully in the education process at a sufficient level. As a result, learners' and teachers' lack of sufficient engagement impacts negatively on the extent of learner control over the content and process of learning as well as bars possibilities of pedagogical experimentation with the adoption of new and appropriate teaching methods. In the second section of the chapter the analysis considers the extent to which the adult education programme for migrants under study is characterised by a fixed knowledge and curriculum, or whether knowledge is fluid, and the content is negotiable with migrant learners. It argues that the language course is of limited relevance to migrant learners' experiences and fails to build on their knowledges and skills. The third section analyses the techniques and activities that are utilised in the classroom with migrant learners. It proposes that the ultimately teacher-centric learning process employed in the course can be seen as a defensive strategy: both the learners and the educator were not prepared to enter or, more crucially, to produce a space of intercultural interactions. In the final section the chapter analyses the relationships between educators and migrant learners in the Greek language programme under study. It argues that the seemingly positive climate and the frictionless learning process of the Greek language course are mainly the consequence of keeping distance, rather than engaging with, of maintaining boundaries rather than challenging them.

Finally, the chapter presents some tentative conclusions and reflect on the extent to which LCE is practiced in adult education programmes for migrants in Cyprus, trying to reflect on possible paths for further research.

4   Motivation

Motivation in second language learning has been the focal point of many theoretical models (Dorney, 2005; Lamb, 2004; Oxford, 1996; Noels, 2001). Furthermore, motivation is considered as one of the most significant pillars of adult education (Cross, 1981; Knowles, Holton, & Swanson, 2012; Wlodkowski, 1999). The research we conducted revealed some of the problematic dynamics regarding both adult migrants' and educators' motivation to participate and engage in adult education, in general, and in Greek Language Programmes in particular. In the case of the adult migrant learners, the relative lack of intrinsic motivation to participate in this particular course revealed primarily the presence of structural impediments related to the absence of a cohesive national integration policy being implemented by the Cypriot state. In the case of educators, the lack of a strong motivation to work in the course reflects the fact that this is rarely a first-choice profession for them and also the deteriorating working conditions for teachers of adult education courses in Cyprus.

4.1 *Migrant Adult Learners' Motivations*

When asked why they decided to participate in the Greek language course, migrant adult learners felt the need to mostly share their frustrations on the problems they have been facing to access the national labour market and the structural barriers they have encountered in their efforts to integrate in Cypriot society. This finding is in accordance to EU's focus during recent years in linguistic integration of migrants as an essential indicator for their social and economic integration (European ministerial conference on integration, 2010; Kelly et al., 2010; LIAM-programme, Council of Europe, 2014). In spite of the differences in the current legal status that regulates their residence in the country, the three migrant learners' narratives portrayed their learning in the context of this course as not sufficient to lead them to a course of more cohesive inclusion in Cypriot society.

In a paradoxical way, although the successful completion of a course on learning the language of the host society is supposed to signify a decisive step towards integration, the migrant learners depicted the Greek language programme as an embodiment of their arduous and uncertain paths towards integration. For example, two of the migrant learners specifically mentioned that their participation in this particular Greek language course came as a direct result of their dealings with the local District Labour Office. As currently enjoying the status of asylum seekers for a prolonged time period, both are not entitled to equal labour rights in respect to Cypriot or EU citizens, or even recognised refugees; asylum seekers in Cyprus can only gain limited employment rights after a six month period from the date of submission of their application, and are thereafter only entitled to work legally in a few economic sectors, performing mainly manual labour, and only for company/employers that have been authorised by the State (Cyprus Ministry of Labour, Welfare and Social Insurance, n.d.).

For them, one of the main motivations for joining the Greek language course is their desire not to work, to refuse the jobs offered to them by the Cypriot state via the Labour office, jobs that they know are temporary, seasonal, low paid and sometimes even non-existent. This situation reflects findings from other research (Bevelander, 2011; Connor, 2010) showing how refugees and asylum seekers face greater challenges compared to immigrants in their effort to integrate in local societies, these challenges often being the result of their lower language skills. Ahmad, an asylum seeker from Kurdistan, explains this strategy in the following terms:

> Why? When I came here, I wanted to learn do I can leave in this country [...] But in Cyprus it is not like that. It is not about learning, but a way to avoid the Labour Office. In Cyprus they will give you a job, a false job ... to work in a farm or something like that. They will send you to work, although they know that there is no job waiting for you, You will go the employer will ask you: 'Who gave you my address? Why are you here? I will call the police'. It's all lies. I am only giving an example. To escape these problems, I decided to go to school for six months.

Ahmad's decision to participate in the course is a way out of the obligation to enter a labour regime that he considers to be exploitative and pointless; instead of agreeing to continue 'working' in whatever job is proposed to him by the District Labour Office of Larnaca, he opts for learning. His professed willingness to learn the Greek language is considered a satisfactory step by the official state and can thus secure the continuation of the welfare financial benefits he receives as long as he attends the courses.

The interviewees confirmed that this is strategy is also employed by others: there are asylum seekers who attend for successive years Greek language courses at the same level at the Adult Education Centres, so that they can continue to receive the financial assistance of the state. This situation unveils a policy gap in the local level, confirming the unreadiness of Cyprus to deal with the increased influx of immigration (Mainwaring, 2014, 2016), given its size. Moreover, it indicates an immediate need for analysis of the current policies and practices and their reviews as a means to cope more effectively with the emerging complexity of the demographic situation (Lahav & Guiraudon, 2006).

In the case, of Sara, a female asylum seeker from Sudan, the decision to learn Greek through this specific language course was dictated, according to her narrative, by the District Labour Office. Sara, however, along with Aicha, a female migrant from Lebanon, shared more typical explanations of their motivations for participating in the course; they mentioned reasons and expectations that were related to the notion of knowing the local language as a crucial strategy for their integration in Cypriot society: learning Greek is conceived by them as a tool that can widen the opportunities they will enjoy in the labour market, offering them increased possibilities of cultivating social relationships and friendships with locals as well as other migrants, and paving the way for less financial hardships and better living conditions. Apart from the importance of migrants' assimilation in the labour market (Parutis, 2014; Venturini, 2017), research shows that integration is taking place in the local society first (Casey, 2016), an important component of the broader social integration of the migrants. These narratives on what motivates migrant adults to learn the language of the host country have often appeared in the literature as some of the key findings of other similar empirical studies in different settings (Council of Europe, 2014; Simpson & Whiteside, 2015). In our particular case study, however, it is important to note that this discourse on their motivations was mostly articulated by migrant learners in combination with a relatively negative view of the course they were attending in relation to how it curbed their expectations about the importance of learning the Greek language and the benefits that this will bring to their lives in Cyprus. The migrants' initial motivations for participating in such a course were depicted at the time of our interviews as thwarted, or at least partially thwarted motivations, transformed by the very structural realities of the language course they were attending. It has been shown elsewhere (Rossner, 2008) that lessons that do not meet the expectations of the migrants to cope with the real world, often cause frustration and demotivate the learners. On the contrast, as Nieuwboer and van't Rood (2016) found out, the language lessons that use migrants' daily lives as a starting point for learning can support learners linguistic and social integration.

Sara, for instance, recognised that this specific programme might not be enough for her to speak and write fluently and to facilitate her integration because of its lack of intensiveness, its limited scope, its failure to connect its learning practices with her everyday experiences and the challenges she has been facing in adapting to her new life. Instead of sticking to a critique of these deficiencies, Sara expressed a quite distinct view of what successful integration through learning Greek means for her: in her understanding, it signifies her capacity to fully practice her religious beliefs in her current local setting, exemplified by her as the ability to read the Bible in Greek and to spread its message to others in the Greek language. In her own words:

> I need to stay to this country and I need to know the language, because I need to learn Greek. The Bible, I need to learn the Bible. I love Jesus, I need to bridge people [...] And for this, I need to know sharing the Bible. This is my desire. [...] I'm not happy. I told you, I need to learn the Bible in Greek language, but I didn't. I didn't.

Aicha, in turn, who expressed the strongest motivation to learn Greek through this language course of all of our interviewees, was also critical about how the particular course will not help her to integrate in practice. Although, Aicha was still motivated to learn as much as she can through her participation in the language course, she still expressed her negative views on the lack of an associated qualification that renders the completion of the programme meaningless, the lack of interest by some of her classmates that prevented the group from progressing in their learning, the absence of a formal assessment mechanism that does not allow one – the Cypriot state particularly – to distinguish who has actually learned Greek and who hasn't. As she explained, her motivation to engage in the learning process was shaken by the:

> I say please change this thing with the diploma [i.e. a certificate of completing the course that is awarded to all students at the end of the year]. Not all students should get the same diploma. Not all the same because then the people get the message that 'Oh, if we study or even if we don't study the diploma will be the same'. When they give me this diploma, I have more problems because the people understand that it means nothing.

It is important to refer, here, to some of the specificities of the motivations of migrant adult learners that have been highlighted in the above analysis. For one thing, differences in their legal status might play a crucial role in shaping the motivations of migrant adult learners, especially when their participation in learning activities might be formally linked, or perceived by them as connected, to the prospect of integration in their host society. In addition, the precarity of their legal status might shape the motivations of migrants in a way that their desire to regularise their stay might negatively affect their motivation for learning as such and for their successful engagement in adult learning.

4.2 *Educators' Motivations*

In the case of the Greek language programmes for migrants in Cyprus, the relatively weak intrinsic motivation of educators seems to be primarily caused by the structural and institutional limitations that shape the field of adult education in the country.

Katerina, the teacher of the class we attended, explained that one of her primary motivation for becoming a teacher in the state-run adult education centres was the opportunity to practice philology, the field of her academic studies, accompanied with a satisfactory financial compensation. Her initial motivation seems, however, to have been challenged by several difficulties that Katerina has been facing in her professional environmental. She particularly mentioned during our discussion the pay cuts she had to suffer since the economic crisis and the diminishing social security rights she is now entitled to as a precarious teacher, but also the rigidity of the adult education programmes provided by the state, which has prevented her from taking organisational and pedagogical initiatives. A similar picture on the problematic position of educators of state Adult Educational Centres was painted by the policymaker we interviewed: he referred to them as 'teachers with qualifications who have not been appointed' to formal education. The policymaker placed additional emphasis on the absence of a cohesive state policy on migrant adult education as a major concern. This lack of policy and pedagogical guidance puts, according to him, educators, and learners in an uncertain path, where the educational process of learning Greek is largely unmapped; it is unclear what the learning activities should involve and how they are expected to benefit all participants of such educational programmes. The whole scenery is contradicting the latest UNESCO's (2016) guideline for rising the quality of adult learning. According to the Global Report on Adult Learning and Education (UNESCO, 2016):

> The focal point is that qualifications alone do not guarantee the professionalism of adult educators; however, ensuring professionalism does entail providing initial and continuing training, employment security, fair pay, opportunities to grow, and recognition for good work in reducing the educational gap in the adult population. In addition to initial training, continuing professional development is important to maintain the quality of educational provision in ALE. (p. 58)

The weak intrinsic motivation of educators of Greek language courses for foreigners in Cyprus is best exemplified, by the teacher's lack of interest and engagement with the reality of a multilingual educational programme and the challenge of participating in an experiment of communicating and learning across languages (Kumaravadivelu, 2007). It is striking that although Katerina gave emphasis to her identity as a philologist, she never expressed a concrete professional interest in this particular language course: all the linguistic and philological challenges involved in teaching such a course were treated by her as problems or even burdens and in no way did they act as sources of motivation for strengthening her engagement in the course.

When we specifically asked questions about the challenges of participating in a multilingual class, Katerina replied with a rather formal statement on her willingness to help migrants integrate in Cyprus through learning Greek. However, in the rest of her narrative multilingualism, the migrant composition of her classroom and the challenges of speaking across languages seemed mostly to cause her uneasiness. The backward position she thinks that she has found herself in surfaces in the following articulation on how others (i.e., Cypriot citizens) view her role in this Greek language programme:

> I try not to get influenced, because … all right, the truth is that especially people working for the state authorities when they hear that you are teaching foreigners, they immediately say 'foreigners! …'. It's a bit peculiar, it's not that they are racists, but they think that teaching to foreigners is different. This is how they view it: 'oh, foreigners!' But I am not influenced by these views, nor have I ever shared them. I believe that all students, all human beings have the right to learn.

5 Epistemology

Schweisfurth's conceptualisation of learner-centred education raises the critical importance of the relevance of the curriculum and of educational practices to the learners' present and future lives, as well as the need that what is taught needs to build on learners' existing knowledge and skills (2013, p. 21). A key question to address in this respect, as she points out is that of 'who decides what is relevant to learners' (2015, p. 264) and one might add also those of 'how this relevance or non-relevance is perceived by all participants in the educational process' and how it is 'negotiated in a piecemeal fashion in the context of everyday learning practices'.

In the context of the adult education for migrants in Cyprus these questions acquire additional complexities. On the one hand, the educational system is highly centralised, allowing limited space for the adoption of open, flexible curricula at all educational levels (Hajisoteriou & Angelides, 2013; OECD, 2016). On the other hand, the question of what is relevant in the particular course of this case study, has to be negotiated in an environment where there is no standard common language and where hierarchies between languages might lead to the silencing of some voices and the dominance of others (Risager, 2007).

5.1 *The Question of Relevance*

The absence of targeted policies on adult education for migrants in Cyprus (Gravani, Hatzopoulos, & Chinas, 2019) acts as a factor that can potentially increase the flexibility and scope of the curriculum and facilitate experimentation in course planning and organisation. As Katerina, the language course's educator, told us there is no fixed, centralised curriculum and no standard textbooks for learning Greek in adult education centres in Cyprus. The policymaker confirmed this, stating that the only official material for the programme is a short handbook that is available only in Greek. As a result, the task of designing a curriculum and the choice of material is open for the educators and the learners of the programme. Katerina's strategy, in this regard is to utilise the framework prepared in the context of the official Examinations for the Certificate of Attainment in Greek:

> I think there is some kind of material in the Ministry's website [i.e., The Ministry of Education's examinations for the certification of Greek language] … There are some guidelines at least. Some sort of guidance that advises you that to reach this or that level you need to cover some specific materials and then take the exam … I follow this, I see what someone who attains level A1 or A2 needs to know. I try to approximate this is as much as possible with the class I have.

Regarding the provision of language lessons for migrants, considerations have been expressed if a standardised course with tests, exams and a structured curriculum can be beneficial for migrants, especially those with low educational level (LIAM-programme, Council of Europe, 2014; Nieuwboer & van't Rood, 2016) and proposals were made for more informal and experiential forms of learning (Morrice, 2007). Nevertheless, in the Cyprus case, lack of centralised planning and control did not result to openness and flexibility in practice. When we inquired on whether Katerina discussed the language programme design and curriculum with others, she only referred to some informal conversations and exchanges of ideas she had with other teachers of the same course in other adult education centres across the country. As a result, in the 90-minute lesson that we attended, the curriculum was prescribed and predetermined by the educator. Adult learners' participation/involvement in deciding about aspects of the course was very limited, while the learning activities did not include any learner-centred dimensions. When asked, for instance, if there was any dialogue, exchange of views or even negotiation about the curriculum, the content of the programme, or its educational goals and objectives all interviewees – including the teacher and the three migrant learners – replied with a categorical 'No', as if this was not a real possibility.

To add to this lack of involvement of migrants in the design and organisation of the Greek language course, the policymaker and educator we interviewed made clear that there is no organised mechanism in place for diagnosing the needs of migrants who participate in the programme at any stage of its implementation. Both the policymaker and the teacher stated that, despite this problem, through their past and current experiences with migrant learners, they have been able to inquire on their needs in what could be termed as '*informal* needs assessment' (Sava, 2012, p. 33). For the policymaker, the learners in the course, 'basically want to learn to speak everyday colloquial Greek and are not interested in obtaining a certification of certain qualifications'. Katerina's attempt to identify her student's needs is far more nuanced, recognising the diversity of subject positions and of the aspirations of migrant learners. Her understanding of this diversity, however, is to a significant extent driven by a 'culturisation of difference': the notion that educational needs are culturally determined, with cultures viewed as internally homogeneous (Lentin, 2004). She often described her students' different needs in the following terms: 'Arabs are only interested in oral language ... they only pay attention to the surface, not to the fundamentals of the language ... they only care about being able to communicate in their everyday dealings'. 'Europeans learn faster and have different demands and expectations ...'.

The absence of an open and flexible curriculum that addresses the needs of migrant adult learners has unsurprisingly led to the design of a Greek language course and the development of learning activities that do not seem to be directly relevant to migrants' past, present and future lives.

Although, the educator recognised the question of relevance as a one of the crucial elements that influences the successful implementation of a language programme, it seems that the migrant learners, but even the educator herself, had serious doubts on whether relevance had been achieved in practice. For instance, Katerina, in her description of a typical day in class, recognised that the fast pace of the course short programme (36 hours per year and 1 ½ hours every week), did not allow for a substantial engagement of her course plan with the diversity of experiences and needs of the migrant learners. According to other research (Norton, 1997, 2013) the lack of engagement of learners' past and present experiences in the language course leads to their demotivation, as the learners are left out of the essential-to-language-learning process of negotiation and re-negotiation of their identities.

Indeed, during the class we attended, there seemed to be no time left or no space reserved to a discussion on how the course material and the learning activities were related or could be perceived as relevant to the everyday experiences and challenges the learners have been facing in their efforts to communicate in Greek.

All the narratives of the migrant learners we interviewed raised the issue of this limited relevance in different ways. Aicha and Sara put emphasis on how they strive on their own to connect what they theoretically learn in class to the everyday communication challenges they face in being understood by Greek speakers and to get things done in the supermarket and other shops, in their dealings with several state agencies, in their efforts to fit in their neighbourhood.

In many cases, these attempts fail and these failures cause frustration, but can also potentially increase their determination to come to grips with the Greek language. Ahmad, the only one who spoke Greek somewhat fluently, pointed to the disparities between the irrelevance of the formal methods used in the context of this course and the informal ways of learning that have helped him to learn the language by communication with neighbours and Cypriot friends in everyday settings.

The main obstacles for increasing the relevance of the learning activities of the course might be even more complex and difficult to address. One can discern at the heart of the question of relevance, as it is being articulated by all participants of the Greek language programme, competing understandings of the social and cultural dimensions of language and of cross-cultural dialogue. As it has been shown by recent research, foreign language education is a privileged domain for intercultural interactions (Lázár, 2003; Sercu et al., 2005). At the same time, foreign language education is a space where the openness and uncertainty of intercultural encounters might be contested by means of trying to re-establish hierarchies or inequalities between languages or between proper and improper uses of the same language. These strategies, in the context of foreign language education, are often adopted by native speakers via a fixed focus on the primacy of syntax and grammar rules, as a means to establish difference and hierarchies between native and non-native speakers (Byram, 2008). The following excerpt from Katerina's interview is typical of this strategy of differentiation and hierarchisation:

> I am trying to adapt their needs, but concomitantly to expand them, to push them to new directions. For example, I am not going to stick to 'καλημέρα' (i.e. Good morning), just because they only need to learn how to say 'καλημέρα'. It's not that just because they need to learn the Greek words for 'good morning', or 'hello', or to read some simple sentences, they shouldn't learn what is an epithet, or how can syntactically correct sentences can be formed, or the correct verb tenses. Even if syntax and grammar seem useless to some of the students, this doesn't mean that the class should not learn them.

5.2   *Building on Migrants' Knowledges and Skills*
It is discussed broadly that migrants hold with them skills, competences and knowledge as a result of their working, social and educational life (Clayton, 2005; Kirk, 2004) which are left unexploited or devaluated (Souto-Otero & Villalba-Garcia, 2015) in the host countries. Moreover, learning strategies that relate language learning to learners' experiences has proved to be beneficial

in similar settings (Knutson, 2003; Mollaei & Rahnama, 2012). Our fieldwork drew contradictory findings on the question of to what extent the Greek language course builds and utilises the existing knowledges and skills of adult migrant learners. One the one hand, Katerina, the adult educator claimed that this is one of her main goals. Her position on the issue was stated as follows:

> Many times, many times. In the lesson on occupations, for instance, we drew from the past and present profession of the learners and in the lesson on family, we did the same with their family experiences. Many times, let's say, there is a discussion that is based on their own, personal experiences ... for example, why they came to Cyprus, what they did before they arrived, what type of job they were doing in their country and so on.

Furthermore, as Boud, Cohen, and Walker (1993) concur that the incorporation of experience in adult learning is not enough, but what is needed is the active engagement with it (p. 9). In the 90-minute course that we observed, however, learning challenges were not built on migrant's existing knowledge to a great extent. It seemed that the educator had pre-designed the entire course and that she wasn't open to any digressions, rarely giving the opportunity to learners to freely express their views or leaving enough time for them to narrate a personal story or to tap on their experiences. The course was driven by the educator, without any serious attempt from any side for opening a democratic dialogue amongst the group. Even though, the choice of the two main Greek texts that the educator used during this lesson, titled 'Excuse me, what time it is?' and 'At the airport' might be deemed as ideal choices for involving migrant learners in an open discussion that could potentially be driven by their knowledges and skills, Katerina never made a serious effort for engaging them. As a result, Katerina did most of the talking throughout the course while the learners remained mostly silent, commenting amongst them on what Katerina was transmitting – albeit using a variety of different languages (Greek, English or Arabic).

Although there is a strong tradition favouring the teaching/learning of a new language monolingually, the complexity in the demography of current language classes let to a shift towards bilingual (Hall & Cook, 2014) and – in some cases – plurilingual instruction (González-Davies, 2017). In the case of the reported course, this multiplicity of languages that are present in the class of such a Greek language course ultimately presents the condition of possibility for migrant knowledges and skills to surface. The point where the learning activities are truly driven by the migrant learners' skills is the moment when the predetermined communication process breaks down or when there is a sense that this break down might be imminent; typically, this moment arrives when the learners do not understand the knowledge that the teacher is transmitting. At this moment, migrant learners take the initiative to act as translators: they can start to lead the discussion, moving freely and sometimes skillfully from language to language, creatively attempting to mix or hybridise the languages they know well, or those that they don't know too well, in the common effort to make everyone understand. Greek, Arabic, English are all used intermittently as the languages of translation in the occasions when the teacher is not understood or at least not understood by all the learners.

This is not to argue that these practices of translation between learners or between learners and the educator are unproblematic. They might as well be viewed as creating obstacles to the efforts of adult migrants to learn Greek and as marginalising the less multilingual learners who are not as competent in moving easily between languages. Despite these potential drawbacks, however, the spontaneous instances when migrant learners take control of the course through these creative translation practices is a moment where space is created for a negotiation of what the learning of the Greek language can involve.

6 Technique

According to Schweisfurth's conceptualisation of learner-centred education, the role of teaching techniques and methods should not be treated in a reductionist sense (2013, p. 12), as if the mere adoption of collaborative methods or group work can automatically lead to active learning. The critical task is to incorporate the question of choosing methods within the wider framework of fostering dialogic teaching, as a set of practices element that can both empower learners and serve their rights of expression and participation as well as enhance their personal and social development (2015). In the context of the Cyprus case study, the key question to address, in this regard, is 'to what extent the discussion in class was dialogic' and 'if as a result, adult migrants took substantial responsibility for their learning'.

During our observation of the 90-minute class, we attended a course that could be described as essentially traditional, shaped largely by a 'chalk and talk' method of teaching. The core of the lesson was formed by the written course materials, a series of brochures with Greek texts and exercises, brought to class by the educator and distributed to the students at selected moments. Most of the talking was done by the educator; explaining the learning exercises and how they should be solved, announcing what activity will come next after these were solved, reading aloud the occasional Greek sentence she had written on the blackboard, translating to English some of the tasks posed by the exercises in the cases when migrant learners could not understand their meanings and so on. The migrant learners were not invited to pose questions or to express their views on the course material and the learning activities. In addition, we observed no instance where the educator allowed the space for any open dialogue to occur in an organised fashion and amongst all participants. The sole event of organised dialogue occurred when two learners were asked by the teacher to read aloud a written text they were handed, documenting a dialogue between two Greek speakers. The implementation of these traditional educational methods prevented open discussion on the usefulness, the repercussions, or alternative approaches to the chosen learning activities, while some learners remained silent during the entire course. As Brookfield (2013) claims the use of democratic dialogue in an adult education classroom is not only a way to empower the learners in the cognitive level, but also in the political level. When we refer to migrants, political empowerment seems even more necessary, as the teacher shall be able 'to prepare people to participate in deciding how they will use the resources available to them and how they will act out in the world' (Brookfield, 2013, p. 4). The issue of power relations and the negotiation of learners' identities in a language learning course is not to be neglected, because according to MacPherson (2005): 'Teaching a language means teaching a culture, with implicit assumptions about the means to, and ends of, a good life. In most cases, this good life is rooted in a particular conception of liberation' (p. 589).

On the other hand, during our interview, Katerina, the course's educator, presented a contrasting picture of the educational techniques she chooses to utilise in the 'teaching of Greek for foreigners':

> Everything. Whatever can suit the goals of the particular lesson or let's, say, of the particular learning unit: it may be dialogue, or maybe role playing, it may be spelling, it can be an oral exercise, a written exercise ... It depends on the unit and even more on the disposition of the students. Some of them may feel bored sometimes or tired or feel psychologically wearied down. You have to adapt ... You have to be a psychologist! There are occasions when students want to play the role of the teacher, they enjoy it and different dynamics are at play. You see how dialogic communication flows between someone who is an Arab trying to teach another Arab ... and trying to teach in Greek.

One way to interpret this discrepancy between observation and claim is to point to the possible contradictory or even hypocritical stance of the educator: attempting, perhaps, to impress or to please academics by professing that she implements progressive teaching methods. A more productive analysis, however, would be to analyse this discrepancy through the prism of the structural dynamics that shape adult education for migrants in Cyprus.

For one thing, adult education programmes in Cyprus are marred by the lack of appropriate infrastructure that discourages the utilisation of collaborative educational techniques. As Norton (1997) notes regarding language lessons for migrants 'the influential role of the teacher is determined not only by the explicit content of the lessons but by the type of materials incorporated into a lesson and the methods' (p. 426). The Greek language programmes, as all the courses organised by the Adult Education Centres, are hosted during the evenings at the premises of a local state elementary school. The educator and the learners are obliged thus to use facilities designed and constructed for other educational purposes and other types of learners. Chairs and desks are too small and arranged in a horseshoe layout, there are few options of teaching aids (a blackboard, no flipcharts, no projector, no computer, no audio system, no internet connection), and to add to this, the classroom needs to be left to its previous state of being when the lesson ends, dissuading thus any initiative for a flexible re-arrangement of the space. According to Mayo, Pace, and Zammit (2008), the use of existing infrastructure for delivering adult education programmes is common in small states with limited resources, a situation that poses challenges for both adult educators and learners as these sites are usually inappropriate for adults.

Second, the extremely tight time frame of this education programme, which officially purports to aim at developing the Greek language skills of adult migrants, acts as a barrier to the possibility of experimenting with teaching methods and to dialogic teaching in general. The restrictive time devoted to lessons has been documented in research (Larrotta, 2017) as being quite a challenge for the successful learning of adults. These time restraints generate the common perception of all course participants that time is always pressing and inadequate; this is the general feeling that was repeatedly raised during all of our conversations with the educator and the learners. 'It is a question of time', 'the time we have on our hands makes this difficult', 'there is no time for ...', 'there is no time to discuss', 'there is no time to share', 'we don't have the time to ...' were some of the phrasings that were used by both educator and learners when we were discussing questions on the dialogic interactions that occur in class, or on how a typical course evolves from start to finish, or if, and if not why not, learners participate in class discussions.

Another structural impediment of the adult education system in Cyprus, which directly affects teaching methods in the particular case of Greek language teaching, but not entirely limited to this, is its lack of engagement with the problematic of intercultural encounters and the challenges these pose to adult learning (Gravani, Hatzopoulos, & Chiina, 2019). For example, as it was stated by both Katerina and the policymaker, there is currently no training programme for adult educators in Cyprus that tackles issues related to intercultural education or that aims at developing their intercultural competences. Consequently, Katerina had so far only the opportunity to attend some seminars on the teaching of Greek as a second language, which was organised, according to her description, mainly as a general orientation training on the specificities of adult learning, without any focus on teaching methods appropriate for multilingual and multicultural classrooms. Nonetheless, dealing successfully with a multicultural class is a highly complex task. As Duff and Uchida (1997) suggest 'in teacher education programmes, student teachers and practicing teachers should reflect on their own teaching foundations and experiences, cultural biases and understandings, and knowledge of what constitutes (and is constituted by) cultural knowledge as well as what current critical perspectives have to offer' (p. 479).

Moreover, the lack of concern with interculturality in the organisation of adult educational programmes, in the design of course curricula or in the debates on teaching methods in Cyprus, can also be associated with how dialogic teaching is discouraged in this particular Greek language course. Language cannot be acquired in isolation, besides, interaction in a learning setting that functions as a community of practice (Lave & Wenger, 1991), not only supports language acquisition but also the renegotiation of learners' identities using the new language (Yates, 2011). During our class observation, but also in the narratives of both learners and educator, attempts to foster collaborative learning practices or dialogic interactions appeared or were portrayed as problematic. In most cases, these failures were signaled by the breakdown of communication, mainly caused by the absence of a common language amongst participants. When dialogue reached this point of incomprehension, all participants seemed more comfortable in instantly reverting to the conventional way of assigning the educator with the role of explaining, talking, and finding a way out of this impasse. From the viewpoint of the learners, this failure of dialogic interaction was often interpreted through the lens of their traditional educational backgrounds, shaped by their past learning experiences in their countries of origin. The influence of these experiences might also explain, to some extent, their very positive views of the educator of the course, expecting from her to be the expert authority who transmits the official, proper knowledge of Greek language. In this traditional mind frame that the learners often exemplified in our interviews, dialogue in the context of the course was often considered as synonymous to wasting time or even as a nuisance, rather than as integral part of the learning process.

Aicha, for instance, remembered how annoyed she was when some of her classmates were 'always talking to each other', or 'always asking the teacher for everything' and thus 'distracting her from learning'. She asked to be transferred to another class and she was now very happy that she was moved to this one. Sara, on the other hand, acknowledged that 'conversations in class are important', and expressed the wish that this could be done by 'working in groups', pointing however to how this was impossible in the current situation, since 'we don't have the skills' to accomplish this. Ahmad wondered, 'how can we have a dialogue?', 'when the teacher asks someone to talk, to say something, they usually remain silent ... in the first place because they don't understand what she said, or even if they did understand, they don't know how to express themselves in Greek'.

Both the learners and the educator were not prepared to enter or, more crucially, to produce a space of intercultural interactions, where a common language was not a pre-given, but that it could be constructed collaboratively through the learning process. The lack of preparedness recorded in the course coupled with a reluctant approach towards opening to the possibilities of intercultural communication made the (over-)employment of traditional teaching methods appealing as a way back to the safety of keeping the learning process going.

7 Relationships

Schweisfurth (2013, p. 21) has highlighted mutual respect between teachers and learners, as well the development of interpersonal relationships amongst them, as one of the key elements of learner-centred education. The relevant question, in respect to learner-centredness, is to assess these relationships along a continuum that ranges from authoritarian to democratic, which reflects the amount of control that migrant learners do or do not have over their learning. The analysis of relationships amongst the programme's participants in the context of the Cyprus case study should consider the specific subject positions occupied by the migrant learners and the educator and how these are challenged or reproduced by the specific decisions that inform how the course is designed and organised and how the learning is pursued.

As observers of the Greek language course we noted, on one level, that a climate of mutual respect and cooperation was prevalent. There seemed to be harmonious relationships between learners and between them and the educator, without any tensions or frictions amongst them. On the part of the migrant learners, even though they predominantly expressed disappointment with the learning outcomes of the course in terms of their unimproved Greek language skills, they still seemed to act with respect towards the educator during the entire class and recognised her efforts to help them learn during our conversations after class. Using Oxford's (2003) perspectives to describe the conditions of learning whether it is taking place or not, it seems that the educator is recognised by the learners as the 'capable other' who holds the potential to provide the learners with the needed assistance in order to advance their knowledge and become self-regulated learners. Echoing Vykotsky's theory, Oxford (2003, p. 86) calls this kind of learning as 'mediated learning'. Mediation refers here to the active interaction between the two parts, namely the learners and the more 'capable other' to the point, that the learners move through their zone of proximal development (ZPD). In the reported case, while the learners acknowledged the educator as the 'capable other', the course didn't result in real learning. We here concur that the course did not result in learning, because two critical components were missing: the first one was the dynamic interaction between the two parts in order for the learners to get out of their ZPD, and the second was the motivation on behalf of the learners, which according to Oxford (2003) stems out of meaningful learning. In this case, even though there had been a positive climate in the group, the educator did not take advantage of it by using the appropriate learning strategies (see Oxford, 1999) to assist the students to evolve.

More so, they seemed to be treating each other with respect in the cases where some learners openly expressed their difficulties in following the learning activities and created, in an ad-hoc fashion, a mutual help mechanism of multilingual translations for serving the needs of those who could not understand what was going on at particular moments in class. From the educator's point of view the positive atmosphere in class was because 'they all have their point of view, they are entitled to say everything, whatever they want, but within a spirit of respect, mutual understanding and dignity'.

Another way to interpret this positive climate, however, would be to contextualise it within the dynamics of this educational programme, where democratic dialogue was relatively absent. The good atmosphere and the frictionless learning process appear in this light as a consequence of keeping distance, rather than engaging with, of maintaining boundaries rather than challenging them. During this Greek language course, intercultural relations never really developed amongst participants and established hierarchies were never really put into question or tested primarily because of its teacher-centred approach and non-dialogic character.

Regarding, the aspect of established hierarchies, as it was discussed in the previous section of the chapter, the learning process was structured along a predominantly teacher-centric approach with clear, distinct, and unequal roles for the educator and the learners. Migrant learners were not empowered to become active participants in co-designing the course or in co-selecting or re-shaping the course materials, they were not given the opportunity to draw extensively from their own experiences (Norton, 1997, 2013) in an open and democratic dialogue in class (Brookfield, 2013), or to re-orient the learning activities conducted in the context of this language course.

Regarding the aspect of intercultural interactions, these were minimal especially if one considers the multi-ethnic and multi-racial composition of the specific class. The relative absence of intercultural interactions was evident in the fixed positioning of bodies inside the classroom and the fixed flows of communication amongst them. Sitting arrangements followed ethnic, linguistic and/or gender lines. In the particular class that we attended – but, as it was explained by the interviewees this was a permanent state of affairs – Iraqis sat together with Iraqis who then placed themselves closer to other Arab-speaking learners, while other non-Arab speaking nationalities sat further down the room and again in groups of either ethnic or linguistic affiliations.

Most dialogic exchanges during class mirrored this sitting arrangement, flowing along ethnic or linguistic affiliations. Even Aicha, the migrant woman from Lebanon, who appeared to be interacting with her neighbour, Sara from Sudan, during class, when we inquired on how they get along and commented that they seem to be in very friendly terms, she replied: 'No, we are not friends, we are translators'. During the 90-minute course that we observed, there were three learners who remained silent for the entire class. Two of them – both Ukrainian speakers sat close and talked to each other, presumably both on and off topic in relation to the parallel learning activities. One middle-aged man sat alone and did not utter a word. When we asked other learners who that was and why he was silent, told us that he comes from Israel.

> When we asked him, where are you from, he said 'from Israel' and all Arabs went like this! I was afraid. I sat back. Really ... afraid. When he speaks he stares like this (i.e. with his head down), but no problem. Inside, he is nervous. We came to Cyprus to forget this! (Aicha)

> He was Jewish. The teacher was struggling to push him to participate in discussions. I don't know why he was that way. Maybe it's his character. The teacher was very good with him, but the man was like that. We greeted him, 'good morning', 'good evening' but he was like that ... silent. (Ahmad)

The pedagogical potentials of these intercultural encounters and these acts of translation are lost. In effect, they are treated by all participants, as existing problems, and not as critical junctures for re-shaping the learning process, for making it relevant and useful to migrant learners, and for igniting open dialogic exchange. Translation as a practice that builds social relationships among ethnically and linguistically diverse learners, that both requires and fosters collaborative skills and that can potentially re-define existing hierarchies among languages is merely treated as a way out of incomprehensibility. The uncovering of the presence of a participant-other, which brings to the foreground collective memories and concerns that can act as a spark for connecting the learning process to existing migrants' knowledges and experiences is pushed aside as a dangerous encounter that needs to be neglected or forgotten in the present circumstances. Conclusively, the ineffectiveness of the course in the level of relation management can be attributed to the absence of the main cultural practices that are proposed as effective strategies in language learning, namely the incorporation and problematisation of cultural representations, the encouragement of active dialogue and the promotion of interculturality (Menard-Warwick, 2009, p. 43).

8 Conclusion

The analysis of the key findings of this case study attests to the very limited engagement with learner-centred practices as a tool for empowering migrant adult learners. In this respect, the absence of formal, standard policies on adult education for migrants in Cyprus is a crucial factor that precludes organised efforts towards the adoption of such LCE practices.

Regarding the specificities of the dynamics that were analysed in the context of this case study, we can observe that the presence of migrant learners poses a significant challenge to the task of contextualising and localising learner-centred education for adult learning. First, the status of adult migrant learners as non-citizens is a critical factor in terms of thinking about relevant and appropriate LCE educational practices. The Cyprus case study reconfirms the findings of existing research (Bevelander, 2011; Connor, 2010) that the precarity of the migrants' residence status, ranging from asylum-seekers to refugees and from legal migrants and to sans-papiers, might significantly affect their motivations to participate in adult learning; it can perpetuate hierarchies between educators and learners or between learners, and it can play a deterring role in their capacity to take control of their learning. Engaging with this discussion on citizenship and precarious livelihoods and integrating it into learning activities, be it in the context of a language course or any other type of adult educational programme, might be a first, positive step towards empowering migrant learners.

Second, dialogic teaching in the context of adult education for migrants is intrinsically associated with a multiplicity of translation practices (González-Davies, 2017; Hall & Cook, 2014). Although in the case of the Cyprus case study, the lack of linguistic homogeneity and of a common language of instruction was overwhelmingly considered by all participants as an impediment to the learning process, spontaneous acts of translation across linguistic barriers constitute instances when migrant learners can potentially take control of their learning and that can open up the space for re-negotiating the structure and content of adult learning as well as their own identities. The lack of appropriate learning strategies (Oxford, 1999) is shown to be an essential constraint that limited the potential positive effects of this plurilingual context.

Finally, learner-centred educational practices in the context of adult education for migrants need to emanate from and to concomitantly enhance intercultural interactions (Lázár, 2003; Sercu et al., 2005). Interculturality in the context of adult education for migrants is crucial for overcoming traditional educational assumptions and methods, which constitute obstacles to democratic dialogue in class and for ensuring that migrant learners have an equal right to express their opinions and to equally participate in the learning process.

References

Bevelander, P. (2011). The employment integration of resettled refugees, asylum claimants, and family reunion migrants in Sweden. *Refugee Survey Quarterly, 30*(1), 22–43.

Boud, D., Cohen, R., & Walker, D. (1993). *Using experience for learning*. McGraw-Hill Education.

Brookfield, S. D. (2013). *Powerful techniques for teaching adults*. John Wiley & Sons.

Byram, M. (2008). *From foreign language education to education for intercultural citizenship. essays and reflections*. Multilingual Matters.

Casey, L. (2016). *The Casey review: A review into opportunity and integration*. www.gov.uk/government/uploads/system/uploads/attachment_data/file/575973/The_Casey_Review_Report.pdf

Charmaz, K. (2006). *Constructing grounded theory: A practical guide through qualitative analysis*. Sage.

Clayton, P. (2005). Blank slates or hidden treasure? Assessing and building on the experiential learning of migrant and refugee women in European countries. *International Journal of Lifelong Education, 24*(3), 227–242.

Connor, P. (2010). Explaining the refugee gap: Economic outcomes of refugee versus other immigrants. *Journal of Refugee Studies, 23*(3), 377–397.

Council of Europe. (2014). *The linguistic integration of adult migrants, from one country to another, from one language to another.* Author.

Cross, K. P. (1981). *Adults as learners. Increasing participation and facilitating learning.* Jossey-Bass.

Cyprus Ministry of Labour, Welfare and Social Insurance. (n.d.). *Employment of asylum seekers.* http://www.mlsi.gov.cy/mlsi/dl/dl.nsf/page5j_en/page5j_en?OpenDocument

Denzin, N. K., & Lincoln, Y. S. (2005). Introduction: The discipline and practice of qualitative practice. In N. K. Denzin & Y. S. Lincoln (Eds.), *The Sage handbook of qualitative research* (3rd ed., pp. 1–32). Sage.

Dörnyei, Z. (2005). *The psychology of the language learner: Individual differences in second language acquisition.* Lawrence Erlbaum.

Duff, P. A., & Uchida, Y. (1997). The negotiation of teachers' sociocultural identities and practices in postsecondary EFL classrooms. *TESOL Quarterly, 31*(3), 451–486.

Emerson, R. M., Fretz, R. I., & Shaw, L. L. (2001). Participant observation and fieldnotes. In P. Atkinson, A. Coffey, S. Delamont, J. Lofland, & L. Lofland (Eds.), *Handbook of ethnography* (pp. 352–368). Sage.

European Ministerial Conference on Integration. (2010). *Draft declaration* (Zaragoza, 15–16 April 2010). http://ec.europa.eu/ewsi/UDRW/images/items/docl_13055_519941744.pdf

Eurostat. (2019). *Migration and migrant population statistics.* https://ec.europa.eu/eurostat/statistics-explained/pdfscache/1275.pdf

González-Davies, M. (2017). The use of translation in an integrated plurilingual approach to language learning: Teacher strategies and best practices. *Journal of Spanish Language Teaching, 4*(2), 124–135.

Gravani, M. N., Hatzopoulos, P., & Chinas, C. (2019). Adult education and migration in Cyprus: A critical analysis. Journal of Adult and Continuing Education. https://doi.org/10.1177/1477971419832896

Gravani, M. N., & Ioannidou, A. (2014). *Adult and continuing education in Cyprus.* German Institute for Adult Education (DIE) & W. Bertelmann Verlag. doi:10.3278/37/0575w

Gravani, M. N., & John, P. D. (2005). 'Them and us': Teachers' and tutors' perceptions of a 'new' professional development course in Greece. *Compare: A Journal of Comparative Education, 35*(3), 303–319.

Hajisoteriou, C., & Angelides, P. (2013). The politics of intercultural education in Cyprus: Policy-making and challenges. *Education Inquiry, 4*(1), 103–123.

Hall, G., & Cook, G. (2014). Own language use in ELT: Exploring global practices and attitudes. *Language Issues: The ESOL Journal, 25*(1), 35–43.

Kelly, P., Damsbaek, N., Lemoine, M., Fang, T., Preston, V., & Tufts, S. (2010). *Language skills and immigrant labour market outcomes* (TIEDI Analytical Report 11). Toronto Immigrant Employment Data Initiative.

Kirk, R. (2004). *Skills audit of refugees.* Home Office. 37/04. www.homeoffice.gov.uk/rds/pdfs04/rdsolr3704.pdf

Knowles, M. S., Holton III, E. F., & Swanson, R. A. (2012). *The adult learner*. Routledge.

Knutson, S. (2003). Experiential learning in second-language classrooms. *TESL Canada Journal, 20*(2), 52–64. https://doi.org/10.18806/tesl.v20i2.948

Kumaravadivelu, B. (2007). *Cultural globalization and language education*. Yale University Press.

Lahav, G., & Guiraudon, V. (2006). Actors and venues in immigration control: Closing the gap between political demands and policy outcomes. *West European Politics, 29*(2), 201–223.

Lamb, M. (2004). Integrative motivation in a globalizing world. *System, 32*, 3–19.

Larrotta, C. (2017). Immigrants to the United States and adult education services. *New Directions for Adult and Continuing Education, 2017*(155), 61–69. https://doi.org/10.1002/ace.20241

Lave, J., & Wenger, E. (1991). *Situated learning: Legitimate peripheral participation*. Cambridge University Press.

Lázár, I. (Ed.). (2003). *Incorporating intercultural communicative competence in language teacher education*. European Centre for Modern Languages. Council of Europe.

Lentin, A. (2004). Racial states, anti-racist responses: Picking holes in 'culture' and 'human rights'. *European Journal of Social Theory, 7*(4), 427–443.

LIAM. (2015). Guiding principles. http://www.coe.int/nl/web/lang-migrants/guiding-principles

MacPherson, S. (2005). Negotiating language contact and identity change in developing Tibetan-English bilingualism. *TESOL Quarterly, 39*(4), 585–607.

Mainwaring, C. (2014). Small states and nonmaterial power: Creating crises and shaping migration policies in Malta, Cyprus, and the European Union. *Journal of Immigrant & Refugee Studies, 12*(2), 103–122.

Mainwaring, Ċ. (2016). Migrant agency: Negotiating borders and migration controls. *Migration Studies, 4*(3), 289–308.

Mayo, P., Pace, P. J., & Zammit, E. (2008). Adult education in small states: The case of Malta. *Comparative Education, 44*(2), 229–246.

Menard-Warwick, J. (2009). Co-Constructing representations of culture in ESL and EFL classrooms: Discursive fault lines in Chile and California. *The Modern Language Journal, 93*(1), 30–45.

Mollaei, F., & Rahnama, H. (2012). Experiential education contributing to language learning. *International Journal of Humanities and Social Science, 2*(21), 268–279.

Morrice, L. (2007). Lifelong learning and the social integration of refugees in the UK: The significance of social capital. *International Journal of Lifelong Education, 26*(2), 155–172.

Nieuwboer, C., & van't Rood, R. (2016). Learning language that matters: A pedagogical method to support migrant mothers without formal education experience in their social integration in Western countries. *International Journal of Intercultural Relations, 51*, 29–40.

Noels, K. A. (2001). New orientations in language learning motivation: Towards a model of intrinsic, extrinsic, and integrative orientations and motivation. *Motivation and Second Language Acquisition, 23*, 43–68.

Norton, B. (1997). Language, identity, and the ownership of English. *TESOL Quarterly, 31*(3), 409–429.

Norton, B. (2013). *Identity and language learning: Extending the conversation.* Multilingual Matters.

OECD. (2016). *PISA 2015 results: Policies and practices for successful schools* (Vol. II). Author.

Oxford, R. L. (Ed.). (1996). *Language learning motivation: Pathways to the new century* (Vol. 11). National Foreign Language Resource Center.

Oxford, R. L. (1999). Relationships between second language learning strategies and language proficiency in the context of learner autonomy and self-regulation. *Revista Canaria de Estudios Ingleses, 38*(1999), 109–126.

Oxford, R. L. (2003). Toward a more systematic model of L2 learner autonomy. In D. Palfreyman & R. C. Smith (Eds.), *Learner autonomy across cultures* (pp. 75–91). Palgrave Macmillan.

Parutis, V. (2014). 'Economic migrants' or 'middling transnationals'? East European migrants' experiences of work in the UK. *International Migration, 52*(1), 36–55.

Patton, M. Q. (1999). Enhancing the quality and credibility of qualitative analysis. *Health Services Research, 34*(52), 1189–1208.

Patton, M. Q. (2002). *Qualitative research and evaluation methods* (3rd ed.). Sage.

Risager, K. (2007). *Language and culture pedagogy: From a national to a transnational paradigm* (Vol. 14). Multilingual Matters.

Rossner, R. (2008). *Quality assurance in the provision of language education and training for adult migrants-Guidelines and options.* Council of Europe.

Sava, S. (2012). *Needs analysis and programme planning in adult education.* Barbara Budrich Publishers.

Schweisfurth, M. (2013). *Learner-centred education in international perspective: Whose pedagogy for whose development?* Routledge.

Schweisfurth, M. (2015). Learner-centred pedagogy: Towards a post-2015 agenda for teaching and learning. *International Journal of Educational Development, 40*, 259–266.

Scott, D. (1996). Ethnography and education. In D. Scott & R. Usher (Eds.), *Understanding educational research* (pp. 143–158). Routledge.

Seale, C. (1999). Quality in qualitative research. *Qualitative Inquiry, 5*(4), 465–478.

Sercu, L. et al. (2005). *Foreign language teachers and intercultural competence.* Multilingual Matters.

Simpson, J., & Whiteside, A. (Eds.). (2015). *Adult language education and migration: Challenging agendas in policy and practice*. Routledge.

Souto-Otero, M., & Villalba-Garcia, E. (2015). Migration and validation of non-formal and informal learning in Europe: Inclusion, exclusion or polarisation in the recognition of skills? *International Review of Education, 61*(5), 585–607.

UNESCO Institute for Lifelong Learning. (2016). *Third global report on adult learning and education*. Author.

Venturini, A. (2017). Immigrant assimilation in the labour market: What is missing in economic literature. In A. Weinar, A. Unterreiner, & P. Fargues (Eds.), *Migrant integration between homeland and host society* (Vol. 1, pp. 21–42). Springer.

Wlodkowski, R. J. (1999). *Enhancing adult motivation to learn: A comprehensive guide for teaching all adults*. Jossey-Bass.

Yates, L. (2011). Interaction, language learning and social inclusion in early settlement. *International Journal of Bilingual Education and Bilingualism, 14*(4), 457–471.

PART 3

Comparative Analysis & Reflections

∴

CHAPTER 8

Learner-Centred Education and Adult Education for Migrants: A Cross-Case Analysis of the Cypriot, Estonian, Maltese and Scottish Cases

Pavlos Hatzopoulos, Maria N. Gravani, Bonnie Slade, Larissa Jõgi and Maria Brown

Abstract

This chapter focuses on a comparative analysis of the four case studies presented in Part 2. Hatzopoulos, Gravani, Slade, Jõgi and Brown provide a critical interpretation of the data drawing on Schweisfurth's (2013) four conceptual axes of the LCE framework outlined in Chapter 1. The cross-case analysis of the findings revealed significant divergences amongst the four adult language programmes across the four countries in relation to the motivations of adult migrant learners for participating in adult education, the relevance of the curriculum and the extent to which the courses build on the migrant learners knowledges and skills, the utilisation of teaching techniques and methods within the wider framework of fostering dialogic teaching, and ultimately the degree of control that migrant learners do or do not have over their learning. Importantly, the status of adult migrant learners as non-citizens is a critical factor in terms of thinking about relevant and appropriate LCE educational practices. The precariousness of the migrants' residence status, ranging from asylum-seekers to refugees and from legal migrants and to sans-papiers, might significantly affect their motivations to participate in adult learning, it can perpetuate hierarchies between educators and learners or between learners, and it can play a deterring role in their capacity to take control of their learning. Engaging with this discussion on citizenship and precarious livelihoods and integrating it into learning activities is a critical step towards empowering migrant learners.

Keywords

learner-centred education – cross-case analysis – motivations – epistemology – techniques – relationships – adult education – social change, migration

1 Introduction

This chapter proposes a cross-case analysis of the four case studies that were conducted in four European cities, Glasgow (Scotland), Malta, Larnaca (Cyprus) and Tallinn (Estonia). The findings of the four studies were organised around the issues of motivations for participation, the organisation of the course, teaching practices that are employed in class, the learning climate/atmosphere, and evaluation practices that correspond to the four elements which comprise LCE practice, according to Schweisfurth's approach, namely: techniques, relationships, motivation, epistemology (2013, p. 11). Along these lines, the cross-case analysis will reflect this categorisation, attempting to highlight the extent to which LCE is used in adult education as a tool for social change across different contexts, but also to offer reflections on LCE as a pedagogical approach, about LCE as a field of research, as well as on migration as a social process and migrant adult students as co-creators of educational programmes.

2 Motivations

The four case studies examined the motivations of adult migrant learners for participating in the language learning programmes under study, but also of other participants to the educational process. The studies adopted the view that learning is best achieved through internal rather than external motivation and learners need to be intrinsically motivated to be involved successfully in the education process (Schweisfurth, 2013, p. 12). Indeed, adult learning theory suggests that people tend to feel uncommitted to any decision or activity that they feel is imposed on them (Cross, 1981; Knowles, 1980; Wlodkowski, 1999).

On a first reading, two initial observations stem from a comparative reading of the findings of the four studies. First, the existence of disparities regarding the level of intrinsic motivation of adult migrants for participating in the learning programmes (it is strong in the cases of Scotland and Estonia, relatively strong in the case of Malta, and almost non-existent in the case of Cyprus) tends to mirror the extent to which these four adult education programmes for migrants are learner-centred. In the case of Estonia, for instance, the strong intrinsic motivation of migrant learners correlates with the evidence that the main components of learner-centred education (LCE) are implemented in the context of the language learning programme. As our study concluded, 'here is concrete evidence that the language course for adults with migrant background encourages collaboration, dialogue and motivates cooperation between learners by giving them possibilities to control their own learning process' (Jõgi & Karu, Chapter 4, this volume).

In contrast, in the case of the Greek language programme in Larnaca, adult migrant learners and educators participating in the course were not intrinsically motivated to be involved successfully in the education process at a sufficient level. As a result, our study found, that learners' and teachers' lack of sufficient engagement impacts negatively on the extent of learner control over the content and process of learning as well as bars possibilities of pedagogical experimentation with the adoption of new and appropriate teaching methods (Gravani, Hatzopoulos, & Papaioannou, Chapter 7, this volume).

Second, the level of intrinsic motivations on the part of adult migrant learners tends to be directly affected by the motivations of the other participants to the educational process. One such positive influence was inspired by the role of the charismatic educator in the 'Language training' in Estonian module: 'The role and personal motivation of the language teacher in supporting motivation of adult learners with the migrant backgrounds was significant because of her personal motivation to be a language teacher for migrant adults, her enthusiasm and openness, the nature of interactions with the students, her ability to create an open atmosphere of trust in the class. She enabled learners to feel and experience an open and emotional atmosphere, enjoy the dialogue and small progress in tasks and active participation' (Jõgi & Karu, Chapter 4, this volume).

Another positive instance relates to the work of volunteers in the ESOL programmes for migrants in Glasgow (Scotland), who join the classes and offer one-to-one support for the less able learners. While the presence of a significant variance of language literacy skills amongst migrant classmates is generally viewed in negative terms by all the participants to the educational process in other settings (Cyprus and Malta), in the case of Glasgow, though the work of these volunteers acts as an enabling factor for strengthening the intrinsic motivation of migrant adult learners (Slade & Dickson, Chapter 5, this volume).

2.1 *Contextualising Research on Motivations to Participation*

The cross-case analysis of the four case studies raises the critical importance of contextualising research on learner-centred education. In regards to the exploration of the motivations to participation of learners, the findings of the project illuminate the crucial role of the economic, social and political dynamics shaping the identities and lives of this particular group of learners (i.e. migrants), but also the interrelation between their motivation to participate in educational practices and the general conditions shaping their social integration in different national and local contexts.

Migrant learners might face intense challenges and display distinct desires and expectations in the context of their participation in adult learning in comparison to citizens, due primarily to the distinctiveness of their legal and political status. In general, the potentially precarious living conditions of migrants in the respective host societies has a direct impact on the ways they value and experience learning.

The significance of identifying and addressing the particularities of the migrants' living conditions, complex needs and desires by adult education providers was documented in detail by the Glasgow research team. Their analysis of the gradual expansion of the Glasgow's organisation range of services for migrants brings to light an innovative approach, which connects the ESOL language programme to other services that are deemed crucial for enhancing the successful local integration of migrants.

In fact, the experimental policies initiated in Glasgow, enable and support the motivation of migrants to engage with learning by constituting its ESOL programme as an integral part of a wide range of services, which address immediate needs and enhance prospects for integration. These services include:

- An in-house 'ESOL café', where a free meal is offered after each class and which acts as a space for informal learning (migrants can practice their conversational English, there) and for boosting sociality.
- The provision of family support services in cooperation with local government. Government representatives are invited by the organisation's staff to inform and advise migrant learners about Scotland's housing policy, health service, social benefits, and children's education.
- A crèche, providing childcare service, which is deemed especially important for the participation of migrant women, as most migrants living in Glasgow would not normally have access to childcare due to the prohibitive costs and limited availability of child-minding services (Slade & Dickson, Chapter 5, this volume).

In most settings, however, the complex migrant needs and desires and the precarity of migrants' lives tends to act as a principal barrier to their engagement with adult education. These dimensions were illustrated in the findings of the case studies in Malta and Glasgow. In Malta, for instance, the motivations of migrant learners were found to be largely shaped by external pressures of fulfilling the generalised other's expectations concerning linguistic competence, particularly peers' expectations – peers who, notably, might not necessarily be of the same nationality as that of the migrants. These external pressures were also gendered: migrant women tended to be seen as more likely to quit the language courses as their identities as active learners were thought to be incompatible to their traditional gender roles as the primary carers of their family and children (Brown, Chapter 6, this volume). A similar gendered barrier to the engagement of women migrant learners was observed in the Glasgow case, though this was mitigated through the initiative of providing on the spot childcare services, but also by allowing and adapting to the presence of children in class, as long as they are not too disruptive. In general, however, also in this case the chaotic home lives of migrant learners and the extremely difficult family dynamics were identified as posing a significant obstacle to the motivation to participate in adult education (Slade & Dickson, Chapter 5, this volume).

In Cyprus, the precarity of migrants' lives constitutes a more extreme deterrent to their free and purposeful engagement in adult educational settings. As our study showed, for one thing, differences in their legal status might play a crucial role in shaping the motivations of migrant adult learners, especially when their participation in learning activities might be formally linked, or perceived by them as connected, to the prospect of integration in their host society. In addition, the precarity of their legal status might shape the motivations of migrants in a way that their desire to regularise their stay might negatively affect their motivation for learning as such and their successful engagement in adult learning (Gravani, Hatzopoulos, & Papaioannou, Chapter 7, this volume).

3   Epistemology

Following Schweisfurth's conceptualisation of learner-centred education, the four case studies examined the relevance of the curriculum and of the observed educational practices to the learners' present and future lives, as well as the need that what is taught needs to build on learners' existing knowledge and skills (2013, p. 21). A key question that was addressed in this respect, as Schweisfurth points out is that of 'who decides what is relevant to learners' (2015, p. 264), and additional inquiries on 'how this relevance or non-relevance is perceived by all participants in the educational process' and how it is 'negotiated in a piecemeal fashion in the context of everyday learning practices'.

In a corresponding fashion to the inquiry on the motivation to participate in adult education, the findings revealed wide divergences amongst the four adult language programmes across the four cities in relation to the relevance of the curriculum and the extent to which the courses build on the migrants' knowledges and skills. These divergences can be tentatively explained through the lens of the disparate types of the adult education providers of these four language programmes for migrants. Where non-governmental organisations assumed that role (the NGO, Expat Relocation Estonia, in Tallinn and the community organisation, the housing association in Glasgow) the curriculum of the language course was considered by all participants as tailored to meet the perceived information needs and interests of the migrants, while it also managed to be satisfactorily associated to their existing skills and knowledge, albeit in occasions where the lack of a shared language amongst participants of the course acted as a barrier against this effect. Where, in contrast, the role of the adult education provider is assumed by the state (Malta and Cyprus), the language programmes were characterised by a largely fixed knowledge and curriculum, while there was very limited engagement of the educational activities with the current knowledges and experiences of migrant learners.

An additional layer of explanation can be related to the lack of concrete policies on adult education for migrants in all four countries (Brown, Gravani, Slade, & Jõgi, Chapter 3, this volume). The lack of formal, centralised and standardised policies produces a vacuum that can potentially increase the flexibility and scope of the curriculum of the language programmes under study and facilitate experimentation in the course planning and organisation and in the educational activities that are included in the programme. This space for experimentation with learner-centred practices is not, however, utilised in many occasions as the decision ultimately rests with the language programme's educators or course designers, who might not be even sufficiently self-driven to perform this role, nor are they necessarily professionally trained for participating in adult education for migrants in intercultural environments. In the cases of Malta and Cyprus, the language courses for migrants precisely reflect these problematic dynamics, limiting the involvement of migrants in the design and organisation of the language course and the employment of educational activities.

In Malta, our research concluded that the content-driven character of the language courses limits the value attributed to migrants' existing knowledge by the teacher and other learners; as well as the extent of which learners are asked about their learning needs and expectations. The study pointed to the existence of arbitrary and ad hoc self-developed teacher practices, rather than a formal standard policy, which ultimately allowed for small-scale learner-centredness (Brown, Chapter 6, this volume). The Cyprus study argued that the curriculum was prescribed and predetermined by the educator. Adult learners' participation/involvement in deciding about aspects of the course was very limited, while the learning activities did not include any learner-centred dimensions. The absence of an open and flexible curriculum that addresses the needs of migrant adult learners has unsurprisingly led to the design of a Greek language course and the development of learning activities that do not seem to be directly relevant to migrants' present and future lives (Gravani, Hatzopoulos, & Papaioannou, Chapter 7, this volume).

In the cases of Glasgow and Tallinn, in contrast, the creation of an open space for experimentation produces very different results in relation to the role of the migrant learners in co-deciding what is constituted as the knowledge that is relevant to them. The non-governmental character of the organisations that provide these language courses for migrants might be relevant to account for this difference, since it is with presence of committed, intrinsically motivated educators and course organisers, for whom contributing to the linguistic integration of migrants in their host societies has a special educational and even political value.

The study in Estonia showed how the choice of what exactly and how to teach in each concrete topic remains for the organisers and the teacher to decide. It attributed to this factor the reasons why the language programme is flexible and enables the teacher to take into consideration the learners' needs. In the Estonian context the curriculum is carried out with the application of learner-centred principles. Based on the analysed data, the research concluded that the language training programme and the language course are designed according to the real needs of adult migrant learners and involve to a large extent their experience, needs, interests and expectations. The general aim of the language course is to support the integration of adults with the migrant background in society and everyday life. Therefore, during the language course the language teacher supports the acquisition of knowledge and skills that can help and support the learners to cope with their lives. In the teaching process an individual approach was used. For instance, learners were encouraged to train the skills that may be necessary in their everyday life (for example, writing their CVs to apply for a job, writing an e-mail) (Jõgi & Karu, Chapter 4, this volume).

In the Glasgow language course, the study found that there is no fixed curriculum for the migrant adult learners as the course content is fluid. The staff adopt a responsive and flexible approach to the migrant learners and work responsively, depending on the identified needs of the people accessing the services. The curriculum has been developed by the staff to reflect the 'real life' experiences of living in Glasgow. The staff work with the migrants to explore their information needs by tailoring the curriculum to ensure relevant information is conveyed through the classes. they are better equipped to use the services provided in the city of Glasgow, such as health or social care (Slade & Dickson, Chapter 5, this volume).

The findings of the case studies echo prior research that has emphasised the critical importance of connecting the educational curriculum to migrants' real-life situations as a main source of motivation for adult learners (Rossner, 2008) and as a key supporting process for their linguistic and social integration in their respective European host societies (Nieuwboer & van't Rood, 2016).

3.1   Highlighting the Tensions between Shared Languages and the Multiplicity of Languages

At the heart of the question of epistemology in the context of the four case studies on adult language programmes for migrants lie competing understandings of the social and cultural dimensions of language and of cross-cultural dialogue. As it has been shown by recent research, foreign language education is a privileged domain for intercultural interactions (Lázár, 2003; Sercu et al., 2005). At the same time, foreign language education is a space where the openness and uncertainty of intercultural encounters might be contested by means of trying to re-establish hierarchies or inequalities between languages or between proper and improper uses of the same language. These strategies, in the context of foreign language education, are often adopted by native speakers via a fixed focus on the primacy of syntax and grammar rules, to establish difference and hierarchies between native and non-native speakers (Byram, 2008).

In the context of the adult education for migrants the question of what is relevant in the particular courses of the four case studies and the extent to which the existing knowledges and skills of migrant learners should be valued, has to be negotiated in an environment where there is no standard common language and where hierarchies between languages might lead to the silencing of some voices and the dominance of others (Risager, 2007).

The lack of an a priori standard common language in the well-organised, flexible and learner-centred adult education course in Glasgow is perceived as an additional complication that needs to be solved. Along these lines, all participants tend to stress the importance of developing the correct English vocabulary, the importance of pronunciation of English words and so on. Drawing from knowledges and experiences of migrant learners outside of language acquisition is portrayed as problematic; educational activities focus thus on providing the appropriate language tools for the adult learners so that a shared language amongst the entire group of participants (migrants, tutors, other staff and volunteers) can emerge (Slade & Dickson, Chapter 5, this volume).

In the educational setting of Cyprus, characterised with very limited engagement with learner-centred practices our research highlighted, in contrast, how the existence of a multiplicity of languages that are present in the class of such a Greek language course ultimately presents the condition of possibility for migrant knowledges and skills to surface. The point where the learning activities are truly driven by the migrant learners' skills is the moment when the predetermined communication process breaks down or when there is a sense that this break down might be imminent; typically, this moment arrives when the learners do not understand the knowledge that the teacher is transmitting. At this moment, migrant learners take the initiative to act as translators: they can start to lead the discussion, moving freely and sometimes skilfully from language to language, creatively attempting to mix or hybridise the languages they know well, or those that they don't know too well, in the common effort to make everyone understand. Greek, Arabic, English are all used intermittently as the languages of translation in the occasions when the teacher is not understood or at least not understood by all the learners (Gravani, Hatzopoulos, & Papaioannou, Chapter 7, this volume).

4   Techniques

Adopting Schweisfurth's conceptualisation of learner-centred education, the four case studies investigated the role of teaching techniques and methods within the wider framework of fostering dialogic teaching (2013, p. 12), as a set of practices that can both empower migrant learners as well as enable their rights of expression and participation and enhance their personal and social development (2015). The key questions addressed, in this regard, were 'to what extent the discussion in class was dialogic' and 'if as a result, adult migrants took substantial responsibility for their learning'.

Concurring with the cross-case analysis on epistemology, divergences observed in the four language programmes reflect a distinction between the state of affairs emerging in the context of non-governmental providers (Scotland and Tallinn) and that of state-run adult education (Malta and Cyprus). In the case of the former, the lack of a national and formal centralised approach on appropriate pedagogies leaves the space open for an innovative utilisation of collaborative teaching techniques and methods that tend to empower migrant learners. In the latter, the same openness leads, instead, to the adoption of essentially traditional techniques, shaped largely by a 'chalk and talk' method of teaching which, results to a limited degree of responsibility for learning taken by migrant learners.

As thoroughly discussed in the Estonian case study, the Tallinn language programme utilised teaching methods that followed a learner-centred approach, fostering open dialogue in terms of two-way communication between the educator and the migrant learners or between learners. The language teaching was based on the active and interactive principles, on previous learners' (language learning) experiences, considering their needs, expectations and interest. In the Estonian case, teaching practices adopted a three-way approach in order to open space for dialogue and collaborative educational activities: (a) social/ interactive/dialogue-based interactions (e.g. group discussion, asking and answering questions, group work, pair work), (b) emotional/activating (e.g. games, jokes, sociometrics) and (c) situational (e.g. enhanced lecture, case-study, role-plays, practical exercises) (Jõgi & Karu, Chapter 4, this volume).

In Glasgow, in turn, a wide range of techniques were employed to communicate and engage with the migrant learners. Language was taught, for instance, through song; adult learners were encouraged to sing English sentences to learn the rhythm of the words. Role play was utilised by the teacher for generating interactive exchanges in the classroom. Group activities were undertaken to facilitate the understanding of the complexities of the Scottish dialect. Overall, teaching techniques attempted to innovatively meet the challenges posed by the particularities of this language course, such as the potentially disruptive presence of small children in the classroom or the low literacy of some students. The use of visual props, such as pictures and photographs, at times twinned with song, or the viewing and discussion on short films were employed to actively engage migrant learners, especially in the critical instances where the lesson plan was seemingly unsettled (Slade & Dickson, Chapter 5, this volume).

In Malta and Cyprus, in contrast, traditional techniques were largely utilised during the language courses, such as rote learning, counting and comparing marks of listening comprehension, or the use of lecturing for the transmission of pre-established course content and the discouragement of open dialogic exchanges due to perceived time constraints and limitations. The over-reliance on traditional teaching methods was seen in both cases as a safety option from the uncertainties that could emanate from potential disruptive instances associated with dialogic teaching. In a way, both educators and migrant learners tended to seek through traditional teaching comfort zones, which make them feel safer when they have to take limited responsibility for learning (Brown, Chapter 6, this volume and Gravani, Hatzopoulos & Papaioannou, Chapter 7, this volume).

4.1 Technology-Based Teaching and the Development of Learner-Centred Practices

Schweisfurth, is relatively cautious in welcoming the role of information technology as necessarily a positive drive, facilitating the transition towards more learner-centred educational practices (2013, p. 33). Findings, however, from the four case studies highlight the potential contribution of technologic-based teaching methods and of online resources as key for enhancing learner-centredness as they can significantly strengthen the degree of responsibility for learning taken by adult migrant learners. In all language programmes, except from the course in Larnaca, the multifarious integration of digital technologies and digital tools in the educational process had such a positive impact.

In the case of Estonia, the learning process utilised extensively a specialised e-learning platform designed to introduce users to Estonian history and culture, and support independent learning of the Estonian language, called Kultuuriklikk.[1] The engagement of migrant students in this interactive digital environment is assessed as a catalyst for creating the space for the learners to make their own choices, which, in its turn, supported the formation of a culture of independent inquiry amongst the group and contributed to sharing responsibility for the educational process with migrant learners (Jõgi & Karu, Chapter 4, this volume). The data of the Malta case study also shows that the techniques that more effectively capture the interests of adult migrants and enhance their participation are those that deploy technological resources, even in the cases where non-specialised digital resources are utilised such as Google search, Facebook chat, or YouTube videos. Even more significantly, the use of technology-based resources contributes to the expansion of language learning practices beyond the space of the classroom, via a process that is predominantly driven by the migrant learners' motivation and that strengthens their independent learning. Instances of this process were documented, for instance, in the Glasgow study, where the migrant learners utilised outside the classroom mobile technologies and educational 'Apps' suggested by their Tutor with such productive results (Slade & Dickson, Chapter 5, this volume). In Malta, the even more independent initiative undertaken by migrant learners for creating WhatsApp discussion groups for communication beyond the classroom, socialising, but also practicing their language skills stands out as a key moment of empowerment for migrant learners in taking control over their learning (Brown, Chapter 6, this volume).

4.2 *The Challenge of Interculturalism*
In the Cyprus context, as our study showed, the lack of utilisation of collaborative technology-based resources and tools can, at least partially, be attributed to the absence of intercultural teaching methods. As it was argued the lack of concern with interculturality in the design of course curricula or in the debates on teaching methods can also be associated with how dialogic teaching is discouraged in this specific Greek language course. During class observation, but also in the narratives of both learners and educator, attempts to foster collaborative learning practices or dialogic interactions appeared or were portrayed as problematic. In most cases, these failures were signalled by the breakdown of communication, mainly caused by the absence of a common language amongst participants. When dialogue reached this point of incomprehension,

all participants seemed more comfortable in instantly reverting to the conventional way of assigning the educator with the role of explaining, talking and finding a way out of this impasse. Both the learners and the educator were not prepared to enter or, more crucially, to produce a space of intercultural interactions, where a common language was not a pre-given, but that it could be constructed collaboratively through the learning process. This lack of preparedness coupled with a reluctant approach towards opening to the possibilities of intercultural communication made the (over-)employment of traditional teaching methods appealing as a way back to the safety of keeping the learning process going (Gravani, Hatzopoulos, & Papaioannou, Chapter 7, this volume).

5 Relationships

The case studies followed Schweisfurth's approach by considering mutual respect between teachers and migrant learners, as well the development of interpersonal relationships amongst them, as one of the key elements of learner-centred education (2013, p. 21). The relevant question, in respect to learner-centredness, along these lines, was to assess these relationships along a continuum that ranges from authoritarian to democratic, which reflects the amount of control that migrant learners do or do not have over their learning. The analysis of relationships amongst the educational program's participants in the context of the four studies tried also to consider the specific subject positions occupied by the migrant learners and the educators and how these are challenged or reproduced by the specific decisions that inform how the course is designed and organised and how the learning is pursued.

Considering as a starting point that the four adult education programmes for migrants under study face the additional challenge of managing the co-existence of a group of participants characterised by primary inequalities (educators, who are citizens as opposed to migrant learners, who are predominantly non-citizens), the general conclusions drawn from the studies stress the importance of fostering democratic relationships as an integral part of enhancing learner-centred educational practices. The production of democratic relations amongst formally unequal participants to the educational process was found to be even more complex and challenging, since it often comes at odds with the past educational experiences of migrant learners in their country of origin or their current experiences of suffering unequal treatment in the wider context of their lives in the respective host societies.

The case study in Tallinn, for instance, observed that in the context of the language course the relationship between the teacher and the learners developed in a supportive and open atmosphere. The programme placed value to the open communication, cooperation and establishment of close contacts between the educator and the migrant students. The course environment was characterised by a friendly atmosphere of trust, supporting thus a positive and dialogue-based culture amongst all participants. During the language courses, migrant learners felt safe and respected, as issues and topics that could lead to conflicts were consciously avoided (Jõgi & Karu, Chapter 4, this volume).

In parallel, the Glasgow study argued that the positive attitude of the Tutors, their welcoming approach and friendly and accessible manner was critical to the success of the language programmes and the centre as a whole. The relationships nurtured by the centre's staff were recognised as a key strength, building a culture of mutual respect and equality amongst the migrant learners and between them and the educators. The classroom was consistently promoted as a place of tolerance and acceptance, while negative attitudes towards cultural difference and concomitant tensions among migrant communities of different ethnicities were not tolerated (Slade & Dickson, Chapter 5, this volume).

5.1   *Going beyond Tolerance and Mutual Respect*

In contrast, the cases of Malta and Cyprus brought into light instances where the cultures of tolerance and respect might also act as appearances that reproduce boundaries and hierarchies between native and migrant cultures rather than challenging them. These findings, in this respect, reflect the growing critique that problematises the negative impact of the Western discourse on tolerance in reproducing cultural, racial, ethnic, and sexual inequalities across the fields of radical political and feminist theory and postcolonial studies (Brown, 2006; Mahmood, 2004; Scott, 1999).

The Malta study analysed, in detail how, on the one hand, the language courses were shaped by visible democratic features, consisting of the 'open-door' practice of the teachers, the proactive approach and practices whereby teachers do not wait for students to approach them with difficulties but 'chase' students to verify if there is need for further support, as well as the confidence and reassurance that adult migrant learners experience when seeking support and assistance beyond standard lesson times. Additionally, the study drew attention to evidence indicating that the educators and the management team of the lifelong learning centres were willing to go that extra mile, beyond their job description to consolidate the educational milieu framed by the learning programmes by transforming it into a vivid learning community that also voices subaltern cultures and discourses.

At the same time, however, in class, there were few occasions when these subaltern voices surfaced, particularly to avoid jeopardising the authenticity of institutional discourses. The democratic component of the relationships amongst the program's participants in Malta was limited, since the nature of the gauged dialogue did not necessarily translate to dialogue with critical potential, restricting thus the amount of control that migrant learners can have over their learning. The lack of a shared, common language was identified as the main impediment to open communication and critical democratic dialogue amongst the course's participants and in this sense, particularly some adult migrant learners of non-western ethnic backgrounds or nationalities with seemingly more difficulties in learning to use this shared language were even more marginalised (Brown, Chapter 6, this volume).

The Cyprus case study also illustrated the ambivalent dynamics of the observed climate of mutual respect and cooperation amongst participants to the language programmes. On the one hand, there seemed to be harmonious relationships between learners and between them and the educator, without any tensions or frictions amongst them. On the part of the migrant learners, even though they predominantly expressed disappointment with the learning outcomes of the course in terms of their unimproved Greek language skills, they still seemed to act with respect towards the educator during the entire class and recognised her efforts to help them learn during our conversations after class. More so, they seemed to be treating each other with respect in the cases where some learners expressed openly their difficulties in following the learning activities and created in an ad-hoc fashion a mutual help mechanism of multilingual translations for serving the needs of those who could not understand what was going on at particular moments in class. Another way to interpret this positive climate, however, would be to contextualise it within the dynamics of this educational programme, where democratic dialogue was relatively absent. The good atmosphere and the frictionless learning process appear in this light as a consequence of keeping distance, rather than engaging with, of maintaining boundaries rather than challenging them. During this Greek language course, intercultural relations never really developed amongst participants and established hierarchies were never really put into question or tested primarily because of its teacher-centred approach and non-dialogic character (Gravani, Hatzopoulos, & Papaioannou, Chapter 7, this volume).

6   Conclusions

Adult education for migrants remains a relatively underdeveloped field of inquiry, in both existing research and policy debates. The research project attempted to address this relative lack through a comparative investigation on the extent to which learner-centred education is used as a tool for enhancing adult teaching and learning in the field of adult education for migrants by conducting four case studies in the cities of Glasgow, Malta, Tallinn and Larnaca.

The cross-case analysis of the four studies on the findings of these studies revealed significant divergences amongst the four adult language programmes across the four cities in relation to the motivations of adult migrant learners for participating in adult education, the relevance of the curriculum and the extent to which the courses build on the migrant learners knowledges and skills, the utilisation of teaching techniques and methods within the wider framework of fostering dialogic teaching, and ultimately the degree of control that migrant learners do or do not have over their learning.

This chapter has attempted to emphasise, on the one hand, the potentialities of learner-centred education as a motor for social change through the empowerment of adult migrant learners. As the findings of the case studies have illustrated, in the context of adult language learning programmes for migrants, the capabilities of LCE are best served when:

- The absence of formal and centralised policies on adult education for migrants leaves the space open for increasing the flexibility and scope of the curriculum of the language programmes and facilitates experimentation in the course planning and organisation and in the educational activities that are included. In turn, these processes are closely intertwined with the presence of committed, intrinsically motivated educators and course organisers, for whom contributing to the linguistic integration of migrants in their host societies has a special educational and even political value.
- Technology-based teaching methods and online resources are employed as a key component for enhancing learner-centredness as they can significantly strengthen the degree of responsibility for learning taken by adult migrant learners.
- The intrinsic motivation of migrants to engage with adult learning is enabled and supported by constituting language education programme as an integral part of a wide range of social services, which address their immediate needs and enhance the prospects for their integration in host societies.

The potentialities of LCE for empowering adult migrant learners should be directly connected, however, to addressing the challenges of contextualising and localising learner-centred education practices. As this cross-case analysis has demonstrated in the particular context of adult language programmes for migrant learners in the four European cities under consideration, this localisation and contextualisation of LCE needs to the face three principal dynamics.

First, the absence of formal and centralised policies on adult education for migrants might lead to what can be termed as the paradox of proactive learner-centred pedagogy. In other words, the lack of centralised and standardised epistemology and techniques targeting learner-centredness can generate a space where the educators' ad hoc creativity can draw on their commitment, knowledge and experience to successfully design and implement learner-centred educational practices. Despite the empowering effects that these pedagogical experimentations might achieve, they can still be considered to materialise at the expense of uniform educational delivery for all migrant learners and the possibility of standardised adult teaching, monitoring, and evaluation.

Second, the status of adult migrant learners as non-citizens is a critical factor in terms of thinking about relevant and appropriate LCE educational practices. The precariousness of the migrants' residence status, ranging from asylum-seekers to refugees and from legal migrants and to sans-papiers, might significantly affect their motivations to participate in adult learning, it can perpetuate hierarchies between educators and learners or between learners, and it can play a deterring role in their capacity to take control of their learning. Engaging with this discussion on citizenship and precarious livelihoods and integrating it into learning activities, be it in the context of a language course or any other type of adult educational programme, might be a first, positive step towards empowering migrant learners.

Third, learner-centred educational practices in the context of adult education for migrants need to emanate from and to concomitantly enhance intercultural interactions. Interculturality in the context of adult education for migrants is crucial for overcoming traditional educational assumptions and methods, which constitute obstacles to democratic dialogue in class and for ensuring that migrant learners have an equal right to express their opinions and to equally participate in the learning process.

Note

1 See https://www.keeleklikk.ee/en/

References

Aleandri, G., & Russo, V. (2015). Autobiographical questionnaire and semi-structured interview: Comparing two instruments for educational research in difficult contexts. *Procedia-Social and Behavioral Sciences, 197*, 514–524.

Brown, W. (2006). *Regulating aversion: Tolerance in the age of identity and empire*. Princeton University Press.

Byram, M. (2008). *From foreign language education to education for intercultural citizenship: Essays and reflections*. Multilingual Matters.

Charmaz, K. (2006). *Constructing grounded theory: A practical guide through qualitative analysis*. Sage.

Council of Europe. (2014). *The linguistic integration of adult migrants, from one country to another, from one language to another.* Author. https://rm.coe.int/16802fd54a

Cross, K. P. (1981). *Adults as learners: Increasing participation and facilitating learning.* Jossey-Bass.

Kumaravadivelu, B. (2007). *Cultural globalization and language education.* Yale University Press.

Lázár, I. (Ed.). (2003). *Incorporating intercultural communicative competence in language teacher education.* European Centre for Modern Languages, Council of Europe.

Lentin, A. (2004). Racial states, anti-racist responses: Picking holes in 'culture' and 'human rights'. *European Journal of Social Theory, 7*(4), 427–443.

MacDonald, C. (2012). Understanding participatory action research: A qualitative research methodology option. *The Canadian Journal of Action Research, 13*(2), 34–50.

Mahmood, S. (2004). *Politics of piety: The Islamic revival and the feminist subject.* Princeton University Press.

Merriam, S. B. (1989). Contributions of qualitative research to adult education. *Adult Education Quarterly, 39*(3), 161–168.

Risager, K. (2007). *Language and culture pedagogy: From a national to a transnational paradigm* (Vol. 14). Multilingual Matters.

Rossner, R. (2008). *Quality assurance in the provision of language education and training for adult migrants: Guidelines and options.* Council of Europe.

Schweisfurth, M. (2013). *Learner-centred education in international perspective: Whose pedagogy for whose development?* Routledge.

Schweisfurth, M. (2015). Learner-centred pedagogy: Towards a post-2015 agenda for teaching and learning. *International Journal of Educational Development, 40*, 259–266.

Scott, D. (1999). *Refashioning futures: Criticism after postcoloniality.* Princeton University Press.

Sercu, L., Bandura, E., Castro, P., Davcheva, L., Laskaridou, C., Lundgren, U., Del Carmen Méndez García, M., & Ryan, P. (2005). *Foreign language teachers and intercultural competence: An international investigation.* Multilingual Matters.

Simpson, J., & Whiteside, A. (Eds.). (2015). *Adult language education and migration: Challenging agendas in policy and practice.* Routledge.

Wlodkowski, R. J. (1999). *Enhancing adult motivation to learn: A comprehensive guide for teaching all adults.* Jossey-Bass.

CHAPTER 9

Reading the Migrants' World through Emancipatory Learner-Centred Education: Parting Reflections on the Micro Pedagogical Contexts

Carmel Borg

Abstract

This chapter sets out to provide parting, critical and comparative reflections on the qualitative data generated by the four, LCE-focused case studies that feature in the book. Set against a pan-European backdrop, characterised by nation-states struggling to reconcile their moral obligations with electoral exigencies stemming from the populist call to assimilation, at best, and exclusion, at worst, the analysis of the case studies reveals a repertoire of adult-education provision that genuinely attempts to address individual migrant needs while singing from the assimilationist choir book of the state. In response, this chapter foregrounds an emancipatory vision of LCE (ELCE). ELCE is human-rights driven and represents a pedagogical ecology where education, perceived as a social act, meets the concept of the student as an independent and autonomous learner. The reconciliation of the two strands is premised on a conception of pedagogical hospitality on the learners' terms, and on a participatory notion of education that serves both self and mutual transformation.

Keywords

Emancipatory Learner-Centred Education (ELCE) – comparative adult education – migration

1 Introduction

The research project in question brings to the fore a contested pedagogical approach: Learner-Centred Education; a pedagogical stance glorified by liberals for its focus on the individual learner and maligned by radicals who read the same pedagogy as too individualistic and in conflict with their collectivist understanding of the educational process. A social-justice-oriented reading of

LCE reconciles the two strands, locating the approach in a third space where the individuals' interests and immediate needs can be productively fused with the social and communal dimension of learning. Rooted in social justice, Emancipatory Learner-Centred Education (ELCE), a term coined in the context of this chapter, is human-rights driven and represents a pedagogical ecology where education, perceived as a social act, meets the concept of the student as an independent and autonomous learner, challenging the 'the student as consumer' model (Newson, 2004). The reconciliation of the two strands is premised on a conception of pedagogical hospitality on the learners' terms, and on a notion of teaching that serves both self and mutual transformation (Borg, 2017). Against this conceptual backdrop, this chapter is meant to provide parting reflections on the project while advocating for the urgent need for an emancipatory vision of Learner-Centred Education in response to the liberatory call for social solidarity as resistance to compulsive, dog-eat-dog individuality.

2 Europe as the Overarching Context of the Research Project

While the research project deals with four micro-educational habitats in different geographies, two of them situated in frontier EU countries, the overarching context of the comparative study is Europe, a continent which is not immune to the encroachment of a global economic model that has eaten into the ideal of solidarity and the common good. The lack of solidarity, exacerbated by exploitative social relations, is exemplified by how the European continent is dealing with the migration flow, the sub-theme of this book. Many European states have shown great ambivalence towards migrants, are overly cautious in their expression of solidarity with countries constituting Europe's peripheries, and play the nation-state or the security card in refusing solidarity with migrants. Meanwhile, and mainly due to electoral expediency, the European inertia around migration has normalised a fortress mentality, where it is legitimate to openly fear the other, publicly attribute society's ills to the 'foreign invasion', and vote to specifically stem the 'tide of migration'.

While the Covid-19 pandemic has brought a level of forced reprieve in relation to the retreat of the state from its social obligations, the international, monumental, and angry response to the alleged murder of George Floyd in the hands of the police has reminded us all that slavery and race subjugation is not history. Monuments of colonisers, slave owners and slave traders are not relics from the past but living reminders that democracy in Europe and beyond is continuously distancing itself from social justice, diluting its strength as an ideal space for the affirmation of human-rights-based quality of life. Increasingly, the state is perceived by the millions of protestors who took to the streets to protest against racial discrimination, and by those who toppled and defaced monuments that symbolise asymmetrical relations of power, that for long it has been dragging its feet in championing the plight of the most vulnerable while generating consent around political processes and legal frameworks that favour trans-national capital, wealth and power (Borg & Grech, 2017). The social contract that many European states had negotiated and renegotiated with their peoples, starting soon after the second world war, in a trans-national context marked by mass mobility of people, has been substantially eroded by a world economic order, officialised, on the European front, by a political leader who in October 1987 declared that 'there is no such thing as a society. While generating unimaginable wealth, such a world economic order has weakened social cohesion and the value system that had supported it, sacrificing the dignity and humanity of millions of Europeans and internationally-mobile workers on the altar of competitiveness, flexibility, growth at all cost, balanced and surplus budgets, austerity measures and labour pacification. In the process, partially as a result of their softness and appeasement when faced by the ruthlessness of such an economic order, European states, to varying degrees, are facing a legitimacy crisis marked by increasing citizen frustration, exhaustion, distrust, antipathy, indifference towards politics and politicians, and a shift to far-right politics with strong, nationalist, nativist and xenophobic content.

For the socially initiated, the street and square protests, in the wake of the Floyd's incident, represented a volcanic explosion that reminds the state that the destitute and their empathisers are not to be taken for granted. The millions of people on the street, protesting against multiple forms of oppression, is an indication that hegemony is never complete and that cracks in the world economic and political order do exist. Also, pockets of potential hope, as illustrated by the micro-opportunities analysed in the book, constitute a concrete possibility. Within such pockets, of which very few receive any publicity, questions are being asked and problems are being posed by socially committed agents of social change. Questions that challenge the politics of walls, barbed wire, calls for push backs, deportations and resettlements, all symptomatic of a paranoia that has gripped Europe in relation to the most vulnerable of its citizens and residents, the most materially deprived and socially-excluded 'others' within the Europe. Questions that situate migration in the larger picture of exploitative social and economic relations. They include: Why has Europe, in different ways and in varying degrees, failed the moral and ethical test of social justice? Why has Europe fallen behind in promoting social solidarity and communal understanding? Why social Europe seems incapable of providing an alternative model to the destructive ideology of profit first dignity and well-being later? Why has Europe abandoned social class as a point of reference and allowed itself to fragment and to turn common interests into specialised interests, dividing society into irreconcilable groups? Why has Europe softened its stance on the politics of redistribution? Why are people losing faith in politicians? Why so many people believe that politics is inherently corrupt? Why do many people are convinced that the economy is stacked against them? Why has collective action become such a dangerous word? Why is it becoming ever more difficult in Europe and elsewhere to build majority coalitions/movements of solidarity and win elections? Can predatory economic practices such as the outsourcing of precarious work be challenged and reversed?

In general, the 'official' educational response to migration, in a Europe that popularly perceives itself as being invaded, and its grand cultural narrative as being attacked and diluted, is primarily characterised by a deficit approach whereby, as quickly as possible, the migrant 'other' is to be assimilated into the hegemonic 'us', with language and general acculturation seen as the two main instruments of the rapid educational intervention. While the book reveals micro educational moments imbued with cultural, emotional, and pedagogical empathy, the grand curricular narrative in relation to the perceived needs of migrants is essentially transmissive, and generally answers to the anxieties of a state that is responding to demographic gaps in the economy while comfortably numb to the substantial overtures for genuine economic, social and cultural inclusion. The book underscores the recurrent tension that characterises educational sites where individual educators, who are aware that a one size-fits-all, bureaucratic and administratively efficient approach to education is not in the migrants' best interests. While subverting the grand narrative of assimilation, wrapped in the discourse of quick-fix 'integration' through liberal notions of learner-focused approaches, the collective needs for consciousness building, mobilisation and emancipatory action are often lost in individualistic acts of life-saving educational episodes, unfolding in a wider context that promotes individuality.

3   Learner-Centredness in the Age of Individuality

Against a global backdrop characterised by exploitative human relations, of which many migrants, the protagonists of the book's story, find themselves situated at the extreme end of the receiving continuum, personalised learning, the very core of the learner-centredness movement, also largely seen as the future of global education, is located in the producer-consumer nexus of human relations, where education is experienced as a set of individual diagnoses, remedies or choices, mirroring social relations on a wider scale. As ubiquitous artificial intelligence, algorithms and data analytics continue to eat their way into education, measuring anything from learners' emotions to gaps in learning, and providing personalised solutions to the mathematical reading of performativity in various aspects of their life, relations are bound to become more personal, individual, tailor-made, introspective and self-centred. Left unproblematised, learner-centredness, situated in an increasingly automised and digitalised post-Covid world, while surgically performing its personalised act on the learner may have the effect of educating the mind to act individually in an already socially unhospitable space.

A space where growth is heavily dependent on rates of individual consumption, increasing numbers of Europeans are becoming ever more alienated from their neighbour, worker, homeless, precarious, poor 'other'. Spaces, meant to be communal and collective, are becoming ever more fragmented into micro-habitats which are reduced to private zones of delusionary or real consumption. Within such ecologies, consumption dictates the value of people. Citizens reduced to private consumers, competing with the known or 'unknown other' for visibility through consumption rates and patterns, and the commodification of anything ranging from education and health to relationships and one's own body and identity. Such a context, characterised by multi-directional bombardment of perceived needs and consumables as objects of desire, defies solidarity by emotionally and physically distancing human beings from one another, turning vulnerability into a distant spectacle that at best ends with momentary, even if formidable, acts of charity, as seen in the months defined by the outbreak of Covid-19, that do nothing to challenge the asymmetrical status quo fuelled by individualism, competition, short-term gratification and disposability.

In his book *Work, Consumerism and the New Poor*, the late Zygmunt Bauman (1998) remarks that to be poor in a consumer society is to be totally unnecessary. In Bauman's terms, the construction of the 'poor other' as a burden is exacerbated by the fact that social-class consciousness and international solidarity have largely evaporated on many fronts. The poor, a category which includes millions of destitute migrants are struggling on their own, frozen in material, emotional, psychological, and social wilderness. Unfit for the consumer treadmill, as cynically described by the Polish sociologist and public intellectual, the humanity of the migrants becomes disposable, bureaucratised, and invisible to many. As the migrant are dehumanised, in the political theorist Hannah Arendt's words, quoted in Bauman (1998), they become the responsibility of no one.

In response to the above critique of human obsolescence and disposability in a world of plenty, Emancipatory Learner-Centred Education seeks to transform education spaces into possibilitarian sites of liberatory practice, where individual needs become communal needs, where marginalised voices become centred voices in all aspects of the curricular experience, and where education for survival is transformed into education for active engagement with the world.

4 Emancipatory Learner-Centred Education

ELCE responds to the need for transforming top-down, educator-learner (read migrant) relationships into opportunities for genuine collaboration. For this to happen, the process of knowledge production needs to be revisited, challenging the almost exclusive legitimacy given to specialised knowledge, at the expense of other forms of knowledge production, and questioning why 'official knowledge', perceived by authorities as indispensable for purposeful living in a culturally-different society, does not include the daily experiences, intuitions and cultural expressions of migrant adults as 'worthwhile knowledge' or as valid ways of knowing.

While interrogating top-down models of educator-educatee relations, ELCE makes a strong case for educational encounters informed by a curricular experience that is built collectively with learners; a curricular process in which the themes for eventual exploration and discovery within the community of learners are co-generated, and where co-production of knowledge with adult learners, rather than production of knowledge for educatees, is normalised (Kirkwood & Kirkwood, 2011).

As the paradigm shifts to encounters rather than abstract notions of migrant needs, migrants shift locationally from objects of interest to active subjects, from material of professional generosity to co-participants, problem-posers, co-investigators, creative and critical thinkers, and co-discoverers of knowledge.

ELCE builds on a liberatory vision of education; an education process which is morally informed and committed to action. ELCE creates opportunities for educator-migrant encounters with a view to generating counter-narratives to the popular perception that educational spaces are professionals' territory and, therefore, migrants are expected to assume a secondary or submissive role in relation to the qualified educators who offer remedial action in the name of state-informed notions of 'integration'.

ELCE, community-based, adult education projects aim at addressing the immediate needs of migrants (and other adults) while engaging in consciousness-raising, confidence-building, networking, and transformative action. ELCE initiatives are rooted in participatory democracy, rather than abstract rhetoric and academic bravado, and revolve around the pedagogy of authentic dialogue. This pedagogy contrasts heavily with the transmissive pedagogical model, often the pedagogical tradition that would have schooled and socialised migrants and possibly the dominant pedagogy within the recipient country. The transmission model is based on the assumption that the academic, professional or trainer, is expected to transmit knowledge while learners passively consume the esoteric information imparted by the expert source of knowledge.

Freire (1996) argues that dialogues become real and productive when they reject hierarchy, when educators assume an 'authoritative' role without becoming 'authoritarian', when the act of knowledge production and discovery is done in communion with participants, and when nobody is reduced to a purely spectatorship role. Authentic dialogues committed to liberation and emancipation promote critical consciousness by making critical connections between the immediate need for literacy, personal experiences and the oppressive structures that perpetuate discrimination. Such dialogues are the natural pedagogical choice where there is commitment to critical literacy as social action. Course programmes informed by the principles of ELCE are meant for educators to open themselves to transformation as much as it is meant for migrants to experience critical consciousness and transformative action.

Moving into a situation characterised pedagogically by a dialogical approach is not easy in the case of disenfranchised learners, deeply steeped in the 'culture of silence' and where verticality is assumed as the best way forward to avoid conflict and channel information without resistance. Fully aware of the effects of such a pedagogical ecology, creating an emotional context that engenders meaningful dialogues (as opposed to superficial chatting) constitutes an important principle of ELCE. In such a situation, the role of the educator is crucial in modelling the art of dialogical encounters and in creating a safe and trustworthy environment.

While focusing on the immediate practical needs of learners, ELCE-driven programmes challenge perceptions of migrants and migration, problematise assumptions about learning in the context of migration, challenge the perception that the expert's is the only source of knowing, generate empathy with all migrants, but especially with those who are struggling as a result of social injustices, border-cross emotional roadblocks to mutual understanding, and overcome fatalism by building confidence around the possibility that human injustices can be reversed through collective engagement with the world.

While ELCE-informed programmes operate within a preconceived framework, the core themes/experiences for the curricular programme will always be generated by the educators and the learners. Through such an approach, curriculum design and development respond to the 'dynamic present' of migrants and their concrete material realities; curriculum design is transformed into an act of mutuality and reciprocity, where migrants become co-designers and co-developers of the curricular experience.

5   The Four Projects through the Eyes of ELCE

The four programmes that constitute the comparative study of this book address the often-perceived need by the state to integrate, read assimilate, migrants, at times referred to by the law as 'aliens', into society. This emergency, explained above as symptomatic of a hegemonic conception of migration as disruptive to the social and cultural fabric of a country and as threat to identity, generates the need for quick-fix programmes that are meant primarily, albeit not exclusively, to initiate migrants into the dominant society, with clear instructions by the supplier state of what are the basic skills and knowledge needed to survive life in the recipient country. Within such a context, Learner-Centred Education (LCE), at its best, becomes an on-site, practical response to cohort situations which are marked by heterogeneity in terms of migrants' cultural, social, and economic capital, self- and social location, and years of experience in mobility outside the migrants' home country. While all four case-studies report varying degrees of on-site, student-focused measures, aimed at matching needs with actual curricular experiences, the state's intentions, and its reasons for initiating such programmes are rarely contextualised and problematised.

Given the short-termism of the programmes, what can generally be achieved beyond the first-response goals, as pre-determined by the programme, is limited. This is confirmed by Sara and Aicha, two interviewees in the Cyprus case study, who claimed that the programme they attended will not be enough for them to achieve fluency and to improve their chances for real integration. The latter also lamented of the lack of a formal qualification and assessment at the end of the programme that, in her view, renders the programme meaningless. The linguistic goals of the Estonian programme, ranging in scope from 'use of everyday expressions and simple phrases', to introducing oneself and others, to asking simple questions, are indicative of a possible common, course denominator in this regard.

While constituting a possible beginning, such programmes rarely achieve the level of empowerment needed for participants to become productive members of a community rather than peripheral survivors. Tracer studies are needed to determine the participants' educational trajectory and the community's ability to facilitate access to follow-up educational programmes available within the geographic reach of the migrants.

In contrast to the short-term approach of most of the programmes under review, inductive ELCE programmes, as described above, call for long-term, programmatic commitments that serve the ethical and pedagogical need for educators to familiarise themselves with the multiple challenges and realities that define the different types of migration and the intersection of the receiving context with the past and present lived realities of migrants. Such familiarisation is crucial for educators to equip themselves with the necessary information needed to facilitate real access to the programme. The language cafés mentioned in the Scottish case study provide a concrete example of how educators can use informal spaces to familiarise themselves with migrants' realities and their real needs, including logistical needs, such as childcare facilities that are indispensable for women wanting to access adult education in a patriarchal society. Also, in ELCE programmes committed to venturing beyond the teaching of skills sets, time is needed to build the trust and safety that is crucial for educators to engage with learners in problematising and challenging the status quo, in collectively generating goals and themes for the curricular experience, in developing meaningful dialogues and other educational encounters with the learners, and in transforming educational experiences into concrete emancipatory collective action. Engaged in slow learning, ELCE's curricular range transcends survival to enable migrants to gain 'powerful knowledge' that will transform their self as well as their collective life rather than reinforce their status quo. Such an educational experience requires time and long-term commitment rather than a conveyor-belt approach to normalisation.

Prescribed timeframes, at times inevitable, as hinted in some of the case studies, exercise unmeasurable stress on the participants, who often have to reconcile the tight and ambitious schedule of the educational programme with personal, family and work-related pressures. Surprisingly, in the case of Estonia, where the stress factor was mentioned by the participants, retention rate was high, with no reports of dropouts. While participants described the educators as enabling and supportive, two good reasons for participants to maintain good levels of attendance, the high retention rate can also be attributed to the high stakes associated with such programmes and their deliverables. In comparison to programmes that move on fixed rails, given the slow-learning attributes of ELCE-informed programmes, the education process has built-in flexible mechanisms that are sensitive to the plight of migrants, and usually revolve around the participants' timetable as well as educational needs.

The tension between the practical need for learner-focused approach to education and centrally dictated programmes is thrown into sharp relief when programmes are required to produce summative results at the end of the programme's proceedings. The accountable state demands proof that the individual migrant is fit for permanent living within the country and that s/he and society can profit from her/his stay. With this expectation, the summative assessment procedure is perceived as a transparent, inductive benchmark by the state, the Ministry for Home Affairs, in the case of Estonia. Such assessment, for which the programme is originally designed to build up to, may limit the flexibility and adaptability of the programme to genuinely serve migrants first before the state. The contrast in this regard between the Estonian programme and the Scottish provision is stark, with the former responding to a very clear set of official goals and the latter answering to very fluid and unpredictable variables. In the case of Cyprus, the lack of assessment was construed as a form of rudderlessness by the interviewees and, by association, the programme was perceived as meaninglessness, bordering on the irrelevant.

What is reassuring is that none of the observers reported assessments based on rote learning. Where summative assessment was required, as in, for example, the case of Malta, it was complemented by formative assessment, with educators providing personalised assessment notes. ELCE-informed programmes, while acknowledging the need for accountability and transparency, build towards assessment procedures that are deeply rooted in the migrants' reality, allow for multiple ways of registering growth, development, and transformation, promoting reflection and experiential knowledge as well as collective action as a result of communal reflection. The portfolio that migrants accumulate by the end of the ELCE programme is personal rather than standardised, needs-driven rather than pre-determined, and participatory in that peer assessment forms an integral part of the assessment procedures.

The programmes under review generally locate the educator, often acting on behalf of the state, as the dispenser of expert knowledge, especially in the realm of linguistic skills. Given the fact that most programmes cater not only for new arrivals but also for migrants with years of experience within the country, it is rather intriguing that the potential for migrant-to-migrant learning is generally under-explored as a fixture of the programme. In the Scottish case study, streaming was used to differentiate learning. While streaming served the purpose of creating different levels of intervention, depending on individual and group needs, such an approach bars learners from engaging with inclusive pedagogies such as peer tutoring and cooperative learning. ELCE programmes thrive on pedagogical communality where teacher-students and student-teachers enter a pedagogical reality that blurs the pedagogical distance created in an expert-learner situation. Peer tutoring and other possibilities for mutual learning and transformation are promoted through an educational milieu which recognises migrants as co-producers of knowledge rather than consumers/clients of what is officially perceived as worthwhile knowledge.

As indicated above, some of the programmes populated by migrants are imposed as a minimum requirement for permanence or status acquisition. Such is the case, for example, with the programme 'I Belong' in Malta, referred to in passing, in one of the chapters. The imposition of the Maltese state, coupled with the possibility of status refusal or withdrawal and, in extreme cases, expulsion, generates fear, suspicion and frustration on the learners' part who, in some cases occupy positions of high responsibility, with years of high-level service to the community. Such feelings certainly do not constitute the ideal emotional climate for learning and, in fact, are often counterproductive in the context of what they set out to achieve. In addition, state imposition also tends to fashion the relationship of the learners with their educators, the latter construed by the former as functionaries of the 'repressive' state. ELCE programmes contrast sharply in this regard, with participatory notions of curriculum design, development and evaluation contributing to a genuine sense of belonging, ownership of the means of educational production and to self-understanding that the educational experience is meaningful as much as it is self-identifiable and intrinsically motivating.

Regarding teaching resources, where referred to in the book, such resources are often made available or recommended through the course programme, as pre-prepared packages, limiting further the learners' participation in influencing the curricular experience. In this regard, the resources used in the Maltese case study reflect a content-driven approach to teaching and learning. ELCE programmes, informed by a commitment to participatory educational action, build on themes generated with the participants, encourage learners to create and share resources as part of a collective endeavour to build a portfolio of learning materials that guard against irrelevance, childish content, or culturally insensitive texts. Within ELCE programmes, materials are seen as 'codifications' that serve critical literacy.

The importance of quality teachers, who are competent in their respective field, favourably disposed towards diversity, internationalisation and interculturality, empathetic, multifunctional, and willing to accommodate, is mentioned, to varying degrees, in all case studies. Participants spoke highly of the commitment, care, and willingness to accommodate, shown by the educators. Of significance to LCE approaches is that participants felt that educators went far beyond their call of duty and acted as multifunctional enablers, ranging in tasks from counsellors to career and course advisors. Some expressed the view that they attended the programme because of the educator-student friendships that developed within the programme. The intimate educational environment, characterised by small classes, as in the case of the Maltese programmes, added to the level of educators' care, attention, flexibility, pace-matching, positive reinforcement, and pedagogical empathy, as mentioned by the observer. While such qualities feature prominently in educators committed to ELCE, the pedagogical stance in question adds a strong and overt social-justice dimension to the repertoire of educators' indispensable qualities. Such a quality ensures that the teaching-learning process responds to the liberatory call for equitable access to education as a platform for a human-rights-informed access to the common good.

The case of Cyprus throws important light on the plight of teachers. Educators there felt that their dedication is not matched with proper remuneration and social security, initial and in-service training and a clear policy framework that provides direction and clear goals as to what such programmes should aim for and achieve. Such a situation frustrates and demotivates educators who work in educational environments which require from teachers a high level of motivation.

While migrants are often referred to in totalising discourse, the Scottish case study searchlights the importance of creating educational spaces that respond to multiple accessibility issues. The Scottish case study mentions language cafés that are patronised by large family groups. Interaction with migrants in such spaces provided educators of the ESOL programme with opportunities to interact with prospective participants, encounters which revealed personal stories, struggles and roadblocks to personal development. For example, through such encounters, it became crystal clear that without childcare facilities, most migrant women, often solely responsible for family care, including the extended family, would not be able to attend the language programme. Such a need is very different from the needs of a male professional attending the 'I Belong' programme in Malta, where the immediate need is neither lunch nor a childcare facility, but proximity to the medical facility he works in. What the two stories illustrate is the need for accessibility to be 'negotiated', long before the start of the programme, through informal encounters that reveal who the migrants are, where they are coming from and what could be blocking their participation. The pre-programme stage, a period of informal familiarisation with the plight of migrants, through multiple encounters, is of the essence in the quest for wider accessibility.

The Scottish and the Estonian case studies refer to learning outside the confines of the designated space. The use of digital devises to amplify learning is a commendable LCE strategy because it multiplies the possibilities for further learning as well as adds flexibility in terms of access outside 'office hours'. The Maltese case study reveals efforts to combine language teaching with teaching of IT skills and with helping students to maximise the use of the Internet for language-development purposes. Also, regarding extending accessibility, the Maltese case study also reveals efforts to increase accessibility by outreaching to voluntary organisations which are community-based, and often more cognisant of the immediate needs of migrants. LCE as community development is a feature of ELCE. Education programmes articulated within an ELCE framework, consciously and strategically set their educational goals to address community regeneration and development, securing further access to common goods.

The social dimension of the programmes was particularly emphasised by the women attending the ESOL programmes in Scotland. For women, often located in the private realm of the family, such programmes are liberatory in that they offer the opportunity of meeting other women, literally seeing the world and interacting with others in public spaces. ELCE programmes consciously seek to help migrants emerge from the culture of isolation that reproduces marginalisation and peripherality. Helping migrants to occupy public spaces is generally an important first step in gaining the necessary confidence to live in and interact with the world.

In terms of motivation to learn, of particular interest is the case of Cyprus, where some of the participants claimed that they enrolled to avoid work which, when available, in their view, is precarious, underpaid, seasonal and temporary. One migrant also refers to 'false jobs', that come complete with threats of police intervention. This is an interesting case which provides insights into enrolment as a form of resistance, indicating that migrants come to educational spaces with a level of consciousness that ELEC programmes regard as the raw material for their curricular experience. In emphasising the quotidian as the initial phase of collective knowing, ELEC programmes speak to the lived experiences of participants as texts for critical literacy.

The Scottish as well as the Cypriot case studies highlight the precarious plight of the migrants who often must choose between putting food on the table and attending an educational programme. Attendance tends to become fluid or negligible where chronic precariousness competes with attendance. Such is the case of the Romanian men whose attendance for ESOL programmes dwindled significantly when knowledge of English was dropped as a requirement for selling the magazine 'The Big Issue'. In such precarious situations, liberal notions of LCE are viewed with suspicion and often considered as worthless. ELCE programmes, situated in the raw context of migrants, welding critical reflection of the immediate world with concrete action that announces the world, which may include job matching and further education constitute such programmes' definition of learner-centredness.

6 Conclusion

The chapter set out to contextualise the four case studies in the larger political context. What emerges from the parting reflection is a European scenario marked by ambivalent and contradictory relations with migrants, and an educational intervention that is located somewhere between the assimilationist-integrationist dialectic. The four cases reflect the aforementioned tension, generally responding to the learners' needs on the ground while rarely problematising the ideological stance of the state in relation to the educational plight of migrants. Emancipatory Learner-Centred Education is hereby presented as an ideologically-informed and pedagogical approach that goes beyond course adaptations to address learners' needs. ELCE is an educational process that welds the collective reading of the world with ongoing communal action for personal and social change. ELCE's vision is overt and clear, it foregrounds the notion that migrants and educators act in communion and are both protagonists in a process of mutual and reciprocal transformation.

References

Bauman, Z. (1998). *Work, consumerism and the new poor*. Open University Press.
Borg, C. (2017). Reclaiming social Europe in the shadows of a global predatory economy. In *Arraiolos Malta 2017, 13th Meeting of the Heads of State of the Arraiolos Group* [Proceedings] (pp. 17–31). Mediterranean Academy of Diplomatic Studies. https://www.um.edu.mt/library/oar/bitstream/123456789/46571/1/Reclaiming_social_Europe_in_the_shadows_of_a_global_predatory_economy_2017.pdf
Borg, C., & Grech, M. (Eds.). (2017). *Pedagogy, politics and philosophy of peace. Interrogating peace and peace making*. Bloomsbury.
Freire, P. (1996). *Pedagogy of the oppressed*. Penguin Books.
Kirkwood, G., & Kirkwood, C. (2011). *Living adult education: Freire in Scotland*. Sense Publishers.
Newson, J. A. (2004). Disrupting the 'student as consumer' model: The new emancipatory project. *International Relations, 18*(2), 227–239.

Index

acceptance   94, 95, 163
accessibility   33, 86, 112, 179, 180
Action Aid   31
active learning   11, 30, 60, 136
actors   9, 25, 62, 124
adaptability   177
adult education   4–8, 12–15, 19, 21, 26, 29, 31–35, 43, 44, 47–51, 56, 61, 66, 72, 95, 98, 106, 115, 119, 121–123, 125–127, 129–132, 137–139, 143, 144, 152–156, 158, 159, 162, 164–166, 174, 176
Adult Education Centres   7, 8, 33, 50, 122, 127, 129, 131, 132, 138
adult learner   4, 5, 8, 9, 12, 14, 15, 31, 32, 36, 61, 66, 68, 72, 75, 80, 81, 83–92, 94, 95–97, 98, 104, 105, 113, 117, 123, 126, 129, 132, 133, 143, 153, 155–158, 160, 173
adult learning theory   10, 152
adult literacy   31
adult migrants   5, 7, 8, 12–15, 33, 36, 44, 48–51, 62, 66, 67, 74, 80, 81, 85, 87, 96, 98, 101–110, 112–119, 121–123, 125, 126, 128–130, 133, 135, 136, 138, 143, 152–157, 159, 161, 163–166, 173
Afghanistan   81, 92
Africa   VIII, IX, 24
analytical thinking   11, 24
andragogical principle   XIV, 11
Angelides, P.   131
Arab   VIII, 137, 142
Arabic   92, 103, 135, 136, 159
Arnesen A. L.   33
assessing learning   89
assessment   9, 60, 73, 74, 86, 89, 90, 110–112, 119, 129, 133, 175, 177
assisted learning   23
Asylum, Migration and Integration Fund (AMIF)   14
asylum-seekers   15, 143, 166
austerity   170
authentic dialogues   174
authoritarian   11, 23, 72, 93, 115, 140, 162, 174
autochthonous   X
autonomous learner   16, 169

Bauman, Z.   172
Bevelander, P.   126, 143

Bible   128
Biggs, J.   22
Borg, C.   13, 16
Boud, D.   135
Bowles, S.   127
Brockett, R. B.   22
Brookfield, S.   11, 137
Brown, M.   13–15, 155, 156, 160, 161, 163, 164
Buiskool, B. J.   33
Byram, M.   134

capable other   141
capitalism   VIII, X, 24
cartographies   6, 7, 13, 43, 51
case studies   5–8, 12–16, 19, 33, 43–46, 48, 51, 152–155, 157–160, 162, 165, 175, 176, 178, 180, 181
Casey, L.   128
certificate   60, 74, 89, 129, 132
Charmaz, K.   123
childcare   82–84, 90, 94, 98, 154, 155, 176, 179
China   123
citizen   57, 170
citizenship   15, 44, 46, 50, 56, 57, 74, 108, 143, 166
Clayton, P.   134
Cleveland-Innes, M.   30, 31
climate change   IX
Coben, D.   31
cognitive   4, 26, 28, 137
cognitive injustice   X
college   48, 83, 89, 90, 94
colonial   24
common language   91, 131, 139, 140, 144, 158, 161, 162, 164
communication   9, 30, 35, 51, 56, 59, 60, 63–65, 67–69, 72, 73, 75, 88, 118, 124, 133–135, 137, 139, 140, 142, 159, 161–164
community   29, 31, 36, 51, 80, 81, 83, 84, 87, 89, 90, 93, 116, 139, 156, 163, 173, 174, 176, 178, 180
comparative analysis   15, 47, 51
competences   30, 34, 45, 134, 139
competitiveness   57, 170
conceptualisation   10, 11, 13, 62, 124, 131, 136, 155, 159
Connor, P.   126, 143

control   4, 10–12, 15, 21–23, 26, 45, 69, 72, 74, 80, 116, 118, 125, 132, 136, 140, 143, 144, 153, 161, 162, 164–166
Council of Europe   122, 126, 128, 132
Covid-19   16, 169, 172
Cross, K. P.   125
cultural difference   63, 105, 163
cultural expectations   97, 98
culture   X, XIV, 4, 56, 58, 59, 69, 85, 91, 92, 94, 102, 103, 112, 116, 117, 122, 133, 137, 161, 163, 174, 180
curriculum   9, 10, 14, 15, 20, 21, 23, 24, 26, 29, 30, 32, 33, 51, 66, 69, 71, 86–88, 98, 101, 106, 108 ,109, 112, 115, 119, 122, 125, 131, 132, 138, 155–157, 165, 175, 178
Cyprus   VIII, XV, 4, 6, 7, 13, 15, 44–46, 48–51, 113, 121, 122, 125–131, 135, 136, 138–140, 142–144, 152, 153, 155, 156, 158–161, 163, 164, 177, 179, 180

democratic   3, 11, 20, 23, 26, 27, 72, 93, 95, 111, 115, 116, 135, 137, 140–142, 162, 163, 166
democratisation   25
demographic   IX, 6, 13, 14, 44, 79, 110, 119, 127, 171
Denzin, N. K.   123
Dewey, J.   20, 21, 26
Dialogue   IX, 9, 27, 62, 66, 69–71, 73–75, 115–117, 124, 132, 134, 137, 139–144, 152, 158–161, 163, 164, 166, 174, 176
Dickson, N.   14, 50, 79, 153, 154, 157, 158, 161, 163
Directorate for Research, Lifelong Learning and Innovation (DRLLLI)   7, 101, 109, 114, 116
District Labour Office   126, 127
dominant framework   32
Dörnyei, Z.   65
Duff, P. A.   139

Early School Leavers (ESL)   34, 48, 108
education providers   6, 81, 132, 154–156
educational 'Apps'   93, 161
educational activities   23, 156, 158, 160, 165
educator   XIV, 11, 15, 23, 27, 61, 66, 86, 91, 101, 103, 107, 111, 113, 114, 117, 119, 123, 125, 131–133, 135–142, 153, 159, 161–164, 173–174, 177, 179
educators' motivations   129
English as a Foreign Language (EFL)   7, 101

English for Speakers of Other Languages' (ESOL)   7, 14, 80
emancipatory education   13, 16, 22, 169, 171
Emancipatory Learner-Centred Education (ELCE)   16, 169, 173, 181
Emerson, R. M.   124
Emes, C.   30, 31
employment   IX, 7, 35, 44, 49, 50, 55–57, 85, 89, 97, 126, 130, 140, 156, 162
empowerment   XIV, XV, 31, 137, 161, 168, 176
epistemological limitations   112
epistemology   9, 10, 13, 62, 66, 80, 82, 86, 106, 112, 119, 123, 124, 131, 152, 155, 158, 159, 166
established hierarchies   141, 164
Estonia   XIV, 4, 6, 7, 13, 14, 44–51, 55–58, 61, 63, 74–76, 152, 156, 161, 177
ethnic groups   VIII, 98
ethos   IX
European Union (EU)   34, 47, 57
Europe   VIII, IX, XIV, 4, 13, 32, 34, 45, 122, 126, 128, 132, 169–171
European Commission   33, 34
European Ministerial Conference on Integration   126
European Social Fund (ESF)   14, 57
Eurostat   32, 44, 45
everyday learning practices   10, 131, 155
expectations   28, 67, 69–71, 97, 98, 102, 103, 107, 109, 127, 128, 133, 154, 156, 157, 160, 177
experiential learning   11, 23

Farsi   92
Fejes, A.   6
female adult learners   83, 85
flexibility   5, 20, 71, 86, 90, 115, 131, 132, 156, 165, 170, 177, 179, 180
France   33
Freire, P.   XV, 21, 26, 27, 31, 174,
Fretz, R. I.   124

Gates, P.   28
gendered learning   84
General Medical Council (GMC)   29
Glasgow   XV, 4, 7, 14, 29, 80, 87, 98, 152–158, 160, 161, 163, 165
Global Report on Adult Learning and Education   130
globalisation   24, 25
globalised market   30

INDEX

Gramsci, A.   x, xv
Gravani, M.   13, 15, 50, 122, 123, 131, 155, 156, 159, 160, 162, 164
Grech, M.   170
Greek   viii, 7, 8, 15, 19, 50, 114, 122, 124–141, 156, 158, 159, 161, 164
Greek language for foreigners   7, 50, 122
Gu, Q.   28
guidance   96, 130, 132
guiding principles   44
Guiraudon, V.   127
Guo, S.   5
Guthrie, G.   10, 24

Hajisoteriou, C.   131
Hall, G.   135, 144
Hatzopoulos, P.   xiv, 13, 15, 50, 123, 131, 139, 153, 160
hegemonic   ix, 171, 175
hidden agenda   25
Hiemstra, R.   22
higher education   xiv, xv, 19, 28–30, 48, 50
higher-order thinking   11, 24
homeless   85, 172
Houle, C. O.   22
human capacity   6, 44, 47

identity   ix, xiv, 89, 108, 130, 172, 175
ideology   23, 24, 25, 171
inclusivity   93
informal familiarisation   179
information needs   87, 88, 156, 176
initial training   130
integration   5, 7, 12, 14, 32–34, 45, 49–51, 55–57, 59, 67, 74, 76, 80, 81, 85, 87, 103, 126–129, 153–155, 157, 158, 161, 165, 171, 173, 175
interaction   9, 23, 62, 63, 66, 73, 92, 103, 104, 109, 124, 125, 134, 139–142, 144, 153, 158, 160–162, 166, 179
intercultural competences   139
intercultural interactions   125, 134, 140, 142, 144, 158, 162, 166
interculturalism   161
internal pressures   10, 64, 102
International Master in Adult Education for Social Change (imaesc)   xiv, xv, 13
internationally-mobile workers   170
interviews   7–9, 13, 61, 67, 80, 101, 106, 107, 123, 124, 128, 139

intrinsic motivation   64, 129, 130, 152, 153, 165
intrinsic-extrinsic continuum   102
Ioannidou, A.   123
isolation   98, 139, 180
IT skills   134, 180

Italy   33

Jewish   142
Jõgi, L.   x, xiv, 13–15, 50, 153, 156, 160, 161
Jones, R.   3, 12, 35
Jordan, R. K.   29
justificatory   4

Karu, K.   x, xiv, 14, 153, 157, 160, 161, 163
Kirk, R.   134
Kliebard, H.   10, 24
knowledge   x, 4, 5, 8, 10, 11, 15, 20, 21–24, 26, 27, 29, 30, 57, 59, 60, 65–68, 70, 72, 74, 76, 86, 90, 91, 98, 104–107, 115, 117, 119, 125, 131, 134, 136, 139, 141, 155–157, 159, 166, 173–178, 180
Knowles, M.   10, 11, 21, 22, 31, 62–64, 72, 102, 125, 152
Korean   102, 107
Kumaravadivelu, B.   130

Lahav, G.   127
language learning   4, 5, 7, 8, 14, 35, 50, 59, 62–66, 68, 69, 72–75, 125, 133, 134, 137, 143, 152, 161, 165
Lattimer, H.   8
learner   3–6, 8–16, 19, 22, 24, 29–31, 56, 59–62, 64–76, 80–85, 87, 89–95, 98, 101–112, 114, 115, 117–119, 121, 124, 125, 131, 132, 136, 140, 143, 144, 152, 153, 155–160, 162, 164–166, 169, 171, 172, 177, 178, 181
Learner-Centred Education (lce)   3, 8, 10–13, 16, 19, 23, 24, 31, 43, 62, 80, 81, 124, 151, 152, 166, 168, 169, 173, 175, 181
learning climate   9, 123, 152
learning outcomes   22, 62, 117, 141, 164
learning setting   75, 139
learning strategies   22, 134, 141, 144
legal migrants   15, 143, 166
Lentin, A.   133
Libya   ix
Lifelong Learning   xiv, xv, 5, 7, 34, 48, 49, 57, 74, 101, 105, 106, 116, 163
linguistic affiliations   142

linguistic barrier 118, 144
Linguistic Integration of Adult Migrants (LIAM) 126, 157, 165
living conditions 56, 128, 154
locality x
Lundahl, L. 33

MacPherson, S. 137
Mainwaring, C. 122, 127
Malta xv, 4, 6, 7, 13–15, 33, 44–51, 101–104, 106, 108, 110, 114, 119, 122, 152–154, 156, 159–161, 163–165, 177–179
Martin, P. 33
Mayo, P. ix, xv, 12, 31, 138
Maltese as a Foreign Language (MFL) 7, 101, 105
medical education 29
Merriam, S. B. 21, 22
Mezirow, J. 22
micro-habitats 172
Middle East viii, 122
migrant adult learners' motivations 5, 8, 12, 14, 15, 33, 36, 49, 50, 62, 67, 87, 98, 101–110, 112–119, 122, 123, 125, 126, 129, 133, 135, 143, 152, 153, 155–157, 161, 163–166
migration vii–xi, xiv, xv, 5, 6, 13, 14, 16, 19, 32–34, 36, 44–47, 49, 51, 55, 56, 80, 82, 121, 152, 169, 170, 171, 174, 175, 176
Ministry for Education and Employment (MEDE) 7, 101
Ministry for Home Affairs 48, 177
Ministry of Education and Culture (MoEC) 122
'modes of thought' 25
motivations 9, 10, 15, 82, 84, 85, 98, 102, 104, 123–126, 128, 129, 143, 152–155, 165, 166
Mtika, P. 28
Multicultural 14, 80, 139
multilingual 50, 130, 136, 139, 141, 164
mutual understanding 91, 141, 174

narrative 4, 5, 23, 26, 107, 117, 126–128, 130, 133, 139, 161, 171, 173
national ix, x, xiv, 3–6, 12, 14, 20, 33, 35, 36, 44, 46, 55, 96, 126, 159
National Health Service (NHS) 88
National Records of Scotland (NRS) 44, 79
native 91, 102, 112, 134, 158

Non-governmental Organisation (NGO) 7, 31, 109, 155
Not in Education, Employment or Training (NEET) 35
neo-liberal 25
new ways to learn 23
Newson, J. A. 169
non-verbal communication 9, 124
North vii, viii

objects 9, 62, 104, 124, 172, 173
observation 7–9, 13, 24, 29, 32, 33, 61–65, 67, 70, 75, 76, 87, 92, 101, 104, 106, 108, 123, 124, 136, 137, 139
online resources 114, 115, 119, 165
Open Schools 123
Organisation for Economic Co-operation and Development (OECD) 33, 131
Ozga, J. 3, 12, 16, 35

Pakistan 46, 61, 81, 85, 87, 89–92, 94, 98
Papaioannou, I. xv, 15, 153, 155, 157, 159, 160, 162, 164
participation 5–7, 9, 11, 15, 30, 32–35, 49–51, 56–58, 60–66, 80, 107, 112, 122, 123, 126, 129, 132, 136, 152–156, 159, 178, 179
patron saint 20
Patton, M. Q. 123, 124
pedagogical experimentations 125, 153, 166
pedagogies 5, 6, 26, 35, 50, 119, 159, 178
peers 102, 154
Pépin, L. 34
periphery states 24, 25
Phillips, D. 12, 36
philology 123, 129
Pisani, M. 33
Plowden, M. 20
Poland 44, 45, 91
polarisation 24
policymaker 4, 5, 7–9, 20, 26, 28, 61, 65, 67, 68, 70, 71, 76, 101, 109, 114, 116, 123, 124, 131–133, 139
political artefact 24
Portugal 33
postmodern 26
powerlessness ix
practitioner xiv, 4
precariousness 15, 166, 180
pre-school children 94

INDEX

problem-based learning 11, 23, 29, 30
problem-solving skills 11, 24
professional XIV, 29, 50, 61, 66, 67, 101, 102, 113, 117, 120, 129, 130, 156, 173, 179
professionalism 130
Programme Coordinator 55, 65, 71, 73, 80, 81, 83–88, 90, 94–97
Programme for the International Assessment of Adult Competencies (PIAAC) 33, 36

quality of educational provision 130

refugee VIII, 15, 35, 46, 47, 49, 57, 59, 101, 126, 143, 166
relevance 10, 15, 68, 86, 87, 102, 105, 116, 119, 125, 131, 133, 134, 155, 165
research XIV, XV, 4–9, 12, 13, 19, 25–27, 29, 33, 35, 36, 43, 44, 46, 48, 51, 58, 62, 64, 76, 80, 81, 84, 85, 86, 92, 94, 96, 101, 103, 120–125, 128, 133, 134, 138, 143, 152, 154, 156–158, 164, 166, 169
residence status 15, 143, 166
respect 6, 9–12, 14, 15, 22, 23, 27, 71–73, 94–96, 98, 117, 118, 126, 131, 140, 141, 143, 155, 162–164
Riddell, A. 31
rights 3, 11, 31, 33, 49, 50, 55, 58, 96, 126, 130, 136, 159, 169, 170, 179
Roma 35, 85, 87, 94
Romania 44, 81, 83, 84, 86, 89, 95

sans-papiers 15, 143, 166
Sava, S. 133
Saville, N. 5
Schweisfurth, M. 3, 4, 9, 10, 12, 13, 15, 19, 20, 22–25, 27–29, 31, 32, 36, 62, 66, 69, 72, 73, 80, 91, 93, 102, 115, 117, 123, 124, 131, 136, 140, 152, 155, 159, 160, 162
Scotland 6, 7, 13, 14, 44–51, 79–81, 83, 87, 96, 152, 153, 154, 159, 180
Seale, C. 124
self-directed learning 11, 21, 22, 29
self-sought informal strategies 116
Shaw, L. L. 124
shifting identities IX
Simpson, J. 128
Slade, B. 13–15, 50, 79, 153–156, 158, 160, 161, 163
social act 16, 169, 174

social change XIV, XV, 4, 5, 9, 13, 19, 22, 26, 31, 35, 43, 124, 152, 165, 170, 181
social inclusion 33–35
society 5, 20, 24, 35, 47, 51, 55, 57–59, 62, 64, 67, 69, 74, 85, 117, 126–129, 155, 157, 159, 170–173, 175, 177
solidarity 122, 169, 170–172
South VIII, IX, 4
space 9, 62, 71, 80, 81, 97, 116, 119, 124, 115, 131, 133, 134, 136–138, 140, 144, 154, 156–162, 165, 166, 169, 170, 172, 180
Spain 33
Spencer, J. A. 29
standardisation 15, 108
student cohorts 119
summative results 117

Tabulawa, R. 24
tailor-made 172
teachers 6–9, 11, 14, 21–23, 25, 27, 30, 48, 57, 60, 61, 65, 69, 72, 74, 87, 110–112, 115, 116, 119, 122–126, 130, 132, 139, 140, 153, 162, 163, 178, 179
teaching activities 93
technology-based teaching 160, 165
Thompson, P. 28, 69
time XIV, XV, 4, 9, 10, 12, 23, 28, 34, 44, 45–51, 61–64, 66, 70, 73, 81, 84–86, 91, 95, 98, 101–103, 105–107, 110, 112, 113, 116–118, 120, 124, 126, 128, 133–135, 138, 139, 158, 160, 163, 176
tolerance 94, 163
Tough, A. 21
training programme 59, 65, 67, 139, 157
travelling policy 3, 4, 12, 35, 36
Turkey VIII
Turkish invasion VIII
tutor 8, 80, 84–89, 91–98, 158, 163

United Kingdom (UK) 14, 20, 28–30, 44–48, 50, 79, 113
unawareness 20
United Nations Educational, Scientific and Cultural Organization (UNESCO) 3, 62, 130
United States of America (US) 20, 26, 30

Villalba-Garcia, E. 134
Vykotsky, L. 141

Walker, D. 135
Welcoming Programme 7, 14, 55, 57, 58, 61, 69, 73–76
Whiteside, A. 128
Wildemeersch, D. 6
Woodward, C. A. 29

Workers' Party 31

Yates, L. 139

zone of proximal development 141

Printed in the United States
by Baker & Taylor Publisher Services